THE GERMAN QUESTION
AND EUROPE

THE GERMAN QUESTION AND EUROPE

A History

PETER ALTER

A member of the Hodder Headline Group
LONDON
Co-published in the United States of America by
Oxford University Press Inc., New York

First published in Great Britain in 2000 by
Arnold, a member of the Hodder Headline Group,
338 Euston Road, London NW1 3BH

http://www.arnoldpublishers.com

Co-published in the United States of America by
Oxford University Press Inc.,
198 Madison Avenue, New York, NY10016

British Library Cataloguing in Publication Data
A catalogue record for this book is available from the British Library

Library of Congress Cataloging-in-Publication Data
A catalog record for this book is available from the Library of Congress

ISBN 0 340 74153 8 (hb)
ISBN 0 340 54017 6 (pb)

1 2 3 4 5 6 7 8 9 10

Production Editor: Rada Radojicic
Production Controller: Iain McWilliams
Cover design: Terry Griffiths

Typeset in 10 on 12 pt Sabon by Cambrian Typesetters, Frimley, Surrey
Printed and bound in Great Britain by MPG Books, Bodmin, Cornwall

What do you think about this book? Or any other Arnold title?
Please send your comments to feedback.arnold@hodder.co.uk

Contents

List of maps and figures   vii
Preface   ix

1 The German Question and Europe   1
2 Vienna 1815: the quest for stability   14
3 Economic progress and political failure   35
4 German unity: first attempt 1870–71   58
5 The German Question in war and peace   78
6 The nemesis of dictatorship   93
7 Germany in the Cold War   112
8 The German Question 1989–90: a dream come true?   129

Notes   145
Chronology   154
Select bibliography   160
Index of names   171

List of maps and figures

Maps

2.1 Germany in 1815 after the Congress of Vienna 24
3.1 Development of the Prussian–German Customs Union 40
4.1 The German Empire, 1871–1918 65
5.1 Germany in 1919 85
6.1 The Sudetenland 98
6.2 Growth of Hitler's Greater Germany, 1935–1941 100
7.1 Occupation zones in Germany and Austria, July 1945 116
8.1 Germany reunified, 1990 137

Figures

2.1 Meeting of the Federal Diet of the German Confederation in Frankfurt, 1816 31
3.1 First meeting of the Frankfurt National Assembly, 18 May 1848 47
6.1 Defeated Germany, 16 July 1945: Churchill in Berlin 110
7.1 Prime Minister Attlee feeds his valuable dollars to the cuckoo, 1947 118
7.2 The Berlin Wall in 1961 123
8.1 'A spectre is haunting Europe', 1989 134

Preface

In the summer of 1999 the seat of the German parliament and federal government was moved four hundred miles to the east, from Bonn to Berlin. This signified the spectacular end of a protracted process to overcome the political, military and economic consequences of Germany's unconditional surrender in 1945, her loss of sovereignty, the partitioning of the country into two states and the division of the nation under the impact of two bitterly opposed ideological systems. The German nation-state, founded as late as 1871, had been restored against all the odds and had regained its former capital.

Nine years earlier, on 3 October 1990, the unification of the post-war successor states of the Reich, the Federal Republic of Germany and the German Democratic Republic, had been achieved with the consent of the world powers and Germany's European neighbours. In a historical perspective, this was a most remarkable event. Notwithstanding the troubles which the German Reich of 1871 had caused since it was founded, the peoples of Europe welcomed the re-creation of a united Germany with eighty million inhabitants, economically the most powerful state in the European Union and one of the wealthiest in the world. However, amidst all the rejoicing about the breaching of the infamous Berlin Wall, the end of the Cold War between East and West and the renaissance of an undivided Europe, doubts and anxieties remained. Familiar questions resurfaced in the following years. Can the interests of all Europeans be reconciled in the long run with the Germans' desire to live within a single state? What will be the overall policy of the 'new' Germany? Will she continue on her present course and pursue supranational goals? Or will she once again begin to assert herself in Europe? Will the Germans remember the lessons of the past? Will the move from Bonn to Berlin signal a fundamental shift in German foreign policy?

These questions, sometimes worded differently, have worried the Germans' neighbours over the last two centuries. Since the upheavals of the Great French Revolution at the end of the eighteenth century the Europeans have had to live alongside a nation that either existed in a number of states, thus occasionally creating strife or a power vacuum in Central Europe, or, when unified (as between 1871 and 1945) constituted a threat, if indeed she was not an actual source of brutal aggression and war. From the early nineteenth century onwards there have been few periods when the Europeans have not had to think about the 'German Question' and their politicians have not been obliged to search for suitable answers to it. The question, put in various guises over the years, and varying in content depending on the political context, and the answers given to it by 'Europe' at crucial turning-points in the continent's history are the subjects of the book.

My survey of the 'German Question', one of the key problems of modern European history, was partly written in Germany, partly in England. This gave me the unforeseen advantage of being able to discuss my interpretations with friends and colleagues in both countries. I also benefited from the services of excellent libraries in both countries, and am particularly indebted to the British Library and the library of the German Historical Institute in London, and the libraries of the Universities in Duisburg and Cologne.

I am most grateful to all who supported me, often unknowingly, in writing on a problem which, according to leading German politicians, has now been resolved for good. My old friends Jane Rafferty and Tony Paris-Simons, in particular, saved me from getting lost in the maze of the 'German Question' by forcing me to find convincing answers to their inquisitive queries and express my thoughts in a language which is not my mother tongue. The Master and Fellows of Trinity Hall, Cambridge, offered me generous hospitality for many years and helped to sharpen my views. In the last analysis, however, my efforts as a chronicler of the 'German Question' and 'Europe's answers' could only be brought to a happy conclusion thanks to the constant encouragement, and almost limitless patience and perseverance of Christopher Wheeler, Director of Humanities Publishing at Edward Arnold. One could not wish for better professional company.

London
January 2000

Peter Alter

|1|

The German Question and Europe

Right at the end of the Second World War, when the despicable Third Reich had surrendered unconditionally to the combined military forces of the Western Allies and the Soviet Union, a small book was published in neutral Switzerland which was to become one of the most important and penetrating analyses of modern German history. Its title was simply *The German Question*; its author the eminent economist and political philosopher Wilhelm Röpke. Röpke had fled the Nazi dictatorship in the early 1930s and subsequently lived and worked in Geneva. In deepening despair he had watched, in close proximity to his former homeland, the criminal and warmongering machinations of the National Socialist regime, the violent destruction of the European state system by Hitler's armies and, finally, the apocalyptic demise of Germany as an independent, civilised and respected member of the European family of nations.

Röpke's book was a scathing condemnation of the course of German history from the early nineteenth century onwards. Modern German history, Röpke argued, represented nothing less than the negation of the idea of a German nation-state. 'We need today to be clear in our minds at last', he wrote, fully aware of the crimes committed in Germany's name, 'that Germany's unification by Bismarck's "blood and iron" policy 1866–71 was a solution by force that pushed Germany in the form of Greater Prussia along the path which inevitably led past the stages of 1914, 1933 and 1939 to the catastrophe of today, to disaster alike for Germany and for Europe.'[1]

Thus what the great Hanoverian historian A. H. L. Heeren had already foreseen as early as 1817 had come true. He had said that the preservation of the loose federal character of Germany, created by the Peace of Westphalia in 1648, was in the 'highest interest of Germany and of Europe'. Indeed, it made this country 'a bulwark of European peace'. A centralised Germany, on the other hand, would not for long resist the temptation, by virtue of her geographical situation and resources, to aspire to hegemony over Europe.[2] These are in fact thoughts repeated and elaborated by the writer Constantin Frantz, an intellectual adversary of Otto von Bismarck whose work is appreciated again nowadays. There has thus been no lack of men who understood the significance which a tightly united Germany had for the freedom of Germany and the peace of Europe.

In his book, Röpke very briefly outlined two alternatives for the political organisation of Central Europe, an issue which since the nineteenth century has been commonly known as the 'German Question'. The German Question was and is one of the major problems of modern European history. There have been times in the last two centuries when it dominated politics in Europe and an answer was considered urgent. At other times it has lain dormant, generally held to be either resolved or to be of no political topicality any longer. The German Question experienced long evolutionary changes in its background and meaning as well as unexpected and swift movements which revolutionised the map and politics of the whole of Europe. It has almost always been, as Röpke made manifestly clear, a question of deep concern to Germans and other Europeans alike. In 1989–90, an answer was found to the German Question once again in its long history: this time through the fall of the Berlin Wall, the collapse of communism, and the unification of the two German states. And once again, contemporaries assumed that this would be the definitive answer. But will the events of 1989–90 really mark the end of some two hundred years of political unrest and turmoil emanating from the centre of Europe? Many observers are reluctant to deny the possibility that the old problem might resurface yet again, although in a new guise.

The history of the German Question must be examined in order to understand the enormous political changes and, of course, challenges of the last few decades, which have confronted Europe in such an astounding way. In 1989–90, as earlier in 1815, 1848–49, 1870–71 or 1918, there was a 'question' which demanded an answer from at least two sides. The German Question was primarily directed at the Germans themselves. 'What and where is Germany?', the writers J. W. von Goethe and Friedrich Schiller asked in 1797, indicating the non-existence of a unified German nation-state, that is, a political organisation which, in German eyes, the French, British, Dutch and Spaniards already had. Over the last two hundred years the Germans have tried time and again to provide answers to the question. Their answers have depended on the prevailing circumstances and very often, of necessity, have remained purely theoretical, deeply rooted in political wishful thinking. In other cases and historical situations, however, the answer has taken on a political shape.

In all their endeavours to find an answer to the German Question, the Germans have found that their answer cannot be given in a vacuum. In other words, the German Question has never been of concern to the Germans alone. It always was a question of fundamental concern to Germany's neighbours. Its recurring topicality was of great interest to them and gave them every reason to comment on it extensively. There were even times when the German debate on the German Question gave rise to fears of ominous developments in Central Europe which could endanger the peace and well-being of the entire continent. Consequently, the German Question was also a question directed at Europe. From the early nineteenth century onwards, whenever the German Question entered the political arena fellow-Europeans asked themselves how Germany would fit into the existing as well as the future geographical, political and mental map of Europe. From about the mid-nineteenth century it was no longer a question for them of whether a German nation-state should be established at all, but rather how it would be constituted and which territories it would include. Occasionally the German Question even turned into an issue of world politics, for example in the twentieth century, especially in the era of the so-called Cold War between 1945 and 1989.

On the other hand, in 1871 in particular, Germans and other Europeans alike shared the strong impression that after the foundation of the German Reich the German Question could finally be consigned to the history books. All that the Germans had wanted, namely the establishment of their own nation-state, had been gloriously achieved. The widely read Prussian historian Heinrich von Sybel expressed the feelings and thinking of his contemporaries in an incomparable way. At the beginning of 1871, only a few days after the proclamation of the German Reich in the Hall of Mirrors at the palace of Versailles, Sybel wrote: 'What have we done to deserve God's grace, that we are allowed to experience such great and powerful things? What for twenty years was our only wish and aspiration has now been fulfilled in such a splendid way! What is there left to do in my lifetime?'[3] Well, Sybel found a new purpose in life by writing a seven-volume work on the foundation of the new German Empire which glorified it as the precious achievement of the Hohenzollern dynasty and the dynamic Prussian Prime Minister Otto von Bismarck.

Today we know that in 1871 the German Question had not been answered for good. To a very large extent it was the Germans' own fault that it soon reappeared on Europe's political agenda. In the late nineteenth century and first half of the twentieth century, Europeans no longer thought of the German Question as a synonym for the Germans' national aspirations. It now came to mean a real or imagined threat emanating from Germany in various shapes and levels of intensity. And after 1945, the German Question once again changed its appearance in the eyes of 'Europe', with the national dimension regaining prominence. Now it referred to both the enforced partition of Germany and the Germans' real or alleged desire for reunification.

By the 1970s, however, the German debate on reunification had more or less petered out. The division of the world between the two superpowers, the United States and the Soviet Union, the apparent consolidation of the communist East German state, and the policy of *détente* had created a *status quo* in Europe which left no room for major political changes such as the reunification of a divided country in the centre of the continent. Moreover, there seemed to be a sort of perverse logic in a post-war situation based on sacrifice, undoubtedly painful, on the part of the nation responsible for the outbreak of two world wars and the Holocaust. Should the Germans living on the two sides of the dangerous demarcation line between East and West not renounce the right to national self-determination in the interests of the balance of power in Europe and European security? In any case, the Federal Republic of Germany and the German Democratic Republic seemed to have accepted, to all intents and purposes, the post-war development against German unity, however unsatisfactory this might have been from a national point of view. After 1949 both German states had turned, at least outwardly, into model members of their respective alliance systems.

Thus the German Question had become a non-issue in German and European politics, only to resurface quite dramatically in the late 1980s. For a comparatively short time it then dominated world politics once again before reaching, in the unanimous view of most Germans and Europeans, a happy conclusion. Completely taken by surprise at witnessing something everyone had thought impossible, historians were not the only ones tempted to see these events as history repeating itself or, with undisguised moralistic undertones, as a second undeserved chance for the Germans to live freely in their own nation-state. The German Question answered at last – this was the verdict of one school of thought and the sigh of relief could hardly be ignored.

However, as early as 1990 representatives of another school pointed to historical experience and hastened to warn of a new German Question. What they had in mind, and to which they readily applied the old term as a catch-phrase, was the fear that the reunited Germany would inevitably establish hegemony over Europe by playing its economic and demographic card. The German government, very conscious of history's fortuitous and unexpected turn in Germany's favour and the country's responsibilities in view of its fateful role in the recent past, was quick to deny any hegemonic ambitions on the part of reunited Germany. Chancellor Helmut Kohl, in particular, never tired of pointing to the country's firm integration into supranational political and military structures on a European and Atlantic level. There is simply no scope, he argued, for a new German Question to take off; Europe's fears are unfounded.

But who is Europe? Prince Bismarck, the founder of the German Reich of 1871 and early Eurosceptic in some respects, once said: 'Qui parle Europe a tort. Notion géographique.'[4] He meant that Europe is a rather woolly term, an easy generalisation and not, of course, an acting, identifiable person. It may conjure up a cultural idea, a geographical notion or a political system. To the question: 'what or rather who is Europe?', the distinguished American historian Gordon A. Craig has given a pragmatic answer. In the nineteenth century and later, he says, Europe simply meant the five European states which, because of their military, economic and other resources and their territorial size, were considered to be great powers: Britain, Russia, France, Austria-Hungary and Prussia/Germany.[5]

Until 1914 these five states constituted, in legal theory and political reality, the so-called pentarchy of the European state system. As a kind of security council they oversaw and, if necessary, ordered the political affairs of Europe, and even occasionally of the world at large. This was achieved by the smooth means of diplomacy (seldom by force), perhaps most spectacularly at glittering international conferences and congresses such as the Congress of Vienna in 1814–15, the Paris Peace Congress in 1856, the Congress of Berlin in 1878, and the Paris Peace Conference in 1919 (though the latter was dominated by the United States).

Seen from the Prussian/German capital Berlin, until 1914 'Europe' primarily meant the other four great powers. When we discuss, in subsequent chapters, Europe's attitude towards the German Question at any given time, we refer mainly to the attitude of these powers. After the First World War the situation became less clear. Austria-Hungary had disappeared as a great power in 1918 and was dissolved into a number of successor states. Russia had lost its great-power status following the October Revolution of 1917, at least temporarily. The European status of the young Soviet Union remained unclear until well into the Second World War. It was watched with suspicion by the Western powers because of its social order, revolutionary ideology and unconventional foreign policy. 'Europe' in the inter-war years effectively meant Britain and France, plus Fascist Italy under Mussolini. After 1945 'Europe' had changed once again. Confronted with the rapid rise of the two superpowers, the United States and the Soviet Union, during the latter phase of the war Europe had virtually lost all its former political importance, although Britain and France still claimed to be world powers, if on a reduced scale. As far as Germany or the German Question was concerned, immediately after 1945 the best that Europe in West and East could hope for was to be consulted by the superpowers, Britain and France certainly a little more so as junior partners of the United States.

Nevertheless, in post-war Europe the French and British attitude towards the German Question and their influence in designing the West's policy towards Germany gradually gained more weight, even though neither Britain nor France was ever able to influence the course of events decisively, let alone determine major moves in American and Soviet strategy. This became obvious once again in the months between the fall of the Berlin Wall in November 1989 and German unification in October 1990, when the governments in London and Paris were reluctant, to put it mildly, in their support for the quickening pace of inter-German rapprochement. Their frantic efforts to influence the great strategic decisions in Washington and Moscow had, all in all, little success.

The term 'question', as used here in a political and historical context, needs an explanation too. It became common usage in political language after the French Revolution, and it meant more than simply 'a question'. In nineteenth-century Europe quite a number of such political 'questions' existed. At times they occupied politicians intensively, occasionally brought Europe to the brink of war, and were even the direct cause of wars. There was an Eastern Question, an Irish Question, a Polish Question, a Jewish Question, and so on. Behind all these questions was hidden, to all intents and purposes, a national problem. In the nineteenth century peoples and nations turned to the ideology of nationalism and demanded their own nation-states. This had been denied them thus far because, for example, they lived in a multinational state. The Irish, or more precisely their national leaders, asked: when and under what conditions can we secede from the United Kingdom and establish autonomy ('home rule'), and, finally, our own independent state? The Poles, another example, persistently asked: when and under what conditions will the three powers, Russia, Prussia/Germany and Austria-Hungary, be prepared to release the Polish territories occupied by them, and accept an independent Polish nation-state? In this sense, the German Question was also primarily a national question up to 1871. Only in the course of the nineteenth century did the term 'question' gain the more general meaning of 'problem' or 'crisis' as in the 'Balkan Question' or 'Schleswig-Holstein Question'. These 'questions' demanded the attention of Europe's leading statesmen. If they failed to find a satisfactory answer the almost inevitable consequence was political unrest, even war and revolution.

Among the many 'questions' of the nineteenth century, the German Question was undoubtedly the most prominent. 'The German question', declared the writer and historian Constantin Frantz rather dramatically in 1866, 'is the most obscure, most involved and comprehensive problem in the whole of modern history.'[6] This statement made it clear that since the early nineteenth century the German Question had been understood and defined in very different ways. When examining some of the definitions by historians and politicians, two observations are striking. First, when the term 'question' is used, this implies not only the political organisation of Central Europe, i.e. the issue as to whether the Germans should live in one centralised state, in a loosely knit federation of semi-independent states or in several sovereign states. Closely linked to this issue was the question as to the constitutional order under which the Germans should live.

Second, while German authors, past and present, show interesting, often wide variations in defining the German Question, definitions by non-German authors are fairly uniform and stereotypical. They understand the German Question primarily as a security problem, namely as the question of how Europe's centre can be stabilised in order to guarantee the 'tranquillity of Europe' – in contemporary diplomatic language, 'le repos de l'Europe'. This expresses a line of political thinking and planning, as well as political activity by European statesmen, which can be traced right back to the Peace of Westphalia of 1648. This approach particularly dominated French policy towards Germany far beyond 1945. The Westphalian Peace Treaty accorded the 'estates' of the Holy Roman Empire far-reaching independence at the expense of the central imperial power in Vienna. From 1648 onwards most of Germany's neighbours, especially France, upheld the principle that granting the German estates far-reaching political freedoms was the best guarantee of Europe's peace and security. The Peace of Westphalia, by making the constitution of the Empire part of the *ius publicum europaeum*, thus cemented the decentralised structure of the Holy Roman Empire with the Emperor as its formal head.

For Europe, the German Question was more or less defined by and reduced to the crucial question: how can Europe's peace and security be preserved without violating German interests, but simultaneously curbing the political ambitions of the Germans? This meant, in practical terms, that Germany's neighbours favoured neither the existence of a strong unified state in Central Europe, nor a power vacuum which could attract unwanted advances from a neighbouring state. Both a political vacuum and a powerful centre in the heart of Europe tended to destabilise the European state system and would consequently represent a security risk for the whole continent. This view of Central Europe developed into a political maxim which guided European diplomacy to a considerable degree, and still continues to do so. From the mid-eighteenth century until the foundation of the German Reich in 1871, Central Europe had indeed come close to being a power vacuum, mainly due to the political antagonism between Berlin and Vienna, the two major German powers. The year 1871 saw the beginning of a short period, in historical perspective, when the European centre was dominated by one strong state and the consequences for the 'tranquillity of Europe' are well known. Germany's unconditional surrender in 1945 and its partitioning into two states can almost be regarded as the logical conclusion, the return to a situation which seemed to be much more conducive to the European balance of power.

The Allied powers had discussed a return to the pre-1871 status in Central Europe as early as the time of the Great War of 1914–18. The idea of a dissolution of the German Reich appeared among the Entente's war aims, particularly at the insistence of France. German territorial losses as stipulated by the Versailles Treaty of 1919, and various attempts at giving autonomy and even independence to certain areas in the following years (Saar region, Rhineland), were also a by-product of such deliberations. However, all these plans came to nothing. Unfortunately, Germany's territorial losses on its western, northern and eastern borders were not understood by Berlin as a warning of worse to come should it disturb the 'tranquillity of Europe' once again. On the contrary, the so-called 'humiliation' of the Versailles Peace Treaty only kindled aspirations of revising the Allies' restrained measures of 1919 to curb German power.

Germany's rapid recovery as a political and military power from the mid-1920s onwards and Europe's experience of National Socialist aggression and expansionism after 1933 brought back with force the notion of Germany as the European troublemaker *par excellence*. The consequences were not long coming. As soon as the tide turned in the Second World War the British and their American ally, in particular, produced memoranda openly arguing for the dismemberment of Germany. During the summit conferences of the Big Three, first in Tehran in 1943, then at Yalta and Potsdam in 1945, the problem of whether Germany should be split up into a number of separate states was discussed in great detail.[7]

Again in 1989–90 it became immediately obvious to the whole world how important the security dimension of the German Question was for Europe when German unity reappeared on the political agenda and a settlement was imminent. To all those responsible for negotiating the terms of German unification it was clear right from the very start of the 'Two-Plus-Four' talks that the old problem of how to protect the 'tranquillity of Europe' against Germany's political ambitions could only be solved within a European framework.[8] The then German government fully recognised the anxieties and resentments of the other Europeans, including the Russians, and in an admirable demonstration of political prudence (so rare in German foreign policy in the past) complied with an answer to the German Question that satisfied Europe. By not pursuing a selfish, nationalistic policy and unreservedly confirming their commitments within the Western alliance and the European Union, the Germans were thus able to persuade Europe to abandon its traditional preference for a politically divided Central Europe. This was, after all, quite a remarkable concession by the superpowers, and even more so by fellow-Europeans, who could still vividly remember Nazi terror, the ruthless persecution of the Jews, the war and German occupation of their countries.

When a German nation-state was created for a second time in 1990 and the concept of an undivided Central Europe once more gained the upper hand, as in 1871, most Germans had the feeling that they were witnessing a miracle. Unification happened against all the odds. The first German nation-state had, after all, existed for a mere seventy-five years – a short span of time compared with those centuries when the political geography of Central Europe was characterised by weak constitutional constructions. Therefore, the journalist and historian Sebastian Haffner, one of many similar voices at the time, had praised the existence of two Germanies in 1972. He asked whether something could be bad for Germany that was good for Europe. 'It's like this: the Germans can live better and more securely in two small states than in one big one.'[9] The famous American diplomat George F. Kennan, a specialist in German affairs, declared as late as in the summer of 1989 that 'the unification of Germany is simply no option'.[10] Well, diplomats, like historians, have never been good prophets.

The German Question may indeed have been the 'most obscure, most involved and comprehensive problem in the whole of modern history', as Constantin Frantz had put it. However, a generally accepted definition of it has never existed since the early 1800s. This is certainly nothing unusual. There are many historical and political terms which defy clear definition. In the case of the German Question it is, in fact, quite illuminating to follow the efforts of writers in their attempts to define the question and to see which aspects they emphasise. Quite obviously, in defining the 'most obscure problem' they depend on their historical experiences and the political situation at the time. The German historian Anselm Doering-Manteuffel, who has written an excellent text-book on the early history of the German Question, refrains from giving any definition at all. He simply adopts the interpretation of contemporaries:

> Contemporaries of the nineteenth century used the term 'German question' for the problem of how to achieve the goal of a national state in Germany given the opposing interests of the great powers, Austria and Prussia. It emerged after the failure of the National Assembly in the Paulskirche in 1849, and recurred throughout the decades until 1871. But the fundamental problem of the 'German question', the existence of a non-national federation of numerous individual states in the age of national movements and nascent nationalism, accompanied the history of the German Confederation from as early as 1815.[11]

One hundred years after the German National Assembly had met at the Paulskirche in Frankfurt, the content of the German Question as described by the modern scholar Doering-Manteuffel had changed almost completely. The antagonism between Austria and Prussia was, of course, no longer an ingredient. For many years now, under the constant threat of Soviet expansionism, the definition given by Wilhelm Röpke in 1945 set the tone. In his influential book, the third edition of which appeared in 1948, he wrote: 'The future of Europe depends on our succeeding at last after this war in attaining what three past generations have failed to attain, the peaceful reintegration of Germany in Europe, and with it the protection of Europe against Germany and of Germany against herself'.[12] Röpke had coined the phrase which, in the years after 1945, became part of practically all definitions of the German Question. Still under the influence of the apocalyptic end of the Second World War, Röpke detailed the essence of the German Question as follows: 'However could it happen that in a great civilized nation all the forces of evil should be let loose, and what now is the just and sensible way of treating the Germans?'[13] This question encapsulates the major problem facing the victorious Allies after 1945 when they tried to implement their occupation policy in Germany.

Fifteen years after Röpke, when the partition of Germany seemed to be solidly cemented and the two German successor states of the vanished Reich consolidated, the conservative historian Walther Hubatsch once again interpreted the German Question exclusively as a national and security problem. In the study *The German Question* Hubatsch asked: 'How can the numerically strongest people of Europe arrive at a common formation of its political will? . . . How can the people become a nation – as this process has occurred in France, England, Poland, Italy and in the Iberian, Scandinavian and Balkan countries – without endangering the peace and freedom of the other European nations?'[14] Hubatsch summed up most succinctly the fact that even after 1945 the German Question was primarily a problem of Europe's security and stability – even in an age overshadowed by the threat of nuclear weapons and the ideological conflict of the Cold War.

However, at almost exactly the same time, other definitions of the German Question were being put forward, all still possible and acceptable. An example is that of Gerhard Ritter, who was one of the leading conservative historians in the newly established Federal Republic. He had grown up in Wilhelmine Germany, started his academic career in the Weimar Republic, and become, during the Second World War, a member of the underground German resistance movement. Ritter combined the German Question with the more general question as to 'how it could happen that a seemingly strong difference in political thinking and forms of political life has developed between us and Western Europe in modern times: a difference which really has made Germany into a "problem" for West Europeans'.[15] This was the question of the notorious German *Sonderweg* ('deviation'), Germany's peculiar path into modernity. In recent decades this has developed into a favourite topic of historical debate, with few convincing conclusions, but always useful as a warning to politicians and scholars who dream of a reunited Germany as a bridge between East and West, or as a country with political options in all directions.

Ritter's discussion of the 'German problem' transcends the German Question as understood in its narrow political sense. His influence is evident in the work of a sociologist who turned to the subject in 1968. Ralf Dahrendorf discussed the German Question in the introductory chapter of his important book *Society and Democracy in Germany*. For him it essentially boils down to the question 'why is it that so few in Germany embraced the principle of liberal democracy?'[16] Dahrendorf's mental proximity to Gerhard Ritter is obvious. He too is concerned with the German *Sonderweg*, i.e. Germany's political development and political culture allegedly so different from that of Western Europe – 'Western Europe', of course, seen as a more or less homogeneous block, which makes the comparison rather an odd one.

Ten years after Dahrendorf, the influential historian Theodor Schieder offered a definition in kindred spirit. For him the German Question is

the question as to the peculiarities that distinguish German history from that of its European neighbours and the consequences to be drawn from these peculiarities. These consequences emerge in the nineteenth century, in the century in which the results of a centuries-long development during the transition of the European nations in the age of 'national' states, economic and industrial revolution and social upheavals became clear. Now a German Question in the narrowest sense seems to be the question of the political shape of Germany in a system of states determined by its citizens, states that are developing economically and expanding politically.[17]

What Schieder here calls the 'German question in the narrowest sense' is a sufficiently accurate description of the subject of this book: the territorial and political organisation of Central Europe since the early nineteenth century, the constitutional order under which the Germans live or to which they aspire, the European balance of power – either strengthened or endangered by German-speaking Central Europe – and the perception of the German state or states on the part of other Europeans.

As a rule Europeans (and Americans) usually prefer the term 'German problem' to German Question.[18] For them the crucial experience since the early nineteenth century is that Germany is a difficult, unruly, even dangerous neighbour. The 'German problem' meant to them political instability in Central Europe, aggressive behaviour on the part of the Germans, militarism, expansionism and a dubious 'national character'. The German 'national character' as perceived by the Western Allies needed to undergo a thorough change after the Second World War. According to Allied assumptions and plans, the Germans were unable to achieve this by their own efforts. They needed help from outside and even had to be forced into a process of prolonged 're-education'. Some methods of 're-education' applied in the Western zones of occupation after 1945 were certainly of doubtful value. However, in retrospect, the sudden, shock-like confrontation with Western political values, Western political thought and Western culture after twelve years of stifling dictatorship was not merely a long overdue eye-opener, but, in the long run, had an altogether salutory effect on the West German population. More than anything else, 're-education' demonstrated to them the nationalistic narrowness of a good many of their political attitudes and their understanding of what constitutes a civil society.

Two eminent non-German historians – one French and the other British – have given a good description of what Europeans mean by the 'German problem' since 1870–71. Jean-Baptiste Duroselle, born in 1917, wrote on the occasion of the hundredth anniversary of the foundation of the German Reich:

> Since the Cold War, in which the Germans virtually stopped being our 'arch enemies', French historiography has, admittedly, changed its tone; but we still have to be clear that most works written in the eight decades since 1866 are based on the dogma of a fundamental and eternal opposition. The fact is that in these eighty years the French have seen the Germans take over their country three times and that they were extremely angry about these brutish aggressors. Three times, on these same three occasions, the Germans, with clear consciences, have broken out of their 'besieged fortress', to defend

themselves against the hated French imperialism or against Franco-Russian encirclement.[19]

The 'German problem' here is nothing more than a very subjective impression of constant aggression by a neighbouring nation. This nation intensified its aggressive policy as soon as it had gained its own nation-state and this policy went on until its state ceased to exist. Moreover, and perhaps even worse, the very act of the Reich's creation was accompanied by the annexation of Alsace-Lorraine from France. How could France, even if it was the aggressor in 1870, ever establish friendly relations with such a neighbour?

A. J. P. Taylor, born in 1906, perceived the 'German problem' in a similar vein to Duroselle. In its exaggeration and vehemence Taylor's perception of the 'German problem' is representative of views to be found in Britain and the United States during the Second World War and its aftermath. This view held the Germans, because of their psychological disposition ('national character'), to be the greatest danger to world peace. In his popular book *The Course of German History*, first published in 1945 and still in print, Taylor boiled the 'German problem' down to the two familiar questions: 'How can the peoples of Europe be secured against repeated bouts of German aggression? And, how can the Germans discover a settled, peaceful form of political existence?'[20]

Taylor ventured the opinion, understandable in 1945, that the Allies in the anti-Hitler coalition should agree on measures that would make German unity impossible for good. According to Taylor, 'only a divided Germany can be a free Germany. A reunited Germany would become a militaristic state in order to resume the march towards European domination, or its power would be compulsorily reduced by foreign interference, if the former allies had the sense to come together again in time.'[21] For Taylor German history is a 'history of extremes' which does not know 'moderation' or 'normality'. 'Geographically the people of the centre, the Germans, have never found a middle way of life, either in their thought or least of all in their politics.'[22] Among the reasons that might explain this imbalance Taylor points specifically to the Germans' delay in becoming a unified nation. He holds this responsible for a collective feeling of insecurity, belatedness and deprivation, eventually causing compensatory aggressive actions towards Germany's neighbours in Europe.

Today much of Taylor's interpretation of modern German history may appear rather dubious or over the top. However, it is easy to find examples which lend support to his ideas. One only has to think of the provocations and vacillations in Wilhelmine foreign policy, when there was much talk of Germany as a world power, the Kaiser wanted to challenge Britain's naval supremacy, and German politicians demanded a 'place in the sun'.[23] On the other hand, it is also easy to point to statements on the German side that clearly indicate awareness of the problems arising from Germany's belated birth as a nation-state in an age of nationalism and imperialism. One of the people who already knew better in Wilhelmine Germany was Theobald von Bethmann Hollweg, Chancellor of the Reich and Prussian Prime Minister from 1909. His tragedy was that he was unable to stop German gunboat diplomacy in the years preceding the Great War. As late as June 1913 Bethmann Hollweg was complaining, albeit in private, about the political inexperience and naivety of the Germans, or more precisely the German ruling class, who were newcomers to global competition:

> We are a young people, perhaps still believe rather naively in violence, underestimate more subtle means and do not yet know that what violence can achieve can never be preserved by violence alone. . . . We are not sure and conscious enough of our inner being, of our national ideals. It may well be rooted in the character of our . . . individualistic and not yet balanced culture that it does not possess the same suggestive power as French and British culture.[24]

After this cursory survey of definitions of the German Question, incomplete as it may be, we can at last come to a conclusion. For the purposes of our investigation in the following chapters a comparatively simple definition may suffice which will, of course, depend on the various elements already mentioned. This definition of the German Question has three main aspects, all closely intertwined. In this study the German Question is understood, first, as the question as to the territorial order of Central Europe; second, as the question as to the political and constitutional order of Central Europe; and third, as the question as to the short-term and long-term effects of the changing nature of the Central European order on Germany's neighbours, their concerns, reactions and responses. In other words, over the last two centuries the German Question has never ceased to be a political challenge to the whole of Europe. Answers given to the question at crucial moments in the continent's troubled history were not only of considerable concern to the Germans, Europe's most numerous people, but also to all Europeans, in 1815 and 1848, as well as in 1871 and 1945–49, and, most recently, in 1989–90. This will be demonstrated in the following chapters.

|2|

Vienna 1815: the quest for stability

On 6 August 1806 the venerable Holy Roman Empire of the German Nation finally ceased to exist. Its last Emperor, the Habsburg Francis II, renounced the imperial crown, thereby succumbing to the intense pressure exerted on him by Napoleon Bonaparte, who, with his revolutionary armies, had conquered practically the whole of Central Europe. The dissolution of the Holy Roman Empire, which had already been a mere shadow of its former self for many years, created the German Question in its modern sense, or as the historian Imanuel Geiss put it: 'The death of the Holy Roman Empire . . . gave birth to the German Question'.[1]

After the rather ignominious demise of the Old Empire in 1806 the greater part of Central Europe became a protectorate under French hegemony, organised in the shape of the short-lived Confederation of the Rhine. The Confederation, founded as early as 12 July 1806, represented a loosely structured union of German princes who were obliged to form an alliance with France and were completely under French control. Napoleon was in fact proclaimed their 'protector'. In nationalist German historiography the Confederation, to which thirty-six German states eventually adhered, has a very bad reputation as a French satellite and product of French expansionism. Its enduring modernising effects on German politics and society in general have only recently been emphasised by historians. Moreover, under French pressure the traditional mosaic of hundreds of states, principalities and free cities in Central Europe was rearranged to give larger units, such as Bavaria, Württemberg, the Grand Duchy of Berg or Westphalia. The price for their territorial enlargement, in some cases their creation, was that these old and new states of the Confederation had to enter Napoleon's political orbit. This aroused the disapproval of later German nationalists, but it could not dispel the reforming impulses in the ensuing process of state-building in these often heterogeneous territories.

However, the feeling that the Confederation of the Rhine was Napoleon's creation and would disintegrate with his fall from power was widespread in the years after 1806. As Central Europe's political organisation, at the demand of France, it could only be an intermediate solution to the German Question. Therefore, almost immediately after the end of the

Old Empire the question arose as to what could replace it as the political framework under which Germans would live. Reacting to the new situation after 1806 and looking to the future, the writer and agitator Ernst Moritz Arndt, an early protagonist of German nationalism, wrote a poem with the famous opening line 'What is the Germans' fatherland?' Arndt, after enumerating various territories which could be considered as the Germans' fatherland, rejected any existing state or historical reminiscence and finally gave the following answer to his own rhetorical question: 'It should be the whole of Germany', and the 'whole of Germany' was, according to Arndt, 'as far as the German tongue can be heard'. This spatial idea of Germany, based on language and culture, was, from then on, to have a somewhat problematic, even dangerous influence on Germans wherever they lived in Europe. It was problematic because Arndt's concept of a German cultural nation implied the political claim that all German-speakers, including the Swiss Germans should form a political nation and live in one single state, whether they liked it or not. At almost the same time Baron vom Stein, the reformer in the service of the Prussian state defeated by France, put forward some much more realistic ideas. He conceived a future German nation-state, liberal and modern, within the borders of the defunct Old Empire, or, if that should prove too ambitious, a state which comprised Prussia, Saxony, Bavaria, Württemberg, Baden, Westphalia and the Rhineland, but not Austria.

Yet the decisions on the future shape and constitution of Germany after the demise of the Old Empire, the dissolution of the Confederation of the Rhine (October 1813) and the final defeat of the Emperor Napoleon at Waterloo (June 1815) were not made either by the writer Arndt or the politician vom Stein, though admittedly their ideas and concepts left a mark whenever the German Question was on the political agenda in the course of the nineteenth century. The political decisions which laid the foundations for a new order in Europe after the turmoils of the French Revolution, the Napoleonic Wars and the Wars of Liberation, when the first stirrings of liberalism and nationalism were felt in Germany, were made elsewhere. At the cradle of the new European order stood the victorious powers of the coalition against Napoleonic France, and that meant primarily Britain, Russia and Austria. However, like Prussia, defeated France (now once again under the Bourbons) and smaller European states were also invited to send representatives to the Congress of Vienna, and it is only correct to say that the re-organisation of Central Europe was deliberated and put into effect by the whole of Europe in 1814–15.

Looking more closely at the decisions of the Congress of Vienna, a characteristic becomes apparent that was typical of later congresses and conferences in European diplomacy and is still valid today. International gatherings of diplomats never start their deliberations from scratch, but discuss an agenda and make decisions for which the ground-work has already been done in the run-up to the meeting. In other words, decisions or agreements made at conferences have, as a rule, a pre-history and do not originate from a *tabula rasa*. Consequently, long before Napoleon's fall the Allies were developing ideas and plans for the future organisation of post-revolutionary Europe, in particular of Central Europe. Indeed, the roots of Allied planning went as far back as 1804–5. Even at that early stage, when Napoleon was still at the height of his power, principles and guidelines had been formulated which were to determine the work of the Congress of Vienna ten year later, and which, to all intents and purposes, the statesmen at the Congress transformed into political and legal reality.

According to these early guidelines, the guiding principle for the shape of post-Napoleonic Europe was, first, to break French hegemony and, second, to erect barriers against a revival of France's expansionist policy. One has to remember that from the seventeenth until well into the nineteenth century it was not 'Germany' but France that was traditionally considered the troublemaker who disturbed the 'tranquillity of Europe', whatever constitutional order she happened to have at a given time. This image of the French still played an important role during the Franco-Prussian War of 1870–71. The French declaration of war on Prussia and her German allies was seen by the 'European public' as no less than another attempt by France to establish herself as the hegemonic power in continental Europe. In 1870–71 this traditional image of the French was greatly to Bismarck's advantage and contributed decisively to the ease with which he was able to found the German Reich, in the shape of a greater Prussia, without the threat of British or Russian intervention.

In 1814–15 it was also clear right from the start of the Congress that the future organisation of Europe and its political stability in years to come had to be founded on a new order in Germany. This is the reason why the German Question, or the search for an answer to it, played such a central role at the Congress. All other problems occupying the statesmen of the great powers in Vienna were, in effect, subordinated to this one issue. Europe's future security and peace were largely understood to depend on a system of checks and balances against France, in which Central Europe naturally had to be accorded a key function. A stable Central Europe would, it was assumed, guarantee a stable continent. At the turn of 1804–5 it had already been stipulated, in an exchange of ideas between the Russian Tsar Alexander I and the British Prime Minister William Pitt the Younger, that the future organisation of Europe should be put under political guarantee by the pentarchy in order to give it stability and protect it from unwanted changes in whatever guise and under whatever pretext. Moreover, in the correspondence between Alexander I and Pitt there were already hints that the political weight of France needed to be counterbalanced by a strengthening of the weakest of the great European powers, namely Prussia, by giving it a strong position on the Rhine. The whole of Germany, including Prussia and Austria, should be organised on a federal basis. The only question still open was where exactly on the scale between power vacuum and power centre the new federal order in Central Europe was to be located. That was left to the Congress to decide.

What Britain and Russia had discussed fairly informally in 1804–5, as something they thought desirable for the future, suddenly, in its political substance, became quite topical in the autumn of 1813 when the peoples of Europe rose up in arms against Napoleon's rule. In those chaotic months it was not yet clear who would ultimately decide Europe's future organisation. Would it be the conservative statesmen of the coalition against Napoleon or, perhaps, a quite new generation of politicians, handed the reins of power by the revolutionary situation of the Wars of Liberation? For many Germans, in particular, the war against Napoleonic France acquired the quality of a fight for national self-determination. In other words, it was seen as a fight which excluded, quite naturally, the discredited leadership of the old authorities. In Central Europe the Wars of Liberation were clearly more than a reaction against foreign oppression and tutelage. They were a manifestation of the ideas of freedom and equality which had had an enormous impact on the people's imagination since the French Revolution of 1789.

The Great Revolution had propagated the self-determination of individuals and nations. The leading statesmen of the age, whose experiences were formed by the revolutionary events of the late eighteenth century in North America and France, perceived these ideas as a threat to their concept of a legitimate order. In their view, a war launched by peoples and nations for the sake of self-determination was dangerously unpredictable and uncontrollable, beyond the calculating power of cool statesmanship; in short, it was merely revolution in another guise. According to the statesmen of the *anciens régimes*, the Wars of Liberation should have the character of a war waged by the cabinets of the great powers against the usurper Napoleon. Consequently, when peace-making and the reorganisation of the continent were again on the agenda, the interests of the states and dynasties should be of primary importance, not those of peoples or nations.

This attitude of mind and political thinking clearly dominated the negotiations between the statesmen of the Allied powers and the peace settlement of the Congress of Vienna. Even before the Congress convened for its first session, Tsar Alexander I of Russia, Austria's Foreign Minister Prince Metternich, the British Foreign Secretary Lord Castlereagh and the Prussian State Chancellor Prince Hardenberg had struck a deal and agreed on what their states' core interests were in a European peace. What surfaced in these mutual agreements was cabinet policy in the old style of the eighteenth century. The interests of the monarchical states were ruthlessly imposed upon the known interests and aspirations of the peoples. So, what were the interests of the victorious powers and how did they reach a compromise amongst themselves which satisfied all sides, including the Germans?

The consensus between conflicting interests was achieved in several stages before the Congress commenced its deliberations proper. On

1 March 1814 the victorious Allies confirmed their alliance concluded in 1813. This was a logical and prudent measure against France, the potential aggressor, still considered as an enemy. The alliance, signed at Chaumont, a small French town between Dijon and Nancy, made the war aims which the Allies had been discussing since 1805 legally binding. First, France was to renounce all conquests and annexations since 1792; second, French influence should be eliminated in Germany, Italy, Spain, Holland and Switzerland; and third, Germany should be organised as a union of sovereign states on a federal basis and with a weak central executive. In the Treaty of Chaumont the general outline of Europe's post-Napoleonic order became visible. It was to be built on a redefined balance of power which basically implied the containment of France, the strengthening of Europe's centre in various ways, and the prevention of Russian occupation of all Polish territories.

In devising the new European order the interests of Britain and Austria were practically identical. Both Castlereagh and Metternich wanted to stop Russia from expanding further westward, since vast territorial gains would give her the chance to take over from France as the continent's dominant power. The two statesmen also agreed on plans for Europe's centre, although with different underlying objectives. Castlereagh's fundamental concept was the British grand design of the balance of power in Europe which should block the hegemonic intentions of any power. Metternich's concept was the narrower and more selfish idea of a Central European balance of power which did not restrict Austria's ambitions as a great power in any way or her role as the leading German power. In Metternich's concept there was no room at all for a unified German state based on the national principle. On the contrary, for him the national and indeed the democratic principle represented revolution in disguise, a deadly threat to the multinational empire of the Habsburgs.

Consequently, the cunning Metternich had taken precautions to prevent the German nation-state from becoming reality. In the weeks before and after the legendary Battle of the Nations near Leipzig (16–19 October 1813), which sealed Napoleon's fate, Metternich had concluded alliances with Bavaria and Württemberg, both then still members of the moribund Confederation of the Rhine. These two states had been enlarged territorially by Napoleon and elevated into kingdoms. Both committed themselves to joining the alliance against the French Emperor. Their motives were, of course, totally selfish and opportunistic. By changing political camps at a crucial moment in European politics they hoped to secure their status and the territorial gains they owed to none other than Napoleon. Their new alliances with Austria guaranteed them their territory and sovereignty as medium-sized German states. The cynical Metternich calculated quite openly that in the years ahead Bavaria and Württemberg would vigorously defend their precarious sovereignty against all national aspirations and those who dreamed of a democratic German nation-state.

Predictably, Metternich's simple calculations worked out well and presented him with the desired outcome. When the German Question was debated at the Congress of Vienna, a Prussian diplomat reported back to his government:

> Bavaria is not the least interested in projects for a German federation which could endanger her political existence by merging her into some German national state. By demanding more territorial gains she rather aspires to the rank of a true European power and is prepared to draw the sword in all directions whence she expects resistance. In this policy there appears the most brutal aggressiveness; it now relies totally on Austria.[2]

At the same time it came as no surprise that Württemberg also opposed any attempt 'to create from various nationalities or peoples, for instance Prussia and Bavaria, a sort of nation'.[3]

Russia, the third of the big victorious powers at the Congress, did not show any marked interest in the political shaping of Central Europe. The Tsar was primarily interested in the restoration of a European state system that was based on conservative principles and would represent a dam against revolutionary ideas. To this extent he could readily agree with Britain and Austria. However, Alexander I had territorial ambitions on Russia's western border which brought him into conflict with his Western allies. More annexations of Polish territory by Russia would inevitably be met by British and Austrian opposition. The governments in London and Vienna were firmly against Russia's drive towards the west which would make her Europe's dominant power. The 'Polish Question' soured relations between the Allies before the Congress had even assembled in the Habsburgs' capital.

The representatives of the four Allied powers signed the peace treaty with France, now under the restored Bourbon Louis XVIII, on 30 May 1814, that is, four months before the Congress opened in Vienna. At the signing ceremony in Paris Prussia and Austria were not only representing the interests of their respective states; they were also acting on behalf of 'Germany', since the smaller German states were not directly involved in the peace-making. The exalted role of Prussia and Austria anticipated two things which became quite apparent in Vienna: first, that Germany as a political entity, like the Old Empire, would remain a passive element in the European state system and would not be organised like a nation-state; second, that the rivalry between Austria and Prussia, as already in the eighteenth century, would continue to be the dominant political factor in Central Europe. The antagonism between the multinational Habsburg monarchy with its German-speaking elite and the predominantly German Kingdom of Prussia turned out to be the characteristic feature of the German Question right up to 1866. In the Austro-Prussian War of that year, the so-called German civil war, this antagonism was eventually resolved in

Prussia's favour. By this time she had become the leading military and economic power in Central Europe.

In September 1814 the deliberations amongst the powers who had participated in the war against Napoleon finally got under way. Strictly speaking, the Congress of Vienna was not a peace conference, because peace with France had already been concluded four months earlier. In Vienna the main topic on the agenda was the establishment of a lasting and stable political order in Europe or, perhaps more correctly, laying the foundations for such an order after a quarter of a century of revolutionary upheavals and Napoleon's almost total domination of Europe. The negotiators in Vienna had the past events on their minds, but their approach was distinctly forward-looking. Their concern was Europe's future, although it cannot be denied that the representatives of the great powers never lost sight of the rather egoistic, very real interests of their own states whenever European matters had to be decided. So the Congress of Vienna was not simply an international gathering which was about to cast off a turbulent past in Europe. Rather it was a joint effort to create the overall framework for a new stable Europe and to block unwanted developments. As far as the statesmen in Vienna were concerned, such developments included the numerous national and liberal movements that were gaining strength everywhere and which, at least in the eyes of conservative statesmen, were aimed only at reviving the revolution that had begun in France with such disastrous consequences. By giving due time and attention to the future structure of Europe, the Congress differed considerably from the Paris Peace Conference a hundred years later, which, in effect, virtually neglected Europe's future and the well-being of all its nations. This is why the political order created by the Paris Peace Conference only survived for a few years; the order devised by the Congress of Vienna endured for several decades.

The Congress was the largest gathering of statesmen and diplomats the world had ever seen, though of course it did not in any way resemble a modern summit conference. Only the Tsar of Russia, the Emperor of Austria and the King of Prussia were present in person, and a fair number of minor German princes. The King of England and the new King of France were notably absent. Nevertheless, all European states, large and small, had sent their representatives to Vienna, with the exception of the Ottoman Empire. The Ottomans, though still in possession of large tracts of the Balkans, were not yet considered members of the European community of states. All in all the Congress was attended by about two hundred delegates who assembled in the Imperial Palace, the Hofburg, between 18 September 1814 and 9 June 1815. The Congress was divided into talks beween the so-called 'Big Four', and later 'Big Five', and meetings of the thirteen special committees which provided the experts in dealing with complicated European matters. The number of problems to be dealt with by the Congress was, of course, considerable. This partly explains why it was so long and why the monarchs were present in Vienna for so many months.

However, the amount of time consumed by the Congress also had some-thing to do with the fact that it constituted a social event, a symbol of relief after decades of political upheaval and war, a public celebration of peace, a return to normality and, hopefully, a new prosperity. This aspect of the Congress remains in the collective memory of Europeans to this day. The well-known description of the Congress by the then almost eighty-year-old Prince and Field Marshal Karl Joseph de Ligne could not have been more accurate: 'Le Congrès danse et ne marche pas'.[4] In Vienna high politics were unmistak-ably made in an outwardly easy-going way; serious diplomacy was closely intertwined with lavish and varied social entertainment. In fact, the French Foreign Minister Talleyrand once complained in a letter to Louis XVIII that two days had passed without meetings: one was spent hunting, the next was dedicated to a great party. To a very large extent, the many balls, banquets and dinners at the Congress can also be explained by the fact that the Austrian Emperor Francis I wanted to appear as a generous host to Europe's leading monarchs and diplomats, and to demonstrate publicly that the Habsburg Empire was not impoverished by the wars or in decline.

The exquisite mixture at Vienna of intense diplomatic negotiations and light-hearted social entertainment suited Metternich very well in the pursuit of his political aims and ideas. He turned the slow progress of the deliber-ations, accompanied by so much fun and pleasure, into a device for further-ing his objectives. For him, the social side of the Congress was a continuation of politics by other means, a form of diplomacy to supplement the official sessions of the Congress. Metternich became the most influen-tial and best-known negotiator at Vienna, outshining even Tsar Alexander I and the versatile French Foreign Minister, Talleyrand. He, more than any other statesman, prepared and forced through the decisions regarding German affairs, and he did so in accordance with strict conservative prin-ciples.[5] Consequently, liberal and nationally minded historians in later times depicted Metternich as a reactionary and the representative of a policy guided by the sterile ideas of restoration and stagnation. An observer of the Congress and its participants, the French Count Pierre Auguste de La Garde, characterised Austria's leading diplomat as follows:

> Metternich has been involved in Europe's massive upheavals for thirty years and has retained that quickness of spirit, that rare perception, that incisive understanding that foresees events and directs them. His judgement, the fruit of long deliberation, is irretractable, and his word decisive, as befits a statesman convinced of the influence of every one of his words. Moreover, Metternich is one of the best raconteurs of our time.[6]

A modern historian, however, judges Metternich far more critically:

> Metternich . . . was a feudalist of the eighteenth century, who dealt with every situation as he found it and solved every problem according

to what was possible – without principle or concept. He flitted from one person to another like a butterfly, promised and repudiated, lied or spoke the truth, and enjoyed to a high degree that which the peoples he governed were largely denied: freedom. He basically did not give a damn about ideals. His boldness, vanity and recklessness got him out of the most difficult situations.[7]

According to this view, Metternich was, without doubt, an opportunist of the first order. What Metternich himself considered to be his supreme political vision and maxim he once expressed as follows: 'In order to strive for a happy future one has, at least, to make sure of one's present; the conservation of things which exist has consequently to be the first and most important of all endeavours'.[8]

All this being said, one has to ask what was finally achieved by Metternich, and by the Congress under his guidance and diplomatic skills. In the first place, the Congress sealed reconciliation with France, the former enemy of the four Allied powers. Of course, peace with France had been concluded much earlier, and had been made considerably easier by the restoration of the Bourbon monarchy. France had thus quickly regained her status as a European great power. The ideological confrontation of the years after 1789 between revolutionary France and the conservative powers had disappeared. At the Congress, the aspiration to restore the allegedly happy pre-revolutionary world in Europe united almost all the diplomats and statesmen. This created a solid common basis for the ensuing negotiations. However, certain reservations about France had not yet completely vanished. Only when the four Allied powers found themselves locked in disagreement at the end of 1814 and beginning of 1815 was the French Foreign Minister Talleyrand admitted to the Allies' Council of Four which decided all major questions. The sources of disagreement amongst the Allies were, first, Prussia's interest in annexing the economically well-developed Kingdom of Saxony and, second, Russia's designs on the entire Polish territory. Prussia and Russia supported one another in their claims to territorial annexation. To counteract these ambitions Austria and Britain signed a formal alliance on 3 January 1815. The war between the former allies that now threatened was only avoided by a compromise which became part of the Final Act of the Congress. This compromise, which involved territorial concessions to both Russia and Prussia, was reached with Talleyrand's assistance. Henceforth France was once more admitted to the pentarchy as an equal partner, a development particularly welcome to the British.

A second major achievement of the Congress of Vienna was undoubtedly the settlement of the German Question within a European framework that established a new balance for the whole continent. Of all the powers in the pentarchy the smallest, Prussia, had the greatest chance of profiting from a European settlement, right from the outset of negotiations. While Britain, Austria and France pursued no open policy of territorial expansion, Prussia had announced very early on her intention to annex the Kingdom of Saxony, which, to the very last, had supported Napoleon's cause and therefore deserved to be severely punished. According to the contemporary interpretation of international law, the victorious powers were free to decide on Saxony's fate. With the annexation of Saxony, Prussia sought not only to enlarge her own territory but also to acquire prosperous industries.

Russia, for her part, supported Prussian aspirations, and this for quite obvious reasons. The Tsar wanted to become King of Poland, and thereby consolidate Russia's grip on that unhappy country, but the other powers would not have any of it. The Final Act of the Congress legalised the compromise between conflicting aspirations. Neither of the greedy powers got all that it was after. Russia gained only some additional parts of Polish territory, and only on condition that she grant more autonomy to her Polish lands. Prussia acquired two-fifths of the Saxon territory, which she incorporated as her new province of Saxony. In addition, as a sort of compensation for her restraint and eventual retreat in the Saxon question, and as a reward for her stand against Napoleon, Prussia also gained, rather unexpectedly, substantial territories further west: Westphalia, the northern parts of the Rhineland and the Saar region. With these gains Prussia doubled her territory; in terms of territorial aggrandisement she was clearly the main beneficiary of the Congress.

Prussia's expansion in western Germany was dictated by more far-reaching considerations on the part of the victorious powers. Apparently the negotiations in Vienna had been conducted in front of a huge map, with whose help Europe was redesigned without any serious consideration of the wishes of its people, let alone its nations. The concept of a stable European balance of power, so much in the minds of the diplomats at the Congress, demanded security against a restless France on the one hand, and the national aspirations of the peoples on the other. Consequently, in return for the northern parts of the Rhineland and the Saar region, Prussia was supposed to hold 'the watch on the Rhine' against French expansionism in some distant future. Along with the newly consolidated states of Baden and Württemberg further up the Rhine, Prussia was to form an impenetrable barrier against French ambitions in Central Europe. The barrier on France's eastern border was extended as far as the Mediterranean by giving Switzerland the status of 'eternal neutrality' and creating the new Kingdom of Piedmont-Sardinia in northern Italy with its capital in Turin. The northern end of the strategic barrier for the containment of France was also provided by a new state: in this case the United Netherlands, comprising Holland and Belgium as well as Luxemburg in a dynastic union.

The settlement of the Congress of Vienna undoubtedly strengthened Prussia's position in Germany and, probably unintentionally, weakened Austria's. Austria confirmed her stronghold in northern Italy by regaining Lombardy and the Venetian territory which Napoleon had removed from Habsburg rule. In addition she was accorded Dalmatia and some Polish

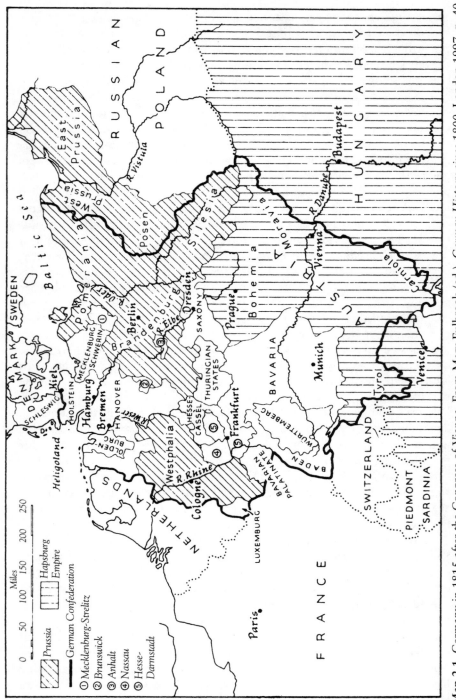

Map 2.1 Germany in 1815 after the Congress of Vienna. From Mary Fulbrook (ed.), *German History since 1800*, London 1997, p. 40.

land. As a consequence of these territorial gains Austria's centre of gravity shifted visibly to south-eastern and southern Europe. Her presence in Germany became less prominent than in the past, the empire less German in composition and outlook. Prussia, on the other hand, increasingly took over the role of the major power in northern and western Germany. From 1815 onwards, Prussia became a Central European power more than ever before. For the German Question Prussia's upgrading as a German power, her political dynamism in the years to come, and Austria's waning influence in Germany turned out to be highly significant. Another fact not yet recognisable in 1815 was also to work to Prussia's advantage as the century progressed. With the unexpected acquisition of Westphalia and the northern Rhineland she had gained the seedbed of industrialisation in Central Europe, which, from about 1840 onwards, became its industrial heartland. This, perhaps more than anything else, helped to tip the scales in Prussia's favour when the German Question was once more on the political agenda in the second half of the nineteenth century.

However, before following this development in more detail we must have a closer look at the handling of the German Question at the Congress. The reorganisation of Germany had, of course, to be based on historical preconditions and political decisions that preceded the Congress. The work of the Congress was far from being a restructuring of Germany from scratch. Rather the reorganisation of German-speaking Central Europe was a mixture of new elements with traditional structures known from the defunct Holy Roman Empire and those which had emerged from the short-lived Confederation of the Rhine. At the same time, any settlement of the German Question in Vienna had to take account of the increased political self-confidence and the sensitivities of a newly won sovereignty now shown by the minor German states which, for good reasons, were all represented at the Congress. The German states and their rulers were understandably quite unwilling to surrender one iota of their sovereignty. This would have deprived them of the spoils so recently gained at the expense of the German body politic. The reaction of the great powers, too, proved to be highly negative when nationally minded men such as the Prussian reformer Baron vom Stein, the journalist Joseph Görres or the writer and political agitator Ernst Moritz Arndt publicly suggested that the Congress should resurrect the old German Empire, though now in the shape of a modern nation-state with a strong central executive.

Most notably, the two great powers to the east and west of Europe, Russia and Britain, thought that a German nation-state based on unity and liberty would concentrate power in the centre of the continent in a way not conducive to its future well-being. Another interested party, France, was determined in any event to follow her traditional policy of keeping the heart of Europe as weak as possible and allowing nothing more than a loose association of German states. And the two major German powers, Austria and Prussia, both members of the European pentarchy, also preferred independence and shunned, for a variety of reasons, the unpredictable entanglements that would inevitably accompany the national solution to the German Question. A democratic nation-state was, in any case, anathema to them, though neither, of course, wanted a power vacuum in Germany.

As a compromise between the idea of a revived German Empire, the almost absurd political fragmentation of Central Europe in a microcosmos of small states as before 1806, and the political exigencies of 1815, the Congress created a new organisation for Germany. This was the German Confederation (*Deutscher Bund*) within the boundaries of the extinct Holy Roman Empire. When the diplomats who redrew the map of Europe in Vienna were called upon to answer the tricky question 'what is Germany?', they reverted rather pragmatically to historical precedent: the geographical shape of the Old Empire which still lingered on in the minds of many people. This meant that the boundaries of the Holy Roman Empire retained a political and international significance until as late as the dissolution of the German Confederation in 1866. Naturally, Austria and Germany became members of the Confederation, which from now on was increasingly equated with 'Germany'. However, as European great powers they both possessed territories outside the Confederation. For Austria this included Hungary, Transylvania, Galicia, Croatia, Slovenia, Dalmatia, Lombardy, Venetia and Istria, and for Prussia East and West Prussia as well as the province of Posen. There was one novelty with notable consequences in the years to come, namely that the number of member states of the Confederation was considerably lower than that of the Holy Roman Empire. The overall pattern of state frontiers definitely represented a significant improvement over the chaotic patchwork of sovereignties and jurisdictions that had characterised the old order.

From 1815 onwards, the former middle-sized members of the Confederation of the Rhine such as Bavaria, Saxony, Württemberg and the Grand Duchy of Baden made up a new group of comparatively large states in the German body politic which were stubbornly to pursue their independence *vis-à-vis* the two German great powers. These states, not yet fully consolidated, became known as the 'Third Germany', referring to their somewhat precarious position between Austria and Prussia. In the nineteenth century, and even up to the present, they continued to uphold the concept of federalism in German political life and state organisation. This very distinct group of middle states was further strengthened by the former electorate of Hanover, which was elevated to the status of a kingdom at the Congress of Vienna, and by Hesse-Kassel and the Grand Duchy of Hesse-Darmstadt. The latter benefited politically from its close family ties to the Russian Romanovs. In addition to these middle states the German Confederation comprised a number of smaller ones such as Brunswick, Oldenburg, the two Mecklenburgs, and the tiny Lippe-Detmold, as well as the so-called free cities of Hamburg, Bremen, Lübeck and Frankfurt am

Main, which still sported the now rather meaningless label of 'Free Imperial City'.

How, then, did the German Confederation, the brainchild of the Congress of Vienna, answer the German Question? How was it seen in a European perspective? On close inspection, it becomes apparent that the answer must be divided into two parts because the German Confederation represented an answer both for the whole of Europe and for the Germans with their familiar idea of a Germany that was fragmented, but also somehow politically united. As the name clearly indicated, the new Confederation was a loosely connected association of states which, to all intents and purposes, were independent and sovereign. The German Confederation was by no means a federal state which accorded its constituent members a certain degree of autonomy on minor questions but transferred all major decisions to a central government. On the contrary, it had no common government and no head of state which would have made it an active player on the European stage. This was a clear signal that the diplomats and statesmen at the Congress of Vienna did not intend to create a strong, unified German state in the centre of Europe. This was, after all, neither the intention of the great powers as the representatives of Europe, nor, at a lower level, of the two major German powers, Austria and Prussia, nor of the multitude of German middle and small states which were jealously guarding their sovereignty. The common denominator which all parties willingly accepted was thus opposition to a centralised German nation-state.

The results of the deliberations on the German Question were legally fixed by the Congress of Vienna in the Act of German Confederation (*Deutsche Bundesakte*). Signed by the then thirty-nine German states and free cities on 8 June 1815, the Act was in effect a resolution of the Congress and thereby an element of international law. To underline this legal quality, on the following day, 9 June 1815, it was made an integral part of the Final Act of the Congress. The main purpose of the 'indissoluble' German Confederation was to guarantee the security of all its thirty-nine members against external and internal dangers. The preamble of the German Confederation stated that the members had agreed 'to unite in a stable union' as they were convinced of 'the advantages which resulted from its firm and lasting bond for the security and independence of Germany, and the tranquillity and balance of Europe'. Against external aggression the members were committed to a common defence policy. Due to the sovereignty of its members the Confederation was, to all intents and purposes, virtually unable to do more than react to external aggression. Only in the event of a unanimous resolution of all members could the German Confederation declare war and actively intervene abroad. This was the case in 1848 when the Confederation asked Prussia to go to war against Denmark in its name and to provide the necessary military means. The Danish War was, in fact, the only war the Confederation ever conducted. In

Act of German Confederation, 8 June 1815

I. General Provisions

1. The Sovereign Princes and free cities of Germany, including Their Majesties the Emperor of Austria and the Kings of Prussia, Denmark and the Netherlands, namely the Emperor of Austria and the King of Prussia for those of their possessions which formerly belonged to the German Empire, the King of Denmark for Holstein, the King of the Netherlands for the Grand Duchy of Luxemburg, unite in a perpetual league which shall be called the German Confederation.
2. The object thereof is the maintenance of the internal and external security of Germany, and of the independence and inviolability of the different German states.
3. The members of the Confederation have, as such, equal rights; they bind themselves all equally to maintain the Act of Confederation.
4. The affairs of the Confederation shall be managed by a Federal Diet in which all the members of the Confederation . . . shall each have one vote either severally, or as representing more than one member, as follows . . .
5. Austria has the presidency of the Diet of the Confederation; every member of the Confederation has the power of making proposals and to bring them under discussion; and the president is bound to submit such proposals for deliberation within a period to be fixed . . .
11. All members of the Confederation engage to assist in protecting not only all Germany but every separate State of the Confederation against any attack, and reciprocally to guarantee to each other the whole of their possessions included within the Confederation. After war has been once declared by the Confederation, no member may enter into separate negotiations with the enemy, nor conclude a separate armistice or peace. Although the members possess the right of alliance of every kind, yet they bind themselves to enter into no treaties hostile to the security of the Confederation or of that of any confederate State. The members of the Confederation also bind themselves not to make war on each other under any pretext, nor to decide their differences by force, but to bring them under consideration and decision at the Diet . . .

G. A. Kertesz (ed.), *Documents in the Political History of the European Continent 1815–1939*, Oxford 1968, pp. 61–3.

the Crimean War of 1853–55 Prussia and Austria concluded a defensive alliance which was sanctioned by the Confederation. In the Austro-Italian War of 1850 the Confederation maintained strict neutrality. According to Friedrich von Gentz, Metternich's adviser and the official secretary of the Congress, the German Confederation was strong enough for the defensive, but too weak for the offensive.[9]

Its military weakness apart, the German Confederation was no subject of international law. This became immediately apparent when, after Napoleon's last stand and defeat at Waterloo on 18 June 1815, a new peace treaty with France had been concluded (20 November 1815). It was negotiated and decided by the great powers amongst themselves, i.e. without the participation of the German Confederation. Such a possibility was not even vaguely discussed, let alone given serious consideration. This is precisely the reason why the German Confederation has rightly been called 'a passive ordering factor in the European state system'.[10] Imanuel Geiss went so far as to speak of the continuity of the German power vacuum.[11] This was perhaps correct, but no other answer to the German Question seemed to be feasible at Vienna, given the international situation and the specific interests of the powers. The nascent national movement in Germany failed to appreciate this. However, the simple reason that the Congress of Vienna dashed all national aspirations in Central Europe is why it was later seen in such a negative light by nationalist historians in Germany. Today, its image has changed. Historians now tend to point to the fact that the German Confederation was constructed in the way it was in order to maintain peace and stability in Europe. They point to its 'forward-looking' characteristics.

> It 'anticipated' modern supranational entities such as the United Nations and the European Union. Moreover, the Confederation succeeded in reconciling a robust and peaceful solution of the 'German question' with the need to meet the security needs of the European great powers in the then-foreseeable future. Viewed from the perspective of our own day, this was a formidable achievement.[12]

Like a leaden weight the Confederation was to prevent the centre of Europe from becoming a restless and potent source of aggression and war. Thus it had both a German and a European dimension. This was undoubtedly its fundamental purpose but in the eyes of many contemporaries also its main weakness in the emerging age of nation-states and power politics.

Ultimately, the rigidity of the Confederation, the lack of any perspective of change towards a national solution, may, after all, be considered as the main drawback of the Viennese arrangements for Germany. In other areas too, where the German Confederation could have played an active role, nothing happened. Neither in legal questions nor in matters of trade and industry were any new solutions put fowards for the whole Confederation in the following years. In short, during the half-century of its existence, the German Confederation completely failed to turn into an organisation that paved the way for a united Germany. It did not even prove capable of strengthening the economic and legal ties of the nation. The sovereignty of the particularist states, perpetually and jealously guarded, blocked even modest moves towards a strengthening of common bonds. And in any case, why should the Confederation become more national? It was clearly a European construct: amongst its members were three foreign monarchs with their German possessions, which made it a unique creation in international law. These foreign sovereigns were the King of England as King of Hanover until Victoria's accession in 1837, the King of Denmark as Duke of Holstein and Lauenburg until 1864, and the King of the Netherlands as Grand Duke of Luxemburg until 1866.

The population of the German Confederation, too, was far from representing an ethnically homogeneous nation, the ideal of the national movements as the basis of a nation-state. The Confederation's population rather resembled that of a multinational empire: Poles lived in the eastern provinces of Prussia, Czechs in Bohemia and Moravia, Slovenes and Italians in Austria, Walloons and Luxemburgers on its western borders. However, as in earlier centuries, the wishes and aspirations of the peoples concerned were not taken into consideration, though the diplomats at the Congress of Vienna did at least have a vague feeling that national aspirations, national tensions and conflicts would play an increasingly important part in the future. Still, they proved to be unable or unwilling to search for political solutions which might diffuse potentially dangerous antagonisms that were already visible on the horizon. The Prussian envoy at the Congress, the brilliant Wilhelm von Humboldt, who had successfully reformed the system of education in Prussia, reportedly held the firm conviction that 'in the long term, no one could prevent Germany becoming, in one way or another, *one* state and *one* nation'.[13]

Let us now look at how the Confederation provided an answer for Germany. Frankfurt, the old Imperial City where the Emperors of the defunct Holy Roman Empire used to be crowned, was destined to be the centre of the German Confederation, not its capital. In Frankfurt am Main the Diet of the Confederation (*Bundestag*) met regularly. It was not a democratically elected parliament, but more a conference of delegates who were appointed and instructed by the member state whom they served. The most famous delegate ever appointed to the Frankfurt Federal Diet was Otto von Bismarck, the future Prussian Prime Minister and German Chancellor, the founder of the Reich of 1871. He served there, as the representative of the Prussian government, from 1851 to 1859. The Austrian delegate chaired *ex officio* because Austria was the permanent presiding power of the German Confederation. Her political pre-eminence in Central Europe was never disputed, at least not until the mid-nineteenth century. Since time immemorial the Habsburg dynasty had been considered Europe's most distinguished royal family and its state the leading German power. The Diet's structure was definitely a clear reference to the old Holy Roman Empire with a Habsburg Emperor at its head. In the nineteenth century, however, it was much more important for Austria to institutionalise visibly her traditional pre-eminence in Germany. It was a position which was increasingly questioned by Prussia, Austria's fast-growing junior partner. When Bismarck became Prussia's delegate in Frankfurt he angered the Austrians by demonstratively behaving like an equal partner. Wherever there was an opportunity, Bismarck made it

Fig. 2.1 Meeting of the Federal Diet of the German Confederation in Frankfurt, 1816. Reproduced with permission from Peter Berglar, *Wilhelm von Humboldt*, Reinbek 1970, p. 120 (Rowohlt Verlag; Historia Photo/Bad Sachsa).

clear to all that Prussia no longer accepted Austria's traditional political role in German affairs.

The Federal Diet could convene either in closed council (*Engerer Rat*) or as a full assembly (*Plenum*). The closed council consisted of the eleven larger German states, all of whom had one vote. The smaller states shared six votes between them. The closed council was where all the major decisions were made, while the full assembly was only able to sanction them. Between 1815 and 1866 the full assembly met only sixteen times in all. Changes in the constitution of the German Confederation were only possible by unanimous vote – a hopeless endeavour since a single small state with a tiny population, like Liechtenstein or the Free City of Bremen, could easily block any motion of this sort. Thus, for half a century, the constitution of one of Europe's most populous 'states' was never altered or amended. In 1816 the population of the German Confederation stood at 32.7 million (excluding Austria, 21.1 million), in 1865 at 52 million (excluding Austria, 33.8 million). Only Russia had a larger population (86 million in 1871).

It was obvious right from its foundation that the German Confederation's well-being and strength depended on close cooperation between Austria and Prussia, its two most powerful members. As soon as these two states saw each other as rivals, which was mostly or increasingly the case, the German Confederation was almost totally paralysed. Whenever they agreed on an issue or a common strategy they had their way. Consequently it is only fair to say that the Confederation's oft-lamented weakness originated to a very large extent from the Prusso-Austrian rivalry, much to the regret of the nascent German national movement.

The German Confederation did not only lack a common head of state. It also possessed neither a central executive, nor a common army, legislature, administration or judiciary. Practically all the rights of sovereignty remained in the hands of the member governments. A contemporary historian therefore emphasised the fact that the supranational German Confederation represented 'a state of peace in a much higher sense', for the simple reason that it was not founded on force, or the threat of force, but on law.[14] However, later and more nationalistically minded German historians saw it in a different light. They had a more negative image of the Confederation as the creation of foreign powers and against the political currents of the age. Heinrich von Treitschke, for example, the popular protagonist of nationalism in Wilhelmine Germany, refused to see in the Federal Diet more than a 'big stock exchange for Europe's subaltern diplomatic gossip'.[15]

Not only nationally minded Germans were disappointed by the German Confederation, but liberals and democrats too. They had hoped for a liberalisation of political life in Central Europe and the creation of a modern constitutional state for the whole of Germany. In Vienna, this option had been discussed by the peacemakers. But the European statesmen at the Congress wanted to create the pre-conditions for stability and order in Europe. This had soon emerged as the overriding conservative interest. With the experience of the revolutionary and Napoleonic years behind them, the diplomatic efforts were directed at the suppression of circumstances which could rekindle unrest and revolution. Once accepted, this concept did not subsequently allow any concessions to democratic, liberal and constitutional ambitions, let alone national aspirations. All these represented 'forces of change' which were opposed by the 'forces of resilience', with Metternich at their helm. Yet the reform movement that had sprung up under the impact of the events in France and during French occupation had not ended with Napoleon's downfall, and the peacemakers were well aware of this. They hoped to meet the expectations of a freer, more democratic Central Europe by making one constitutional concession. Article 13 of the Federal Act of 8 June 1815 had stipulated that all member states of the German Confederation should have modern constitutions, which contemporaries hoped would protect their citizens from arbitrary acts by the authorities and pave the way for a democratic future. However, the reactionary governments found ways and means to dash any hopes of a new departure in constitutional matters. Only the states in southern Germany, where the political example of Western Europe had made the deepest impression, promulgated constitutions which established representative assemblies. They were elected by the propertied classes and their assent was required for the enactment of legislation.

Against this background some of the fundamental problems of the German Question in the years to come were already apparent in the German Confederation from its inception. First, the statesmen at the Congress of Vienna were unable to create a political order in Central Europe that would make change and reform possible and could adapt flexibly to the political aspirations of the age, constantly gaining strength as the century progressed. Only a few of the states in southern Germany acquired constitutions that contained liberal elements. Second, large national minorities lived within the territory of the Confederation. They represented an enormous handicap for the establishment of a homogeneous nation-state as envisaged in 1848–49. Third, the two European great powers, Austria and Prussia, were members of the Confederation, which paralysed it more and more as the rivalry between Vienna and Berlin gradually escalated. Whatever small potential for political development the Confederation's constitution may have offered was thus increasingly prevented from coming into effect. Fourth, the Confederation held an intermediate position between a liberalising and industrialising West and an autocratic and agrarian East, as well as a key function and significance for the balance of power in Europe. This rather odd situation in the heart of Europe was bound to create tensions and conflicts. German progressive intellectual and political culture was largely orientated towards Western Europe. Political thinkers and reformers looked towards England, France, Belgium, Switzerland and even the United States. However, there were numerous factors that weakened Western influences, particularly tsarist Russia's shadow over the political elite in Berlin. Karl Marx once went so far as to call Prussia polemically and rather viciously 'Russia's jackal'. Among the factors which drew Prussia, even Metternich's Austria and some of the smaller German states, towards autocratic Russia was the strengthening of their monarchies with the Tsar's help in 1814–15 and the close family ties between the Romanovs and, for example, the Hohenzollerns and the princely houses in Württemberg and Hesse-Darmstadt. Finally, the structure of landlordism in the agrarian sector, especially the remnants of feudalism in the eastern parts of Prussia, also pointed to close cooperation with economically backward Russia.

In any case, the German Confederation was the brainchild of the Congress of Vienna and thus of Europe. In the early years of its existence it became a stable, as well as manipulative factor in European politics. It never attained, and in fact was never intended to attain, the status of an active player on the European stage. In the 'Concert of Europe', whose conductor was Metternich until the revolutions of 1848, it was not even allowed to play the second violin. The major European powers, for a great variety of reasons, had once again agreed that Europe was best served by a weak centre. The only power not content with this state of affairs soon turned out to be Prussia. Since the 1830s, and then increasingly in the 1850s, she had come to see the German Confederation as a potential area of political advancement to the greater glory of Prussian power and influence. Berlin's policy eventually aimed at two intertwined goals: to destroy Austria's pre-eminence in Central Europe by dissolving the German Confederation which was blocking Prussia's ambitions. In order to achieve this Prussia needed at least the tacit consent of the other European powers since she was not yet powerful enough to recast the German Question on her own. The events accompanying the revolutions of 1848 and the work of the German National Assembly at the Paulskirche in Frankfurt were to show that Europe would always have something to say when the German Question was asked once again.

|3|

Economic progress and political failure

For a long time after the settlement of Vienna the German Question remained dormant. The politics of restoration and consolidation pursued by almost all the European states prevented the slightest change in the direction of a policy which would eventually lead to the creation of a liberal German nation-state, as demanded by the national movement. However, although the loosely knit German Confederation seemed to mark the limit of what would be tolerated politically by the European powers in the centre of Europe, the idea of a united Germany constructed according to the progressive thinking of the time did not entirely fade away. On the contrary, as Greece (1830) and Belgium (1831) gained their independence and the Poles tried to liberate themselves from Russia by means of a revolution (1830), the national movement in Germany became stronger and more public in its agitation. Thus, soon after the end of the Congress of Vienna, the Berlin philosopher Henrik Steffens posed the question: 'Where is Germany, for which we are asked to fight? It lives in our souls. Show us where to find it or we will be forced to find it ourselves!'[1]

The German Customs Union (*Deutscher Zollverein*), in particular, finally gave a new impetus and urgency to those who wanted a revision of the 1815 settlement of the German Question. The creation of the Customs Union added, in their view, a new dimension to the German Question, namely an economic one. At long last the winds of change began to blow once more, and before the century had reached its mid-point even the Germans were encouraged to attempt a revolution. The revolution of 1848 and its political outcome, the Frankfurt National Assembly, were supposed to compensate for what, in 1815, had deliberately been denied to German nationalists, democrats and liberals: adjustment of the national and constitutional development in Germany to the conditions in Western Europe where unified and liberal nation-states with elected parliaments represented progress and modernity. The Customs Union of 1834 and the National Assembly of 1848–49 both revived the German Question and answered it in a way that was to have significant long-term consequences. Europe, on the other hand, did not play an active or high-profile part when the German Question returned to the political agenda. Indirectly, however, Western

Europe provided the impetus and models for reformers in Germany which gradually helped to set the wheels in motion again: the July Revolution of 1830 in France, for example, or liberal parliamentary politics in Belgium and Britain. All this was eagerly studied in Germany, and Britain and the newly created Belgium in particular were recommended as progressive political systems that should be emulated.

By 1830 at the latest there were forces within the German Confederation, especially among the educated middle classes and students, who were questioning whether Germany could or should not open herself up to liberalism, constitutionalism, freedom of the press, freedom of association and equal suffrage for all men. Metternich, the stern guarantor of the Vienna settlement, invariably gave a negative response. Nevertheless, questions such as those levelled by the nationalists and liberals became increasingly topical and urgent as the situation in Central Europe gradually changed.

Such changes took place most visibly on three inter-communicating levels. First, impulses originated from the liberal and national movement that was gaining in strength in the 1830s and 1840s and was organised in Singers', Gymnasts' and Riflemen's Associations. This was, so to speak, the ideological level. Second, political changes followed almost automatically from the remarkable recovery of Prussia as a European power after 1815. This was the political level. And, third, debate on the German Question was provoked in particular by the foundation of the German Customs Union, the decisive new beginning in the sphere of economics and economic policy. This was the economic level.

In retrospect, it was probably Prussia's changing position as a European and German power and the foundation of the Customs Union which had the greatest impact on the resurgence of the German Question. Prussia's rise was so rapid and effective that her economic power already outshone that of Austria by the middle of the century. To all intents and purposes she had now superseded the one German power that had traditionally been by far the strongest politically and economically. The Presiding Power of the German Confederation, Austria, now had to face the fact that her junior partner, Prussia, had become her challenger and later her conqueror when, in 1866, Prussia expelled Austria from Germany and united Central Europe within one state under Prussian hegemony. This was quite an extraordinary sequence of events, a growth of power and stroke of good luck for a state which had hitherto been considered Europe's weakest great power. Only West Germany's rise from destruction and political impotence after 1945 might present a remote parallel.

Prussia's rapid rise to become Germany's leading power also had something to do with the fact that the Congress of Vienna and its territorial arrangements had made her a German power to a much greater degree than had ever been the case before 1815. With the acquisition of Westphalia and the northern Rhineland, Prussia had become a state with two centres, one traditionally in the east, and a new one in the west. The two parts of post-1815 Prussia were separated by non-Prussian territory. In north Germany especially, small sovereign states lay between the Prussian territories or were surrounded by Prussian lands. From the point of view of Berlin this was, in general, a highly unsatisfactory situation because Prussia thus lacked any intrinsic coherence. So, after 1815 geography more or less forced Prussia to focus her attention on north Germany and on slowly 'growing into' Germany. As a consequence of the territorial settlements of the Congress, Prussia quite unexpectedly found herself in a position which allowed the 'national option' to be considered, i.e. pursuit of a policy of uniting Germany under Prussian leadership. The Habsburg monarchy, on the other hand, had lost this option by its territorial gains in the Balkans and northern Italy, which re-enforced the multinational character of its vast empire. Austria 'grew out' of Germany by shifting southwards and consequently becoming a state whose interest and involvement in German affairs gradually, but perceptibly, diminished. After 1815 Austria's *raison d'être* made it practically impossible for her to consider the national option since this would have meant jeopardising her very existence as a pre-modern multinational state.

Prussia's interest in consolidating her newly won position in northern and western Germany had led her to propose, as early as during the Congress of Vienna, that the Federal Act that established the German Confederation should include clauses on a common customs and trade policy. Ultimately, the Prussian proposal would have made the German Confederation a huge free trade area with a common currency and common economic policy. However, the proposal was not adopted and Article 19 of the Federal Act only stipulated that the Federal Diet should deliberate on questions of trade and traffic; decisions binding all member states had to be based on a unanimous vote anyway. Given the diverse interests of the member states this meant, in plain language, that the German Confederation would not provide the overall framework for an economic union of the German states. 'The economic diversity of Germany', commented the economic historian Harold James, 'and the difficulty of moving goods and people, gave a strikingly obvious indication of the absence of unity.'[2]

Still, partial solutions were not excluded and Prussia was quick to seize the opportunity to make the most of what the Congress of Vienna had missed, or was not willing to provide. It soon became clear that the German Customs Union of 1834 laid the foundation for Prussia's growing economic and political power in Central Europe. Without provoking any serious resistance from the European powers, the Customs Union greatly helped Prussia to manoeuvre Austria out of Germany, to weaken the bonds of the German Confederation and to lay the economic foundations of the German nation-state in the shape of the Reich. With the benefit of hindsight one might rightly say that in Central Europe economic nation-building preceded and then accompanied political nation- and state-building.

All this proved to be a development in Prussia's favour which, in the early nineteenth century, not even the wisest Prussian politicians could have foreseen. Initially there was nothing more than Prussia's pragmatic and understandable interest in integrating her diverse territories by creating a unified economic and customs system to facilitate trade. The Prussian customs act was passed on 26 May 1818. In retrospect, this turned out to be a crucial measure that paved the way for future developments and an important step on the long path towards the German nation-state. Those who devised the customs act certainly had more immediate purposes and more practical considerations on their minds. Only later did historians glorify the act as allegedly the first step towards German unity.

Prussia's customs and trade policy was initially extended to some of the small German states either adjoining Prussian territory or forming enclaves within it. For them, close economic cooperation with Prussia was virtually unavoidable. Yet the larger states, especially in southern Germany, strove to remain outside Prussia's economic orbit. States like Hanover, Saxony, Brunswick, or the small principalities of Thuringia feared diminution of their sovereignty and independence should they yield to Prussia's economic superiority. Austria and France supported their stand, and also encouraged Bavaria and Württemberg to go ahead with their own customs union in 1827–28.

The material success of the Prussian Customs Union of 1818, however, soon put an end to all attempts to escape the dynamism emanating from this new and fast-growing economic power in northern Germany. Moreover, when in 1830 the July Revolution in France once again gave rise to a general feeling of political insecurity among the ruling elites, the German states, with very few exceptions, succumbed to Prussia's wooing and agreed to form an economic community with Prussia. Thus the German Customs Union came into being on 1 January 1834. By about 1842 twenty-eight of the thirty-nine member states of the German Confederation belonged to the Customs Union, the most notable non-members being the Kingdom of Hanover (with its British sovereign until Victoria's accession to the throne in 1837) and the major Hanseatic ports such as Hamburg and Bremen. Even after 1834 Prussia still had no proper access to the North Sea.

All this activity on the economic level makes it clear that in the years after the Congress of Vienna the German Question primarily appeared as a question of economic policy in all its aspects. Historians were later to argue that after 1815 clever and forward-looking Prussian politicians were well aware that, on the political level, the German Question had reached a point of virtual stagnation. In Heinrich von Treitschke's view,

> the greatest act of national policy in that long period of peace [after 1815] was exclusively the work of governments and their officials, and it was carried out without the participation . . . of the mass of the nation. . . . Mars and Mercury are the stars which principally determine

the destiny of states in this century of labour. The army and the trade policy of the Hohenzollerns form the two claims on which rests the Imperial dignity of our ruling dynasty.[3]

After the political *status quo* was cemented, Prussian politics had consistently, and indeed realistically, pursued the concept of preparing the ground for greater German unity by practically anticipating economic unity and thus avoiding a direct political confrontation with Europe. With hindsight, this is an exciting, albeit highly debatable proposition which gives great credit to the Prussian leadership.

Grave doubts remain as to whether the politicians of the time did in fact plan developments in Germany in such a long-term perspective and with such a clear objective in mind. In many ways it seems more likely that the politicians simply reacted to the new patchwork shape of Prussia created in 1815 and the demands of incipient industrialisation. Both forced the government in Berlin to initiate certain economic measures which, at first, were only to meet internal needs but were then, in a second step, directed towards including Prussia's immediate neighbours in a wider economic area. The aftermath of the Prussian customs act of 1818 had amply proved the great integrative power of what were apparently purely economic measures. And Prussia's growing economic power was then enough to persuade other German states to seek closer ties with Prussia. In short, the German Customs Union of 1834 was clearly the result of a maelstrom effect which, in the long run, the other German states were unable to withstand, even though it was not always what they wanted. Yet however successful the Union was, contemporaries continued to draw a distinction between economic and political developments. Prussia and Austria, as well as the smaller and medium-sized German states, continued to uphold the loose federal structure of Germany and the sovereignty of the members of the German Confederation in the years after 1815 and likewise after 1834. For the time being even the government in Berlin remained opposed to all plans aimed at German political unity without the explicit or, for that matter, tacit consent of Europe. In official rhetoric the economy and economic unification had nothing to do with politics. The existence of the German Confederation, in the shape given to it in 1815, was not called into question by anyone.

One has, of course, to ask why Austria, which did not join the German Customs Union, had not tried to prevent its very foundation in 1834. It is a difficult question to answer. Metternich, it seems, failed to realise the significance of the Prussian customs act of 1818, a modest and primarily bureaucratic beginning of the progress towards the Customs Union. This misjudgement Metternich shared with almost all contemporaries. Austrian acceptance of the Prussian initiative on the customs issue also had something to do with the fact that at first it was considered an internal matter for Prussia and of no concern to the government in Vienna. By

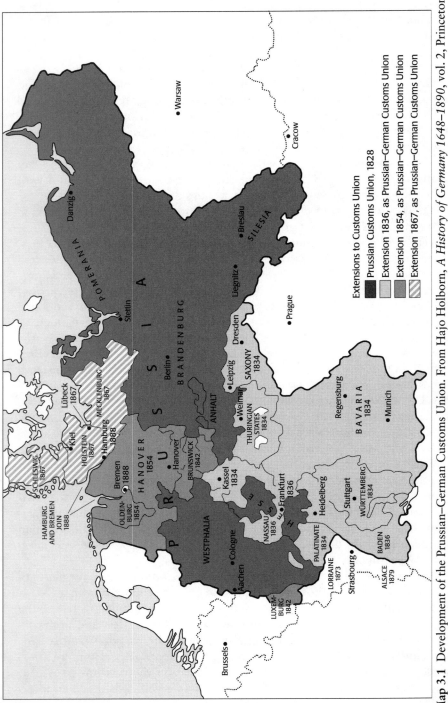
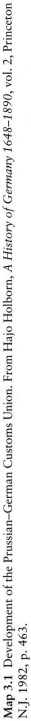

Map 3.1 Development of the Prussian–German Customs Union. From Hajo Holborn, *A History of Germany 1648–1890*, vol. 2, Princeton N.J. 1982, p. 463.

1830, with the unmistakable success of Prussia's customs policy within
the framework of the German Confederation, Austria had, to all intents
and purposes, missed the opportunity to intervene effectively and stop a
development which she had clearly failed to take sufficient notice of.
When, in 1840, Metternich eventually attempted to establish a closer relationship between Austria and the German Customs Union, the Emperor
refused to allow him to lobby Austrian industrialists. They opposed
Austria's joining the Union because they feared Prussian economic competition and considered Austria's markets for manufactured products to be
primarily in the Balkans and in Italy. Then, when Austria reapplied for
membership of the Union, Prussia pointed to the irreconcilability of the
high-tariff policy followed by Austria and the free-trade policy pursued
by the *Zollverein*.

The only conclusion to be drawn is that Austria, in effect, tolerated the
German Customs Union with Prussia as its inspirational leader, and in later
years was prevented from joining it. However, the other European powers
too, who in Vienna had subscribed to the principle of no political change in
the German Confederation without common consent, put up no real resistance to the foundation of the Customs Union. After all, why should be it
of any concern to them? Seen from a distance, the Vienna settlement of
1815 still seemed to be intact. In the British, French and Russian view the
Customs Union was purely the German Confederation's internal affair and
did not in any way affect the territorial *status quo* as devised in 1815.
Certainly, there were some reservations in 1834, but it did not take the
European powers long to come to terms with the Customs Union. Britain,
at that time still the undisputed 'workshop of the world', saw it rather
benevolently as an important trade partner. And why should she turn
against the formation of a larger economic unit in Central Europe which
proclaimed free trade as one of its priorities and repeatedly claimed Adam
Smith's thinking as the ideological basis of its very existence? France, too,
urged the Germans to band together to form their own self-contained
national economy.

In the end, the Customs Union turned out to be a dynamic economic
confederation within a rather static political confederation. Of the thirty-
nine member of the German Confederation in 1842, twenty-eight had
joined the Customs Union, while eleven chose to remain outside it. In fact,
with its foundation the German Confederation gradually started to be
eroded. Metternich, who very soon sensed what was going on, once spoke
with sharp insight of the Union as 'a state within a state' which was upsetting the balance of power in Germany and promoting the 'highly dangerous
idea of German unity'.[4] And, in a way, this was true. In political terms, the
German Confederation represented the face of the present directed towards
the past which was paralysed by the jealously guarded sovereignty of the
German states and their political rivalries.

On the other hand, the German Customs Union looked towards the future. This is how contemporaries saw it. Its foundation coincided with the take-off of industrialisation and the building of railways in Germany. The first German railway began operating in 1835. By 1848 there were over 5,000 km of track. According to Harold James, in 1870 'the railway had been accepted as both the most striking embodiment of the idea of the modern world and the instrument of national integration'.[5] Nevertheless, at the time of its foundation, hardly anyone perceived the Customs Union as the natural forerunner of the German nation-state which, after the futile attempts of 1848–49, finally came into being in 1871. This was certainly not the political objective that inspired the creation of the Union. In the view of contemporaries in the first half of the nineteenth century, Austria would definitely be a partner when 'Germany' or the German Confederation was given a new political shape. However, from 1834 onwards, the course of events clearly favoured Prussia's growing dominance in Germany, and at the same time weakened Austria's influence. In the internal debate on the German Question and its future settlement, the balance, at first almost imperceptibly, was slowly shifting. A modern historian concludes:

> The single outstanding event in all-German politics of these decades was the founding of the German Zollverein. In terms of the development of a German national economy, as well as the history of the formation of a national state and of the struggle for domination between Prussia and Austria, it marked the beginning of a new era. . . . The Zollverein was not concluded by the governments out of 'nationalist' interests, nor even for political motives. The guiding factors were particularist, and in good part fiscal interests. But the Zollverein broke through the German system installed by the Congress of Vienna in 1815, of this there is no doubt. . . . Certainly, the Zollverein did combine the idea of an objective national amalgamation and Prussian hegemony, and was a precursor of the later *kleindeutsch* nation-state. Objectively speaking, the Zollverein would inevitably promote the formation of such a national state. It provided everyone with an alternative model of a workable federation.[6]

Thomas Nipperdey calls the German Customs Union, which formally existed until 1871, 'the single outstanding event in all-German politics' in the years after the Congress of Vienna, but one has to realise that it was later overshadowed by the revolution of 1848 and the convening of the elected German National Assembly in Frankfurt am Main. The National Assembly debated the shape and inner structure of the German nation-state which then, in 1848–49, finally seemed about to materialise. For Europe, this prospect was reason enough to intervene once again in the German Question, more than thirty years after the Congress of Vienna and this time, as before, in a fairly forceful way. Once again the German Question seemed to have taken on a dimension that forced Europe to act. So, when the

German Question was asked between 1848 and 1851, the answer was not provided by the Germans alone as it was in the years around 1834. The European statesmen found themselves confronted anew with the task they had faced in 1815: to settle the German Question in such a way that it would not disturb the 'tranquillity' of the continent.

In Central Europe the revolution of 1848 brought the supporters of liberalism and the national movement a surprisingly quick victory. The revolutionaries held the strong belief that now, at last, the moment had come to establish a polity in Germany that would combine parliamentary government, liberal democracy and national unity. Moreover, they thought that this modern nation-state would easily be compatible with a new and stable peaceable order in Europe. Yet the revolution and the National Assembly failed for various, rather complex reasons. Ultimately, they failed because their hopes and aspirations were too ambitious and could not possibly be achieved in one go and simultaneously. The creation of a German nation-state which would have put an end to the German Confederation and the sovereign existence of more than three dozen states, including Austria and Prussia, was a daunting task in itself. To provide this state, at the same time, with a liberal constitution and democratic institutions was far beyond what was politically feasible.

What is more, the revolution in Germany was part of a European upheaval that encompassed almost the whole continent. It liberated forces which seemed likely, at some point, to bring the threat of war in Europe. During the revolutionary years 1848–49 it therefore became characteristic of the great powers, without exception, to work together in an attempt to prevent such a war, which would inevitably have introduced the incalculable element of nationalism into the relations between them. Once the first revolutionary wave had passed, they were united in pursuing a policy of containment, seeking to return to and confirm the old Viennese order. The leading role in this was played by Britain and Russia, which had been spared revolutionary unrest, despite serious internal problems. While Berlin, Vienna and Frankfurt were locked in battle over what was desirable, and indeed possible, in terms of Germany's political organisation, the governments in London and St Petersburg kept reminding them of the European character of the German Confederation and the settlement of 1815. This diplomatic confrontation about the future of Central Europe dragged on until 1851 and was then settled by the restitution of the German Confederation which had been regarded, rather prematurely, as being outmoded and overtaken by events.

In 1848–49 the German Question presented itself primarily as a national question. Establishing a modern nation-state in Germany had become the overriding topic, a state comparable to those in Western Europe. However, it soon became all too obvious how difficult the foundation of a German nation-state in Central Europe actually was. The National Assembly had just convened in the Paulskirche, a disused church in Frankfurt, on 18 May

1848, when the delegates had to turn their attention to national conflicts, especially between Germans and Poles. As a consequence of the extended debates on national problems, the work on the constitution of the future state was delayed, and this contributed substantially to the eventual failure of the Assembly. The problem facing the Assembly right at the start of its deliberations was that of the borders of the future German nation-state. The question 'where and what is Germany?' was not, of course, a new one.

The so-called Polish debate in the Paulskirche, in July 1848, was marked by its extreme nationalist rhetoric. The majority of the National Assembly were prepared neither to renounce any of the Germans' national rights in Prussia's eastern provinces nor to recognise the national aspirations of the Poles. The national interests of the Germans living in the eastern provinces were given clear priority over the national interests of their Polish neighbours. The Frankfurt Assembly turned a deaf ear to anything concerning the rights of national minorities on German soil. Those who happened to live on the territory of the future German Reich (however its borders were defined) could and should be Germans, nothing else. The concept of the political nation was to determine national identity. Citizenship and nationality were to be identical. Every citizen of the Reich was expected to give it his or her full support and loyalty.

The national problem did not only arise in the eastern provinces of Prussia. Since April 1848, Danes and Prussians had been fighting on the northern border of the German Confederation over the political allegiance of Schleswig and Holstein. The Danes reclaimed the two duchies and demanded that they be incorporated into the Danish nation-state. The main basis of this demand was the existence of a strong Danish element amongst their populations, especially in Schleswig. However, Germans lived there too and the Frankfurt National Assembly therefore wanted the duchies to be part of the German nation-state. Both sides in this escalating conflict paraded political, historical and national arguments. When war became inevitable Prussia was asked by the Federal Diet to intervene on behalf of the German Confederation. This was one of the last acts of the Federal Diet before it more or less abdicated, for the time being, in favour of the National Assembly. The war against Denmark proved, however, that at least in a critical situation the German Confederation could take positive action. The upsurge of national feeling in all parts of Germany enforced the unity of all the Confederation's member states and their common action. Public opinion thus prevailed over particularist interests.

Yet the German–Danish conflict, which had all the potential for becoming a model for similar struggles in Europe motivated by a mixture of national and territorial ambitions, soon alarmed Britain and Russia. The two powers urged the Danish and Prussian governments to search for a compromise. Thus, before the German–Danish conflict, raging since April, could escalate into a European war, the Malmö Armistice was concluded, on 26 August 1848.[7] It was signed only by Denmark and Prussia because neither the German Confederation nor the Frankfurt National Assembly was subject to international law. The Assembly was not even consulted by Prussia. In a situation highly charged with national emotions, the German national movement was forced to keep in the background when vital issues were at stake. For the governments of Europe, the revolutionary, though democratically elected National Assembly did not count, and they once again conveyed the impression that national aspirations did not really matter when the European *status quo* was in jeopardy. The term *Reich* (Empire) alone sufficed to alert the European powers, and this term was used by the Frankfurt delegates whenever they debated the German nation-state. From the point of view of the other Europeans, the historic idea of the empire was closely connected with universalist and hegemonic claims. Consequently, the 'empire' on its own merits threatened the tranquillity and peace of Europe, at least as long as the National Assembly appeared unable to define the exact borders of the future German Empire. At the time, Benjamin Disraeli, later to become leader of the British Conservatives and Prime Minister, spoke of the 'dreamy and dangerous nonsense, called German nationality'.[8]

Politics mirrors and follows realities, and reality was, to all intents and purposes, that the Frankfurt National Assembly was operating in thin air. The so-called 'Provisional Central Government' which it instituted did not possess the power to enforce the decisions of the National Assembly in Germany, i.e. the German Confederation, let alone *vis-à-vis* Europe. It was therefore not recognised diplomatically by any of the European great powers. The Malmö Armistice exposed this all too painfully. The National Assembly's vote to reject the Armistice had no political effect whatsoever, and later had to be scrapped by the delegates. In September 1848 the National Assembly even had to ask for the help of Prussian and Austrian troops to crush an insurrection in Frankfurt. Upset by the 'betrayal of Malmö', the insurgents wanted to force the delegates to take a stronger stance in national affairs and proclaim the democratic German republic.

The difficult problem of defining the territory of the future German nation-state, the Reich, handicapped the work of the National Assembly enormously right from the beginning of its deliberations. However, the task of devising a constitutional structure for the new Reich posed an even bigger problem. The National Assembly confronted the daunting task of laying the constitutional and political foundations of a new order for the whole of Germany simultaneously. Apart from the definite fixing of borders without upsettting European neighbours, this task also demanded decisions as to which elements of their sovereignty the member states of the German Confederation would have to accede to the new Germany and her central government. It was a most delicate matter, not only for medium-sized states such as Hanover, Bavaria or Württemberg, but also, perhaps foremost, for Prussia and Austria. To put the problem another way, the National Assembly, in the course of its deliberations in 1848 and 1849, had to offer two overlapping solutions to the German Question. First, it had to provide an answer to the German Question in terms of its constitutional aspects. Second, it had to find a solution as to the geographical shape of the prospective Germany. Both answers, complex and intricate as they were even individually, had to be worked out simultaneously, *vis-à-vis* a very unsettled political situation in Central Europe and under the watchful eye of the European powers.

The Frankfurt National Assembly, convened for the first time on 18 May 1848, duly elected a central executive which, when the appropriate moment arrived, was supposed to act as a government for Germany, however her territory was eventually defined. The executive, formed by the elected Assembly, was also supposed to weaken the authority of the particularist states of the German Confederation. As its head the delegates elected Archduke John of Austria as *Reichsverweser*, a sort of caretaker Prime Minister. However, in the chilly environment of *Realpolitik* the executive was practically powerless. Real power, and especially military power, remained with the constituent states of the Confederation and in the months that followed the *Reichsverweser* played a more or less decorative role.

Having established a provisional 'government', the Assembly went on to debate and define the human rights of individual citizens, which were meant to be part of the German constitution. Historians later considered that this should not have been a matter of top priority and that it consumed too much of the delegates' time, which would have been better spent on more pressing problems. However, as one of the delegates confessed, the newly elected members of the Assembly felt the need to become acquainted with one another and learn more about each other's political views before turning their attention to the major tasks ahead.[9] With hindsight, too much caution did indeed prove to be a tactical error. At the end of its long-drawn deliberations, the National Assembly eventually passed a comprehensive bill of rights for the citizens of the prospective German state. All Germans were to have equal rights and the bill of rights envisaged provisions intended to protect the individual against arbitrary acts by the authorities. A division of powers along the lines of the Western European and North American model was to guarantee the protection of all citizens against authoritarian measures by the future central government. For the first time in German history the bill of rights, put together by the Frankfurt National Assembly, became a constituent part of a modern German constitution. This was, after all, a rather late achievement. In Britain human rights had been introduced step by step since the seventeenth century; in the United States of America they were included in the Declaration of Independence in 1776; and in France the revolutionaries had proclaimed their declaration of human rights in 1789.

Having discussed and successfully concluded their deliberations on human rights, the delegates turned their attention to the constitutional

Fig. 3.1 First meeting of the Frankfurt National Assembly, 18 May 1848 (contemporary woodcut).

structure of the prospective German nation-state. Again the debate proved to be long and controversial. However, the outcome was a modern constitution based on democratic principles which was intended to introduce into a united Germany a parliamentary system under a constitutional monarchy, though modified by some concessions to the situation under the *anciens régimes*. The constitution of 1849 defined Germany as a federal union with a hereditary emperor as head of state whose powers were rather limited. The 'Emperor of the Germans' was to govern with the aid of ministers, who, in their turn, would be co-responsible for all acts of government. Co-responsibility was the stumbling block, which immediately triggered off criticism. The essence of parliamentarianism is that every minister and the government as a whole are only responsible to the elected parliament, which is the visible manifestation of the sovereignty of the people. And what did the extremely vague term 'co-responsibility' really mean? In the worst scenario it could mean that parliamentarians could be blamed for a bad policy, thereby becoming scapegoats for an incompetent monarch.

Nevertheless, most of the German states accepted without resistance the constitution drafted by the Frankfurt National Assembly, due, probably, to tactical considerations, as soon became clear. They feared new unrest if they rejected the work of the Assembly. Eventually 290 delegates voted for the King of Prussia as Emperor of the Germans, while 248 abstained. The imperial crown was offered to Frederick William IV. The King, however, hesitated, brooded and agonised, before rejecting a position whose authority was, in his opinion, too restricted. A modern constitutional historian has described the scene:

> When the Frankfurt deputation led by Eduard Simson, then president of the Assembly, arrived in Berlin on 2 April 1849 the decision had already been taken. The King simply stated that a parliament had no right to offer a Crown, though when he met the delegation the following day he made his acceptance dependent on the agreement of all the other German princes. The same applied to the recognition of the constitution. This in effect was the end of the affair.[10]

Later, the King is reported to have remarked that the imperial crown offered by the German National Assembly had been tainted by the 'Ludergeruch' (stench) of the revolution. Historians have ventured to suggest that Frederick William's much-deplored rejection of the imperial crown may have been influenced by his anxieties that the European powers would not tolerate a large and powerful German state in the centre of Europe, and may have prevented its creation by military means. The Russian Tsar, in particular, is said to have put pressure on the Prussian King: autocratic Russia did not want a liberal empire on her western border where the unruly Poles lived. However, there is not sufficient evidence to prove whether this proposition has any serious basis. Be that as it may, the Prussian monarch's rejection of Germany's political consolidation under a liberal constitution destroyed any chance of success the German revolutionary movement had.

The territorial shape of the prospective German nation-state was the second important issue which had to be resolved by the Frankfurt Assembly. The delegates in Frankfurt were about to create a constitution for Germany, but what borders should she have? As mentioned earlier, right from the beginning of its deliberations this issue had appeared on the Assembly's agenda. Until the summer of 1848 it was almost unanimous in the view that the new German Reich should cover exactly the area that constituted the existing German Confederation. The concept of the political nation was invoked to underpin this belief. It was often said in Frankfurt that anyone who lived on German soil was a German. At this stage, however, no solution was yet proffered to the question of what would happen to ethnic Germans residing outside the Confederation's borders, particularly those in Schleswig, East Prussia and the Posen province. These last two, though not Schleswig, were included in the German Customs Union.

In the autumn of 1848 the parliamentarians in Frankfurt began to tackle a problem which had likewise been left to one side: how would German-speaking Austrians be brought into the new Reich? Should the entire historic state of the Habsburgs, including those sections of it that lay beyond the German Confederation, belong to the German national state? The answer to this question was soon a resounding 'no'. Equally, no part of the prospective German Reich should be in a union with non-German lands. The Frankfurt parliament rightly felt that the national character of the future German Reich would be impaired if the whole of the Habsburg monarchy, with all its different nationalities, were drawn in. Understandably, the Viennese government voiced its opposition to the idea that Austria could be politically divided, with her German lands joining the Reich. As a result, a compromise, envisaging a confederation of Germany and Austria, was discussed, according to which the German Reich would forgo those parts of the existing German Confederation that lay within the Austrian Empire. With the exception of Austria, all German states would instead form a federation. This Reich would then slot into another federation, with the Habsburg monarchy, governed by the principles of international law. These were the first contours of *Kleindeutschland* ('lesser Germany'), that is, a German state without the German-speaking areas of Austria, which was finally to emerge in 1871. As Prussia went from strength to strength and became the leading force in the unification process after the 1850s, the 'lesser' German option shifted progressively to the fore. *Grossdeutschland*, i.e. a united Germany that included Austria, seemed to have lost its allure.

Gradually a looser conception of the dual confederation evolved, and the original idea of a unitary complementary whole lost currency. As it did so, the Frankfurt parliamentarians became more sympathetic towards a purely 'lesser' German solution. But they were not yet entirely convinced. After the debates in the autumn of 1848, however, there was a majority in favour of a German national state consisting of the territory of the German Confederation, excluding German-speaking Austria, but including Schleswig, East Prussia and the province of Posen. The Assembly realised that this answer to the intricate territorial problem would mean that national minorities were included in the new Germany. Their legitimate rights, including that of the unhindered 'development of their ethnic cultural life', had already been recognised in the declaration on the protection of nationalities proclaimed by the Frankfurt Assembly on 31 May 1848. The essence of the declaration made its way into Article 188 of the constitution of March 1849.[11]

The Schleswig problem was equally difficult. Even contemporaries gave up trying to understand its legal background and dynastic implications. Lord Palmerston, the British Prime Minister, is said to have boasted that only three people ever grasped all the implications of the problem: the Prince Consort (Queen Victoria's husband), who was dead; a German professor, who had gone mad; and himself, who had forgotten all about it.[12] The essence of the debates in the Frankfurt Assembly over Schleswig was that in terms of language the territory belonged to Germany, even though it was also the home of a large Danish-speaking minority. History, moreover, strengthened the alleged legitimacy of German claims: Holstein's membership of the German Confederation since 1815 was stressed, and the so-called indivisibility of the two duchies of Schleswig and Holstein was championed as an inviolable historical principle. Given this attitude, the British historian Sir Lewis Namier has criticised the nationalism of the Assembly as illiberal and related it directly to later, more agressive forms of German nationalism. He referred, in particular, to the Assembly's approach to the Posen problem, to back up his argument.[13] More recent research into the way national questions were dealt with in Frankfurt fail, however, to corroborate the kind of simplistic view offered by Namier.[14] But it cannot be denied that Germany's European neighbours could not hide their fears and apprehensions. As early as 31 July 1848 the French Foreign Minister Jules Bastide wrote to the French envoy in Berlin:

> I believe that the unity of Germany, embracing 40 million people, will be a far more threatening power to its neighbours than Germany is today, and therefore I do not know why we should have any interest in wanting this unity, let alone encouraging it. The urge to expand that is apparent in Germany is not exactly comforting and in the questions of Schleswig and the Grand Duchy of Posen the Frankfurt Assembly offers a fairly pitiable concept of political morality.[15]

Just as Danish nationalists had objected to the proposed position of the German border in the north, Polish and German nationalists clashed over Posen. Early protagonists of nationalism had not envisaged such conflict.

As disciples of Johann Gottfried Herder and Giuseppe Mazzini they proceeded from the assumption that the collapse of the pre-national order in Central Europe would herald the 'springtime of the nations' and a policy of reconciliation among free nations. The eventual fulfilment of national aspirations would create a peaceful world.[16] Yet spring passed quickly. By the end of the revolutionary year 1848 old wounds in Polish–German relations had been reopened and would now fester for decades, adding considerably to the poisonous myth that the two peoples, like the Germans and the French, were hereditary enemies. In the province of Posen, after 1815, Prussia had heeded the recommendation of the Congress of Vienna and allowed the Polish population some national organisations. Now events overturned the German goodwill towards the Poles which had characterised the 1830s, and a new era of tension was inaugurated.

From 1848 onwards the Prussian government in Berlin worked to incorporate East Prussia and the province of Posen into the German Confederation and the German national state, should it materialise. Yet its integration policy was sharply opposed by the Poles in Posen, which in 1846 was inhabited by 1.4 million people. Two-thirds of them were Poles whose political leaders felt that they were the inheritors of a Polish national state yet to be re-created. They rejected resolutely, and with good reason, the idea of living in a German nation-state. As the unforeseen revolutionary consequences of the nation-state principle for the dynastic Prussian state became ever clearer, the Berlin government set sail on an anti-Polish course, involving the suppression of any Polish national aspirations whatsoever. Most delegates in the Assembly in Frankfurt wanted the future Germany to have the upper hand over Polish nationalism and did not voice dissent. In essence they were tacitly condoning Prussia's policy and ignoring Polish desires for independence. On the international level, Prussia's anti-Polish policy created a stable alliance of interests with tsarist Russia, which was also confronted with Polish national ambitions, an alliance that was to last until the eve of the First World War.

A further consequence of the tumultuous events and debates of 1848–49 was that the German national state would not include one of the heartlands of the old Holy Roman Empire, Bohemia, which belonged to Austria and whose inhabitants mainly spoke Czech. The Slav population in both Bohemia and Moravia had adamantly refused to elect delegates to the German National Assembly. In declining this invitation to Frankfurt, one of the leading spokesmen of the Czech-speaking Bohemians, the Prague historian František Palacký, also expressed his commitment to the multinational Habsburg state – 'a state, the maintenance, integrity and strengthening of which is, and must remain, a noble and important duty not only for my people, but for the whole of Europe, indeed for humanity and the civilized world'.[17] Palacký did not believe that there was a place for the Czech nation within a German national state, though there was one in the land of the Austrian Emperor. His stance strengthened the Viennese position in the

German Question. In Bohemia, too, where historic political boundaries did not correlate to the territory of linguistic and ethnic nationalities, the 'springtime of the nations' ultimately caused bitter national conflicts to surface. The more than 300 participants at the first All-Slav Congress that met in Prague in June 1848 rebuffed once again the German National Assembly and its 'greater' Germany. They elaborated upon a conception of a state that presaged the independent Czechoslovakia that was to emerge in 1918.[18]

The attitude of Bohemian and Moravian Slavs in 1848 strengthened sympathy in the German national movement for the 'lesser' German solution that would, at least for the time being, exclude those Germans living in the Habsburg monarchy. The Prussian King may have rejected the suggestion that he be crowned Emperor of a 'lesser' Germany, but this certainly did not prevent Prussia from adopting the national concept of the delegates in Frankfurt, and trying to put it into practice 'from above', initially via a league of mainly north German princes (Erfurt Union). Though Austria, now under her forceful new Prime Minister Prince Felix zu Schwarzenberg, managed to foil Berlin's aspirations to create a federal state in northern Germany under Prussian leadership, once again (in the Punctuation of Olmütz in 1850) the future course of Central European politics seemed to have been set. The option of a 'greater' Germany was faced with too many obstacles and thus had come to nothing. In retrospect, the historian Andreas Hillgruber stated that the best Germans could hope for in the nineteenth century was 'to gain a national state that was unfinished and that never could be finished; even this could only happen under extremely propitious international circumstances'.[19] However, the concept of a 'greater' Germany was to haunt German and Austrian politics until 1938. The 'Anschluss' in that year, forced by Hitler, seemed to be the fulfilment of a national dream which allegedly had lain dormant for years, but it turned out to be only a short and unhappy interlude.

The revolution of 1848 and the debates of the National Assembly on the constitution and the geographical shape of the German nation-state had stirred emotions and given a fresh topicality to the German Question which could not simply be ignored by the governments of the day. After the counter-revolutions had again gained the upper hand in 1849, the governments in Berlin and Vienna tried to use the people's national aspirations for their own selfish purposes and ideas as to how Central Europe should be organised. Both governments had come to the conclusion that the German Confederation was outdated and had to be replaced by a new order in Germany. The undecided question was who would become the leading power in a political gamble which focused even more than in the years prior to 1848 on the Austro-Prussian dualism. Both powers now developed schemes which ultimately aimed at pushing the rival out of the decision-making process concerning Germany's future. All these schemes were more or less directed against the political order of 1815 and therefore challenged

Europe – and Europe was well aware of this. 'Should we desire Germany to become in some respects a single nation, or should it remain an ill-joined aggregate of disunited peoples and princes?', the great political philosopher Alexis de Tocqueville, French Foreign Minister for a few months in 1848, asked at about this time. Bearing in mind Russia's growing power, de Tocqueville answered his own question on a positive note: 'We must change our old maxims and not be afraid to strengthen our neighbour so that he may one day be in a position to help us repulse the common enemy'.[20]

The policies which were pursued by Austria and Prussia from 1849 onwards were clearly directed against Europe and the guiding political ideas of the Congress of Vienna. The Austrian scheme, which was made public by the Prime Minister, Prince Felix zu Schwarzenberg, as early as March 1849, envisaged the accession of the Habsburg monarchy with all its territories (with the possible exception of its Italian provinces) to an enlarged 'German' confederation. This would have created a state with some 70 million inhabitants, a multinational state of a kind already considered anachronistic and out of tune with the *Zeitgeist*. During the revolutionary months of 1848 nationalists and liberals called such states 'prisons of the peoples' and denied them the right to any future. Moreover, a state of 70 million, which would have extended, under Austrian leadership, from Hungary and the Adriatic to the North and Baltic Seas and from the Rhine to East Prussia, would have meant the end of any balance of power in Europe. Contemporaries and later historians knew that

> the keystone of the old order was Austria. . . . If the German-speaking lands of the Austrian Empire were absorbed into a greater German national state, how could the rest of the Empire survive? Indeed, if all the lands included in the German Confederation were welded into a single unitary state, a country of vast extent would be created in the heart of Europe. In terms of the Balance of Power, such a state, whether liberal or otherwise, might prove too large and too powerful for the other countries of Europe to live with in comfort.[21]

Was the Austrian proposal, therefore, nothing more than a propaganda coup, a cunning initiative by Vienna to cover up more realistic ambitions and internal problems? As the Austrian government, almost simultaneously, and much to the pleasure of the national movement in Central Europe, tried to establish closer relations with the German Customs Union, modern historians tend to believe that Schwarzenberg's proposal had to be taken seriously. From the Austrian point of view the future existence, political stability and economic prosperity of the Habsburg Empire made it advisable to seek a much closer association with the other German states than in the decades after 1815. Confronted with the awakening political aspirations of the various nationalities in the Empire, its German-speaking elite could only profit from closer ties with Germany.[22]

Prussia's reaction to Schwarzenberg's scheme was predictable. However,

Alexis de Tocqueville on France and Germany, written in 1851 and first published in 1893

Is it in France's interest that the bonds of a German Confederation should be drawn tighter, or relaxed? In other words, should we desire Germany to become in some respects a single nation, or should it remain an ill-joined aggregate of disunited peoples and princes? It is an ancient tradition of our diplomacy that we must strive to keep Germany divided among a great number of independent powers; that, of course, was obvious when there was nothing on the farther side of Germany but Poland and a semi-barbarous Russia; but is that still so in our day? One's answer to the question must depend on how one answers this other query: how far is Russia a real threat to European independence now? I think that the West is in danger of falling sooner or later under the yoke, or at least under the direct and irresistible influence of the Tsars, and I think that it is in our prime interest to favour the union of all the German peoples in order to oppose that influence. The state of the world is new: we must change our old maxims and not be afraid to strengthen our neighbour so that he may one day be in a position to help us repulse the common enemy.

From his point of view the Emperor of Russia sees what an obstacle a united Germany would be to him. In one of his private letters Lamoricière [General Christophe Léon de L., 1806–65] told me that the Emperor had said to him one day with his usual frankness and arrogance: 'If the unification of Germany, which you doubtless desire as little as I do, should come about, it will require a man capable of things that Napoleon himself could not do to manage; if such a man should come to the fore and all that mass of armed men become a menace, it would be our business, yours and mine, to see to it'.

Alexis de Tocqueville, *Recollections*, a new translation by George Lawrence, ed. J. P. Mayer and A. P. Kerr, Garden City/New York 1970, p. 247.

politicians in Berlin were not bothered about the balance of power in Europe. Far from it. Their immediate concern was the consolidation of Prussia's pre-eminence in Germany by creating a new confederation of all German states under Prussian leadership. This German union or 'empire' should then enter into a loose association with the multinational Habsburg monarchy. In other words, the Prussian plan would have excluded Austria from a Germany united to a greater or lesser degree along national lines. This plan, which openly sought confrontation with Austria, enjoyed the support of the Prussian King Frederick William IV, who only a few weeks earlier had rejected an almost identical scheme. Then it had been the brainchild of the National Assembly, now it entered the stage as the product of princely wisdom and discernment.

Under the circumstances the Prussian plan for a new political order in Central Europe had no real chance of success. It needed the weakening of

Austria in 1866 and a man like Otto von Bismarck to transform it into reality twenty years later. In the middle of the nineteenth century the lesser German states such as Bavaria, Württemberg, Saxony or Hanover still objected vehemently to undisguised Prussian leadership in Germany and the infringement of their sovereignty. The south German states, mainly Catholic, did not want the exclusion of Catholic Austria from German affairs and considered Austro-Prussian rivalry an essential guarantee of their political independence. The European powers, too, could not take wholeheartedly to Berlin's German policy, perhaps with the temporary exception of Britain. The government in London did not conceal its sympathies, both in 1850 and again in 1870–71, for a German nation-state on the territorial basis of the German Customs Union and under the leadership of a Protestant dynasty. A unified Germany which adhered to liberal principles in politics and economic matters was also a prospect to please British politicians. But they made it quite clear that, first, Prussia had to act determinedly as well as quickly, and, second, had to avoid any escalation in her rivalry with Austria which might trigger off a military conflict. Before the year 1849 had ended, however, it had become obvious that the government in Berlin was unable to act swiftly without provoking Austria and offending Russia. Tsarist Russia, not having been touched by revolutionary upheavals in 1848, saw herself as the guarantor of the European *status quo*, which included, in the eyes of her ruler, the restoration of political stability at the very heart of the seemingly restless continent.

The Tsar, Nicholas I, made it quite plain that Russia rejected Prussia's German policy right from the start. In his view it was merely a disturbing continuation of the policy pursued by the National Assembly in Frankfurt, the much-despised product of revolution. Seen from St Petersburg, Berlin's plan to unite Germany under Prussian leadership could only mean that the treaties of 1814–15 had lost their validity as a result of the events of 1848, without the sanction of the great powers. Tsar Nicholas I, Frederick William IV's brother-in-law, therefore had no hesitation in denouncing Prussia's policy in 1849–50 as 'revolutionary experiments'.[23] Prince Schwarzenberg was, of course, quick to agree. France's attitude was more or less identical; she obstructed any political or territorial change in Central Europe as long as she was not one of the beneficiaries, for example if it were a question of extending her eastern frontier towards the Rhine. This had been one of France's barely concealed ambitions since the eighteenth century.

The renewed confrontation between Austria and Prussia over the new order and dominance in Central Europe led the two states to the brink of war in 1850. Yet military conflict, which was eventually to erupt sixteen years later, was ultimately avoided on this occasion. Berlin abandoned its German policy when it realised that the smaller German states would not follow Prussia's lead and the major European powers were objecting to fundamental changes in the German situation. In the Punctuation of

Olmütz, signed on 29 November 1850, the governments in Berlin and Vienna agreed to confer with the other German states on reform of the German Confederation and how to settle their rivalry in a peaceful manner. These conferences took place between December 1850 and May 1851 in Dresden, strategically located half-way between Berlin and Vienna. However, fundamentally opposing concepts of the German states and the paralysing influence of the European powers prevented any new departure in the German Question. Whichever prevailed – Berlin or Vienna – the balance of power in Europe would have been deeply affected. Alarmed by Schwarzenberg's far-reaching answer to the German Question, Britain and Russia, in particular, opposed the inclusion of the entire Habsburg Empire in the German Confederation, which was again on the agenda in Dresden.

The epilogue to all the lofty plans and initiatives for a new political order in Germany in the few hectic years between 1848 and 1851 turned out to be highly sobering, even banal. Accompanied by rather undiplomatic demands that she show restraint in the German Question, the great powers reminded Austria, while the conferences in Dresden were still dragging on, that the German Confederation was a political entity constructed by international law. Its very existence and development (if desired) depended on the consent of Europe. For this simple reason its legal position and political organisation could only be altered with the explicit approval of all the European powers. A reorganisation of the German Confederation by the German states alone and without taking account of its European obligations, as well as its crucial role for the balance of power in Europe, was not possible, at least not for the time being.

The renunciation of all Prussian and Austrian attempts at reorganising Central Europe by the great powers in the spring of 1851 marked the end of the revolutionary era in Europe which had begun in 1848. Challenged in particular by Prince Schwarzenberg's grand design to answer the German Question, Britain, Russia and France returned with determination to the international foundations of the European state system laid in pre-revolutionary times. Austria and Prussia had to comply and to acknowledge once again that the German Question was a European issue. In 1851, as in 1815, the political order of Central Europe was a matter of concern not only to the Germans, but to the whole of Europe. The outcome of the Dresden conferences confirmed the old, though sometimes forgotten experience that any move in the German Question needed the blessing of Europe as an interdependent community of peoples and states. After more than fifty sessions in Dresden the assembled delegates of the German states decided to restore the German Confederation in exactly the shape in which it had existed prior to 1848.

The Germans learned their lesson. Until the late 1860s no one in Central Europe and beyond could imagine the establishment of a German nation-state, comprising all German states except Austria, in the foreseeable future. Only few contemporaries realised in 1851 that the restored German

Confederation no longer was, or indeed could be, the appropriate answer to the German Question. In its existing form the German Confederation completely ignored, for example, the aspirations of the national movement and the popular yearning for greater freedom, civil rights and democracy. The pre-national, undemocratic German Confederation had now, in fact, become a makeshift instrument to stabilise the *status quo*. It was perhaps an essential factor in Otto von Bismarck's greatness as a politician that he realised early and more clearly than most of his contemporaries the fragile and transitory nature of the German Confederation after its restoration in 1851. This conservative Prussian diplomat and politician foresaw the possibility that Europe might eventually be talked into replacing the outdated German Confederation by a different order which, from a German perspective, was more suited to the exigencies of the time. In Bismarck's vision this was an order which gave Prussia, which since 1850 had rapidly been turning into Central Europe's most powerful and economically advanced state, a hegemonic position at the expense of her old rival, Austria.

New political developments in Germany in the 1860s were undoubtedly favoured by the fact that, unlike in the early 1850s, the attention of the great powers was no longer focused on Central Europe. The two world powers in the west and east of the continent, Britain and Russia, were preoccupied with internal problems and challenges outside Europe. For them the German Question had clearly lost its urgency and, in the overall evaluation of their interests world-wide, was now classified as being of only secondary importance. This was the opportune moment for providing a fresh answer to the question – and this time it was given by the Germans themselves.

|4|

German unity: first attempt 1870–71

In 1815 the Congress of Vienna had settled the German Question by following exclusively one simple guideline: the centre of the continent should be organised in such a way as to serve the political interests of the whole of Europe. More than three decades later, in 1849–51, the European powers had masterminded, in a common effort, the containment of revolution which was threatening to overthrow the balance of power in Europe. Now, in 1870–71, the political situation had changed completely. The Germans were about to settle the German Question according to their own ideas. Due to an advantageous international constellation, which had its roots in the outcome of the Crimean War of 1853–56, they were able to keep Europe's intervention at bay, as never before in their recent history.

However, was German unity really achieved by the Germans themselves, that is, by the national movement and its organisations? Is this interpretation not, perhaps, a mere euphemism, a sort of smokescreen designed to conceal the simple truth that in 1870–71 German unity was the achievement of one outstanding man whom contemporaries, and later historians, called the *Reichsgründer*, the founder of the empire?[1] The Prussian King William I, brother and successor of Frederick William IV, had made the 47-year-old Otto von Bismarck Prussian Prime Minister in September 1862. It was a critical time for Prussia, both internally and externally. The role of the monarchy and Prussia's constitution had been called into question. Thus, when Bismarck took office his political guidelines, according to most of his biographers, were clear and simple: first, to secure the undiminished rule of the traditional powers at home and, second, to increase Prussia's influence and status as a European power abroad, at a time when the world powers had disengaged from European affairs. Bismarck's intimate knowledge of European diplomacy enabled him, it has been said, to realise his political aim: Prussia's hegemony in German-speaking Central Europe.[2]

To achieve this aim, Austria's irrevocable explusion from Germany was needed, and Bismarck engineered this through two wars – the German–Danish War of 1864 and the Austro-Prussian War, often labelled the German civil war, of 1866. The birth of the German Empire was thus accompanied by violence and bloodshed, even more so if the Franco-Prussian War of 1870–71 is taken into account. Three major wars within the short time-span of six years, which ultimately led to a fundamental reorganisation of Central Europe, should have provoked a forceful European reaction. At the very least another European congress should have been convened to sanction and legitimise the new order and to remind Bismarck of the limits to Prussia's expansionist German policy. In 1895, when the eighty-year-old retired statesman was looking back on his achievements, Bismarck painted a dramatic picture. The German Empire was founded, he reminisced, 'while the rest of Europe held a gun to its head'.[3] We know that this was certainly not the case.

After the experiences of 1849–51 it could by no means be expected that the founding of a German nation-state, although it excluded the German-speaking lands of the Habsburg monarchy, would be tolerated by the great powers with so little resistance. Apart from the international situation, the creation of a German nation-state benefited from the fact that it was not the outcome of a revolution from below. Instead it was, as contemporaries like Karl Marx and Friedrich Engels had already noticed sagaciously, the product of a revolution from above; at its cradle stood the autocratic Prussian monarchy and the military. However, the new German Empire was not simply a greater Prussia. In many respects it represented a compromise between traditional Prussian power politics and the liberal national movement which was supported mainly by the middle classes. The Reich, by and large, put into practice those constitutional ideas that had been so popular in the months and years after 1848. From that time on, no German policy with aspirations to popular support could not any longer reject notions such as federalism, parliamentarism, democratic suffrage, secret ballot and emotionally highly charged terms such as Reich and Emperor.

But this explains why the young German state of 1871 appeared so strangely ambivalent. It represented, in a very confusing way, an odd mixture of the present and the past, and this made it so difficult for other countries to assess. The modern nation-state of the Germans adopted designations and symbols from the Old Empire. Even if one admits that the superficiality of such notions was obvious and the distance between the modern state and the universal monarchy of the Holy Roman Empire evident, the enforced historical context, from a European perspective, soon turned out to be a handicap, almost a veiled threat to the new Reich's neighbours.

The first German nation-state, the second Empire (1871–1918) was very different from other nation-states. There was still a fiction that the Empire represented a *federation of princes*, though the remaining privileges of the 'states' melted soon under the sun of Bismarckian centralisation and Prussian hegemony within the pseudo-federation. The *legitimist conservatives* did not accept the new nation-state. Even the Prussian King who became Emperor as William I considered the day of his coronation as the 'saddest day of his life'.[4]

On the one hand the Germans had, rather belatedly, finally acquired a comparatively modern form of political existence. What they had aspired to for so long had been achieved, moreover, in the 'lesser' German variant, which Europe found much easier to digest than the 'greater' Germany including the German-speaking Austrians. In 1866 the great decision had been taken that Austria, after more than a thousand years of common history, would leave the German polity. At the time, indeed until well into the twentieth century, many Germans (and Austrians) refused to consider this decision as permanent. In particular Catholic south Germans saw it as a partitioning of the nation and therefore believed it to be transitory. On the other hand, when the modern German state styled itself Reich, its neighbours in Europe feared an expansionist policy and a new era of German uncertainties and German restlessness.

There were indeed sufficient reasons for the rest of Europe to have these anxieties. The German Reich had been founded by the reckless use of military force: in 1864 Prussia, still allied with Austria, had fought against the Danes; in 1866 Prussia waged war against Austria and other German states such as Saxony and Hanover; and finally, in 1870–71, the allied German states (Austria kept her neutrality) fought against France. The rather complex Schleswig-Holstein question which had not been solved in 1849 was used by Berlin in 1864 to trigger off the wars against Denmark and, only two years later, against Austria. The crisis in Prussian–Austrian relations in 1866 had served Bismarck well, allowing him to declare the German Confederation of 1815 defunct. The ignominious demise of the German Confederation was thus not caused by the national movement but by the traditional antagonism between its two main powers. Consequently, the ensuing war between them and their respective allies was strictly speaking a punitive action by the German Confederation against Prussia, demanded and led by Austria. Almost all the other German states supported her.

When, thanks to her military superiority and advanced industrial power, Prussia had prevailed in the conflict of 1866, Bismarck pleaded for a mild peace settlement with Austria. It is well known that Bismarck did not force territorial claims upon the defeated Habsburg monarchy. He saw in her an ally in years to come. However, Bismarck insisted on substantial Prussian annexations in northern Germany, and the victims were Hanover, Hesse-Kassel, Nassau and the old and proud imperial city of Frankfurt. Thus, after almost exactly half a century of impasse, Prussia had finally filled the territorial gap beween her lands in the east of Central Europe and those in the west, won in 1815. All those states north of the River Main that were not annexed, for various reasons, had to join Prussia in the new North German Federation, which had a separate identity from that of the German Customs Union founded in 1834. In retrospect the new North German Federation under Prussia's firm leadership only served as a transient political organisation on the path towards the Reich, established four years later,

---

The French liberal politician and historian Adolphe Thiers after Prussia's victory over Austria, 1866

What has happened is a disaster for France, the like of which we have not suffered for 400 years. . . . I myself consider it necessary to prevent Prussia from becoming predominant; but at the moment I do not want war. In two years time, when Austria is also ready, the moment will have come for France to take up weapons to counter Prussia's ambitions.

J.-B. Duroselle, 'Die europäischen Staaten und die Gründung des Deutschen Reiches', in Theodor Schieder and Ernst Deuerlein (eds), *Reichsgründung 1870/71. Tatsachen – Kontroversen – Interpretationen*, Stuttgart 1970, p. 389.

The French Emperor Napoleon III on the situation in Europe after the Austro-Prussian War; circular note to the French diplomats abroad, dated 16 September 1866

The war that has broken out in central and southern Europe has annihilated the German Confederation and definitively established Italian nationality. Prussia, whose boundaries have been extended by victory, dominates on the right side of the Main. Austria has lost Venetia and broken away from Germany. In view of such considerable changes all states are coming together with a feeling of responsibility; they ask themselves what is the range of the peace recently concluded, what influence it will have on the European order and the international position of each power. Public opinion in France is unclear. It vacillates uncertainly between joy at the destruction of the 1815 treaties and fear that Prussia's power may take on extraordinary proportions; between the desire to preserve peace and the hope of increasing French territory by war . . .

Oskar Jäger and Franz Moldenhauer (eds), *Auswahl wichtiger Aktenstücke zur Geschichte des 19. Jahrhunderts*, Berlin 1893, pp. 461–2.

---

which simply adopted its constitutional framework. The south German states which had supported Austria in 1866 had to pay the price and were forced to conclude military alliances with Prussia, to take effect in a future war. This, the *casus foederis*, occurred fairly soon with the Franco-Prussian War of 1870.

The true cause of this war was not so much the candidature of a Catholic Hohenzollern prince for the Spanish throne, but a clash of smouldering ambitions between France and Prussia and their rivalry for pre-eminence in continental Europe. The outcome of this comparatively short, though bloody war made it clear that 'Germany', now under Prussian leadership, had surpassed France not only in terms of population numbers. She was now stronger than France by virtue of her level of industrialisation, the thorough training of her military and her more advanced infrastructure. Austria-Hungary's inclination to intervene in the Franco-Prussian War on the side of the French ('revenge for Sadowa') was quickly smothered by Russia's threat to take action against the recently reorganised dual monarchy. As an unofficial Prussian ally, Russia had thus proved her eminent political value and highly efficient role behind the scenes during the years of German unification. This could only solidify the Russo-German 'special relationship' that had existed since the early nineteenth century. It had a strong basis in the dynastic ties between the courts in Berlin and St Petersburg.

Like the Austro-Prussian War four years earlier, the Franco-Prussian War could easily have ended after six weeks. On 2 September 1870 the French Emperor Napoleon III and his army surrendered near the town of Sedan in eastern France. But the war went on for another six months, now as a *levée en masse* organised by the new provisional government in France and fuelled by the German demand for the cessation of Alsace and Lorraine. When the German Reich (or 'Germany' as it was also called in the constitution of 1871) was officially founded by the assembled German princes and military leaders in a simple, but later glorified ceremony in the Hall of Mirrors at the palace of Versailles, the annexation of Alsace and Lorraine from France was a foregone conclusion. Why the allied German governments insisted on this unwise annexation is still not quite clear. Bismarck himself seems to have hesitated, but he knew that a territorial sacrifice by the defeated French was a popular issue also favoured by the victorious generals for strategic reasons. To the European public it demonstrated more than the three so-called wars of German unification that the new empire in the heart of Europe readily relied on force and totally ignored the right of self-determination when it did not suit its purposes. Certainly, the newly acquired French provinces had once been part of the Holy Roman Empire and most of their inhabitants were bilingual. However, there was never any suggestion of asking them what they thought of their political allegiance and how they envisaged their own future between France and Germany. This was a big mistake and definitely one of the factors that made the German annexation so unpalatable to European contemporaries.

The question of Alsace and Lorraine, not the three Prussian/German wars within only six years, was to lay as a heavy burden on Franco-German relations from now on until 1918–19. The wars themselves had remained bilateral conflicts and never really endangered the stability of the whole continent. Quite obviously, Britain and Russia did not object to the political developments in Central Europe since 1864 and took only a diplomatic interest behind the scenes. Nothing is known of significant British or Russian intervention in the course of events in 1864, 1866 or 1870–71. How can this surprising attitude on the part of the two great powers be explained? There are at least two likely answers. First, Britain and Russia did not see any reason to be over-concerned by the establishment of a German nation-state, because, from their point of view, this did not disturb the balance of power in Europe and did not affect their political interests where it really mattered. Or, the second possible answer, Britain and Russia accepted the emergence of a German nation-state as something inevitable which could and should not be prevented, and which they ultimately even welcomed.

The British and Russian attitude towards German unification, detached and benevolently neutral, was, in many respects, the reaction of Europe towards the new empire in its midst. In his study on British foreign policy before and during the Franco-Prussian War, Richard Millman points out that the Prime Minister, William Gladstone, and Lord Granville, the then Foreign Secretary, did not wish to see France crushed, whatever their feelings about her being humbled may have been. 'But even if Britain had had the military capacity to intervene and prevent it she might have still lacked the will to do so.'[5] Certainly, around 1870 there were agitated, even hysterical voices in the British public which warned quite vociferously of the political consequences of changes in Central Europe. Best known among them, and often quoted, was the view of Benjamin Disraeli, the Conservative leader and former as well as future Prime Minister. On 9 February 1871, only three weeks after the Prussian King William had been proclaimed German Emperor at Versailles, Disraeli made the following remarks:

> Let me impress upon the attention of the House the character of this war between France and Germany. It is no common war, like the war between Prussia and Austria [1866], or like the Italian war [1859] in which France was engaged some years ago; nor is it like the Crimean War [1853–56]. This war represents the German revolution, a greater political event than the French revolution of last century. I don't say a greater, or as great a social event. What its social consequences may be are in the future. Not a single principle in the management of our foreign affairs, accepted by all statesmen for guidance up to six months ago, any longer exists. There is not a diplomatic tradition which has not been swept away. You have a new world, new influences at work, new and unknown objects and dangers with which to cope, at present involved in that obscurity incident to novelty in such affairs. We used to have discussions in this House about the balance of power. Lord Palmerston, eminently a practical man, trimmed the ship of state and shaped its policy with a view to preserve an equilibrium in Europe. . . . But what has really come to pass? The balance of power has been entirely destroyed, and the country which suffers most, and feels the effects of this great change most, is England.[6]

As already mentioned, Disraeli was leading the opposition at the time, and it is the opposition's tactics in any parliamentary system to depict adverse political events in a more dramatic light than is perhaps really called for and to blame the government of the day for them happening at all. The attitude of the British government of the day towards the political changes in Europe since 1870 was, naturally enough, far more restrained and differentiated. However, Disraeli's speech in the Commons was a spectacular warning of the long-term consequences of German unification which, in a strange way, proved to be largely correct. This is the simple reason why historians like to quote it, thereby often implying that Disraeli's reaction represented the 'official' British view. This is wrong, or at least a distortion. Interestingly enough, in later years Disraeli never again referred to his prophesy made in February 1871. This gives his speech even more the character of dramatic rhetoric and political agitation aimed at the gallery and the electorate at large.

The Liberal government's attitude towards events in Central Europe from 1868 onwards was, on the whole, distinguished by a certain aloofness. After the long-simmering Schleswig-Holstein Question had at last been settled by the outcome of the German–Danish War, Britain withdrew to a position that might best be described as 'non-intervention' in continental affairs and 'isolation' from continental politics. It was not until the turn of the century that this self-imposed isolation came to be styled 'splendid' by Lord Salisbury, the Conservative Prime Minister. In the years before German unification this general attitude towards continental Europe, which one modern author has described as 'mild interest',[7] had strong support in British public opinion. The German Question was certainly not something for the British government to worry about. It considered Prussia an ally and did not have much confidence in French or Russian policy. In London's view, the aggressive powers in Europe were France and Russia, the rivals overseas in the scramble for colonies and zones of influence. Why should Britain put obstacles in the path of a moderately expanding Prussia which, in future, could serve as a bulwark against both France and Russia? Werner E. Mosse writes on the British attitude:

> A strong Germany would be the best safeguard against any repetition of the Napoleonic nightmare. Germany, moreover, having no interests in the Eastern question conflicting with those of England, might prove willing to oppose the encroachments of Russia. The new Germany, therefore, would assist in the defence of Belgium and the Straits. She would also free England from too exclusive a dependence on the French alliance which was popular on neither side of the Channel and ran counter to time-honoured historical traditions. Whereas a French *entente* must always be precarious on account of French restlessness and political instability, the new Germany, especially if grouped around the Prussian monarchy, would prove a solid and reliable partner.[8]

Of couse, there were things that did not go down so well with British politicians. For instance, they did not like Prussian authoritarianism and illiberalism, later often to be called 'Bismarckism', now to be extended over most

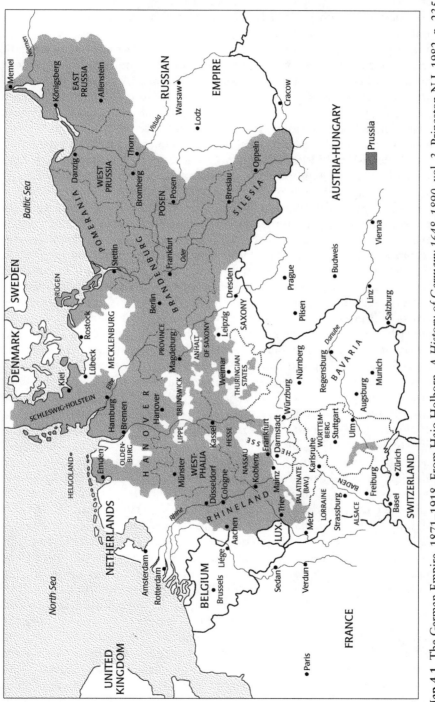

Map 4.1 The German Empire, 1871–1918. From Hajo Holborn, *A History of Germany 1648–1890*, vol. 3, Princeton N.J. 1982. p. 235.

of Germany; they resented the discrimination against the Danish minority in Schleswig; and they criticised, even condemned, the annexation of Alsace and Lorraine by the new Reich. William Gladstone soon became the most influential and articulate spokesman for these critics and an important section of the British public. He openly called it a scandalous crime that in the heart of Europe the fate and nationality of people were decided with the utmost arbitrariness. 'To wrench a million and a quarter of a people from the country to which they have belonged for some two centuries', Gladstone wrote in October 1870, 'and carry them over to another country of which they have been the almost hereditary enemies, is a proceeding not to be justified in the eyes of the world and of posterity by any mere assertion of power, without even the attempt to show that security cannot be had by any other process.'[9]

The Court and the Foreign Office were also dismayed by the German annexation. Sympathies turned rapidly to defeated and humiliated France. In June 1871 the novelist George Eliot wrote to a German friend: 'I think you misconceive the state of English minds generally at the opening of the War. So far as our observation went, English sympathy was mainly on the German side. It was not till after the Battle of Sedan, that there was any widely-spread feeling on behalf of the French.'[10] For Queen Victoria the Prussian Prime Minister Bismarck was 'the wicked man' and Prussian policy 'atrocious'.[11] In the British view Bismarck's work, the national unification of Germany under Prussian leadership, was tainted right from the start; France now appeared as the victim of aggression and brutality. The writer and diplomat Henry Lytton Bulwer may have expressed these sentiments in Britain most aptly when he observed in September 1871: 'Europe has lost a mistress and got a master'.[12]

However, all this moral indignation had little impact on the actual direction of foreign policy in Britain. The annexation did not impair Anglo-German relations for long. When Gladstone returned to power in the spring of 1880, he sought to revitalise the old Concert of Europe that had functioned before the Crimean War. In foreign policy he wanted to 'strive to cultivate and maintain, ay, to the very uttermost, what is called the Concert of Europe; to keep the Powers of Europe in union together. And why? Because by keeping all in union together you neutralize and fetter and bind the selfish aims of each.'[13] It went without saying that in Gladstone's view, too, Germany was a key player in this concert. So, in the last resort, the unification of Germany certainly 'fulfilled one of the chief criteria of British foreign policy since 1815 – it was arguably in the spirit, if against the letter, of the arrangements made at the end of the Napoleonic wars . . . Given the continued dangers of France and Russia, a united Germany would bring the Balance of Power in Europe to a state of virtual perfection.' Come what may in later years, in the early 1870s British public opinion expected that 'England and Germany would not only be liberal but teutonic and Protestant as well – natural allies against the alien values represented in

Paris, St Petersburg and Rome. . . . With its natural ally, the new Germany, Britain would impose peace on East and West alike and decide the affairs of Europe.'[14]

The fateful deterioration in Anglo-German relations only began in the 1890s. For James Garvin, editor of the journal *The Outlook*, after the turn of the century Germany was 'no longer the saturated power of Bismarck's *post bellum* reassurances'. It now represented for him 'an unsated Power' and 'a cause of intensifying anxiety and apprehension to all her neighbours'.[15] German and British historians have repeatedly pointed out that every German government that pursued a policy of restraint and stability in Europe did not represent any threat to Britain and her vital interests on the continent and overseas. On the contrary, under the umbrella of the *pax Britannica* the German nation-state could well exert a stabilising influence in Europe, as a sort of junior partner to Britain, in much the same way as the British had hoped the German Confederation after 1815 or the North German Federation after 1867 would take on this role. In July 1875 Lord Derby, the Foreign Secretary and former Prime Minister, could declare, without being contradicted, that no fundamental conflict of interests existed between Britain and Germany.[16] A year later *The Times* summed up what was the general view in Britain about the new German Reich: 'We have no jealousy of the new Empire. Within its own bounds we wish it every success. But we feel that an enormous power for good or evil has risen up somewhat suddenly in the midst of us, and we watch with interested attention for signs of its character and intentions.'[17]

The attitude adopted by the great power in the east towards the new German Reich was even more positive than that of the British. Russia's neutrality in the Austro-Prussian and Franco-Prussian Wars made her, in effect, into something like the godfather or protector of the German nation-state, which, seen from St Petersburg, seemed to be nothing more than a slightly enlarged Prussia. The official Russian policy towards events in Central Europe did not even waver when, in 1871, the French ambassador to the Imperial Court warned of alleged German ambitions ultimately to incorporate the Tsar's Baltic provinces into the Reich, since they were inhabited by substantial German minorities. Unperturbed by this warning and the anti-German stance of leading Russian diplomats, Tsar Alexander II, a nephew of the Prussian King and now German Emperor William I, had loyally supported Bismarck's German policy since 1866 and did virtually nothing to derail it. Bismarck was not far wrong when he casually remarked in 1871 that he thought the Tsar was Prussia's and Germany's only friend in Russia during those difficult years of German unification.[18]

There is sufficient evidence to suggest that Alexander alone, ignoring all opposing views, defined the official Russian line in Russo-German relations. He was certainly aware that his views were not popular either in government circles or in the Russian press. In the Russian public, as far as it was free to utter its opinions, sceptical voices could not be overlooked. As early as August 1870 an influential paper wrote: 'When France is beaten Central Europe will be turned into a military fortress, into a gigantic barracks whose gates will be guarded by Prussia'.[19]

For the Tsar and his government the best solution to the German Question would undoubtedly have been the enlargement of Prussia's territory and a continuation of the dualistic political structure of Central Europe: Prussia's hegemony in the north and Austria's in the south, with Prussia more powerful and more on a par with Austria than before 1866. This was indeed the prospect which the Tsar adhered to until the Battle of Sedan in September 1870. After that he more or less accepted what could not, in any case, be avoided. He hoped that Russia would have a reliable Prussian ally if Russia and Austria should ever be at loggerheads in the Balkans.[20]

Very much like the other European states, in the event Russia was taken by surprise by the rapid German victory in the war with France, which until then had been considered the strongest military power in continental Europe. The Russians had the impression, the Prussian Ambassador in St Petersburg reported back to Berlin, that the Germans had won 'too thoroughly' in 1870–71.[21] The proclamation of the Reich in the Hall of Mirrors at Versailles was acknowledged by the Russians without much excitement. It is open to question whether the long-term consequences were appreciated in St Petersburg, for the establishment of the German Reich meant that before long Prussia would become an equal, if not superior partner of the Russian Empire. Such a future possibility does not seem to have been on anyone's mind. However, there was suspicion and criticism. There were some fears that Prussia would continue with her expansionist policy, and would now direct it towards Russia's Baltic provinces with their German minorities. After Schleswig, Holstein, Alsace and Lorraine, why should western Russian territory not be drawn into the orbit of German ambitions? This was certainly one of the reasons why Russia, too, criticised the annexation of Alsace and Lorraine. The Russian government described it as a brutal act, damaging to the balance of power and the peace of the whole continent.[22] But in view of her military weakness at the time, Russia had to accept the facts. The only consolation was that, in diplomatic terms, although the balance of power in Europe had been disturbed in 1870–71, it had certainly not been destroyed.

The undeniable apprehensions and reservations which could be observed even in the attitude of the two world powers towards the German unification process between 1864 and 1871, although on the whole they were benevolent and understanding, make it clear that the answer to the German Question in 1871 was heavily mortgaged. It was tainted by the annexation of French territory. This act, compatible with traditional European peace-making though it may have been, was to damage Franco-German relations irreparably for decades. In the following years Bismarck, as the man responsible for German foreign policy, commented on the problem repeatedly.

Some of his comments suggest that initially he was against the annexation and only reluctantly gave way to public opinion, particularly in southern Germany. Various other comments he made indicate that Bismarck considered French hostility towards Germany a given and unalterable factor which German foreign policy, both present and future, would have to take into account whether there had been an annexation or not. This was the pragmatic and seemingly realistic view adopted by the statesman in charge, and from this perspective it was only sensible to protect and strengthen the new Reich strategically against any French ideas of exacting revenge by annexing territory on her eastern border, from which the southern German states could easily be invaded.

This is, perhaps, a plausible explanation for Bismarck's action in 1871. In retrospect, however, it cannot but be described as unwise and fateful. There can be no doubt whatsoever that the annexation of Alsace and Lorraine not only seriously afflicted Franco-German relations well into the twentieth century, but had an extraordinary impact on the history of Europe as a whole. From a European as well as from a German point of view the annexation was a disastrous political decision. It took almost a century to make good the catastrophic damage it had caused. The Franco-German Treaty, signed on 22 January 1963 by Charles de Gaulle (1890–1970) and Konrad Adenauer (1876–1967), finally put an end to decades of fruitless rivalry, perpetual mistrust and enmity. The 'Elysée Treaty', an accord of exceptional political and symbolic significance, truly inaugurated a new era of reconciliation, cooperation and friendship between the two countries, now safely embedded and acting within a broader European context. Seen from Paris, the German Question had at last lost some of its menacing aspects of the past.

Obviously there is not much need to discuss in detail the French attitude towards the founding of the German Reich. This attitude was totally dominated by the fact of France's military defeat, the provocative events in the Hall of Mirrors at the palace of Versailles in January 1871, the harsh German demand for reparations, the transitory occupation of parts of eastern France by German troops and the unexpected loss of Alsace and Lorraine. This loss, so upsetting and shocking to the French people at large, found symbolic expression in the monumental female figure on the Place de la Concorde in Paris representing Strasbourg, which, until the end of the Great War, remained wrapped in black cloth. Georges Clemenceau advised his compatriots that Alsace and Lorraine should always be on their minds but never on their tongues. The French rightly perceived defeat and the founding of the Reich as the end of France's hegemony in Europe. For them, German unity simply meant the decline of France and Germany's rise to political pre-eminence and great-power status after centuries of being used to Europe having a weak centre. However, consternation, dismay and anger at the somewhat sudden changes in European politics did not mean that the French, particularly those to the left of the political spectrum, denied the legitimacy of a German nation-state in any way. The national idea was, after all, a cherished legacy of their Great Revolution. 'L'Empire germanique', a French biographer of Bismarck wrote in 1908, 's'est fait sur une noble idée, l'unité nationale: et le premier effort de ces frères réunis fut d'arracher des Français à la France.'[23]

Even among contemporaries around 1871 there were voices of moderation and dignity. In July 1871 Jules Favre, the Foreign Minister of the newly constituted republic, spoke in this vein:

> Our country has suffered enormously from the misfortune of a war with another power and a civil war. Overcoming our catastrophe by working for peace – this is the republican government's only thought. ... We will strive once again to determine our own fate, not by means of nurturing France's grudge and inciting her to military activity, but by means of supporting her moral forces and appealing to her wonderful ability to work which has earned her such a prominent place amongst her industrial and economic competitors. ... France that governs herself again will be the natural ally of those powers who want peace, and this is a peace which is based on the great principles of the balance of power.[24]

Favre's words were neither aggressive nor hostile, nor did they pronounce a programme of revenge and war-mongering.

Looking back on the now defunct German Reich, historians can soberly assess its weaknesses and strengths. According to Klaus Hildebrand, who has written extensively on modern German history and foreign policy, Bismarck's historic achievement was to accomplish the 'national unity of the Germans within a close compass which was still, though only by a fraction, bearable to the European environment'.[25] Hildebrand refers to the political burdens of the Reich and the fact that it represented the German nation-state in its 'lesser' German variant. Fully conscious of what he could expect of Europe, Bismarck constantly stressed that the Germans in the Habsburg monarchy or the Baltic provinces of Russia should not be incorporated into the Reich. For him the once-fashionable concept of 'greater' Germany was outmoded and not in the interests of Europe as a community of competing states. However, for some historians even the Reich in the shape of 1871 was not an ideal answer to the German Question. Sebastian Haffner once spoke of its 'awkward size': for the continental balance of power the Reich was too strong, for its hegemony in Europe too weak.[26] Both historians point to a natural defect in the German nation-state that was to remain a major issue in German and European politics until 1945.

In evaluating the Reich's position in Europe both authors stress the fact that it did not automatically become France's successor as the leading power in continental Europe. Nevertheless, the potential for achieving that position in the long term could not be denied, simply because of the Reich's territorial size, geographical situation, rapidly increasing population and growing economic power. There was not the slightest doubt that the German Reich, succeeding Prussia, belonged to the European pentarchy of great powers. But the circumstances of its birth, in which violence and military force played such an important role, had given rise to mistrust and suspicion, in varying degrees, among its European neighbours. In the following years this turned out to be a serious handicap to German foreign policy, and Bismarck, who stayed in office until 1890, knew this. Consequently, in conducting the foreign policy of the new Reich, he studiously avoided anything that might have a tinge of expansionism or aggression. In his view, the Reich's future and stability depended on moderation and caution in its dealings with other states, and on not appearing to be Europe's new master. This explains why, immediately after the new nation-state was established, Bismarck declared the Reich to be 'saturated', and defined its foreign policy as 'security policy'. Its priorities were not, he said, egoistic national interests and selfish political pursuits, but the stability and peace of the whole continent. This all sounded soothingly conservative, peaceful and reassuring. Bismarck took delight in presenting himself as 'the honest broker who really wants to strike a deal'.[27] By 'deal', on this occasion, he meant a compromise between the conflicting interests of the various powers and small nations in the Balkans.

After 1871 Bismarck's priority in foreign policy was therefore the consolidation of the Reich. In his view the German Question now appeared in the form of how to secure the German nation-state and integrate it smoothly into the Concert of Europe. This was certainly not an easy task given the new state's potentially dangerous geographical location in the centre of Europe, the smouldering suspicion of its neighbours which could easily be inflamed, and France's desire for revenge and revision of the peace settlement of 1871. Bismarck perceived French hostility as an invariable factor in future Franco-German relations. It is not our task here to analyse in detail how Bismarck designed German foreign policy in the 1870s and 1880s to meet these preconditions so fundamental to the Reich's security. Suffice it to say that his foreign policy followed the guidelines of caution, moderation, securing the *status quo* and searching for compromise with the other powers.

One of the instruments Bismarck used to pursue his goals was an ingenious network of alliances – mainly bi- or trilateral, limited in duration and purpose, and occasionally even mutually contradictory.[28] Avoidance of military conflicts between the great powers in Europe which might endanger the Reich, situated at its heart, was the concept behind all Bismarck's alliances. In other words, in his view the permanence of the answer to the German Question provided in 1871 would not be jeopardised as long as Berlin worked for peace and stability in Europe. Thus, on the one hand, German foreign policy in the 1870s and 1880s had a distinctly European dimension or focus; the well-being of the whole continent had, for very good reasons, to be the immediate, perhaps even foremost, concern of any sensible government in Berlin. On the other hand, its distinctly German dimension consisted, essentially, in efforts to isolate France in diplomatic terms and denying her the opportunity to pursue a policy of revenge with any chance of success. The 'cauchemar des coalitions' (as Bismarck called it in 1877), meaning a system of alliances directed against the Reich and isolating it, should best be avoided by 'an overall political situation in which all powers, except France, need us and will be restrained, if possible, from forming coalitions against us by their adverse relations with each other'.[29] In plain language, Bismarck's maxim, as formulated in 1877 while taking the waters at Bad Kissingen, could only mean that, in Berlin's view, tensions (but not war) between Germany's neighbours were welcome and should even be stirred up. Such a state of European politics would prevent them from forging a common front, possibly even led by France, against the Reich. This policy of alliance-making and isolating France was successfully implemented for almost twenty years until Bismarck was dismissed by the young Emperor William II, who wanted to be his own chief diplomat.

After the fall of Bismarck the government in Berlin inaugurated a foreign policy aimed at headline-catching successes. It was characterised by ill-planned actions and thoughtless attempts at extending Germany's colonial empire overseas. According to Modris Eksteins, the German government

> openly adopted what came to be called *Weltpolitik*, or 'world policy', in contrast to a foreign policy centered hitherto on Europe. *Weltpolitik* was not a foreign policy imposed on Germans by the machinations of a small clique of advisers surrounding the kaiser. It reflected a widespread feeling, promoted by a host of eminent intellectuals and by public associations, that Germany must either expand or decline. This shift in policy, accompanied as it was by the inauguration of a naval building program and an obstreperous pursuit of additional colonies, naturally aroused concern abroad about Germany's long-range intentions.[30]

For Europe, this German policy, soon to be identified with the Kaiser's name, became synonymous with creating a new German Question. Since the 1890s Germany's neighbours had perceived the resurgent German Question as a problem which had to be assessed in the light of the restless 'new course' in Berlin. Thus Bismarck's demise gradually marked the birth of the German Question in a new guise. From now on Germany was seen as a potential threat to the rest of Europe, its tranquillity and stability being put at risk by the upstart among the great powers. In the next twenty years or so, right up to the outbreak of war in 1914, the German Question once again became a European problem, a cause for anxieties and apprehensions.

The young Kaiser William II, grandson of Queen Victoria, had come to the throne in 1888. With his rhetoric and conspicuous public behaviour he was almost the perfect embodiment of the image of German foreign policy around the turn of the century. His random intervention in Germany's relations with foreign powers developed into a force of its own in the diplomacy of the Wilhelmine Reich – uncontrollable, unpredictable and often detrimental to the intentions of the government of the day. During William's reign German foreign policy became a source of trouble and unrest, in sharp contrast to what it had been under the conservative and careful Bismarck in the years after 1871.

However, what were the principal changes when the Bismarckian turned into the Wilhelmine era and what were the repercussions that mattered for the 'repos de l'Europe'? These repercussions were soon felt in Europe in the changed diplomatic climate and the way Berlin proclaimed its political ambitions abroad. But this was only the surface; the changes went much deeper. After the caesura of 1890 the once 'saturated' power more or less liberated itself from being predominantly concerned for the fate of Europe as a whole, which, in Bismarck's time, had been the focus of German foreign policy to a greater or lesser degree. This approach now seemed out-moded and out of tune with the modern world of hastily colonising and expanding European states. The older generation of German politicians had experienced the founding of the nation-state as an unexpected stroke of luck, as the result of an advantageous political environment which had brought a happy ending to centuries of unhappy history. A favourable constellation in world politics had made a long-held dream come true. But all this was soon forgotten by the sons of the founding fathers of the Reich of 1871, and so were the many dangers tied up with its geographical loca-tion at the heart of the continent. The following generation, to all intents and purposes, perceived the German nation-state, so belatedly achieved, as imperfect and unfinished. Compared with other European powers like Britain, it seemed to lack grandeur, a dazzling empire overseas – in short, the prestige of a real world power.

The descendants of the founder generation also applied different stan-dards when they dreamed of Germany's position in Europe and the world at large. It was no longer the continental Habsburg monarchy or the tradi-tional rival, France, that served as the measure for German policy-making. From now on Germany was to compare herself with, and take her guide-lines for conducting foreign policy from, the real world powers, Britain and Russia, and also the United States. The German Reich, in Sir Eyre Crowe's words, 'the heir, or descendant of Prussia', felt the urge to achieve 'the rank and influence of a first class State'.[31] In short, it was clearly Germany's destiny to become a world power, and in the meantime she should behave like one. Those now in charge in Berlin ignored the potential dangers, espe-cially the predictable antagonism which German imperialism and an open military challenge would necessarily create on the part of Germany's power-ful neighbour beyond the North Sea. In the German view, acquiring a vast colonial empire overseas necessitated a grand fleet to protect it. In Britain, however, a German fleet which aspired to rival the British Navy, and the construction of which was accompanied by bellicose rhetoric, was watched

Memorandum by Eyre Crowe (Foreign Office) on the 'Present State of British Relations with France and Germany', 1 January 1907

It cannot for a moment be questioned that the mere existence and healthy activity of a powerful Germany is an undoubted blessing to the world. Germany represents in a pre-eminent degree those highest qualities and virtues of good citizenship, in the largest sense of the word, which constitute the glory and triumph of modern civilization. The world would be immeasurably the poorer if everything that is specifically associated with German character, German ideas, and German methods were to cease having power and influence. For England particularly, intellectual and moral kinship creates a sympathy and appreciation of what is best in the German mind, which has made her naturally predisposed to welcome, in the interest of the general progress of mankind, everything tending to strengthen that power and influence – on one condition: there must be respect for the individualities of other nations, equally valuable coadjutors, in their way, in the work of human progress, equally entitled to full elbow-room in which to contribute, in freedom, to the evolution of a higher civilization. England has, by a sound instinct, always stood for the unhampered play and interaction of national forces as most in accord with Nature's own process of development . . .

So long, then, as Germany competes for an intellectual and moral leadership of the world in reliance on her own national advantages and energies England can but admire, applaud, and join in the race. If, on the other hand, Germany believes that greater relative preponderance of material power, wider extent of territory, inviolable frontiers, and supremacy at sea are the necessary and preliminary possessions without which any aspirations to such leadership must end in failure, then England must expect that Germany will surely seek to diminish the power of any rivals, to enhance her own by extending her dominion, to hinder the cooperation of other States, and ultimately to break up and supplant the British Empire.

Now, it is quite possible that Germany does not, nor ever will, consciously cherish any schemes of so subversive a nature. Her statesmen have openly repudiated them with indignation. Their denial may be perfectly honest, and their indignation justified. If so, they will be most unlikely to come into any kind of armed conflict with England, because, as she knows of no causes of present dispute between the two countries, so she would have difficulty in imagining where, on the hypothesis stated, any such should arise in the future. England seeks no quarrels, and will never give Germany cause for legitimate offence . . .

If it be possible to account for the German Government's persistently aggressive demeanour towards England, and the resulting state of almost perpetual friction, notwithstanding the pretence of friendship, the generally restless, explosive, and disconcerting activity of Germany in relation to all other States, would find its explanation partly in the same attitude towards them and partly in the suggested want of definite political aims and purposes. A wise German statesman would recognise the limits within which any world-policy that is not to

provoke a hostile combination of all the nations in arms must confine itself. . . .
A German maritime supremacy must be acknowledged to be incompatible with
the existence of the British Empire, and even if that Empire disappeared, the
union of the greatest military with the greatest naval Power in one State would
compel the world to combine for the riddance of such an incubus . . .
So long as England remains faithful to the general principle of the preservation
of the balance of power, her interests would not be served by Germany being
reduced to the rank of a weak Power, as this might easily lead to a Franco-
Russian predominance equally, if not more, formidable to the British Empire.
There are no existing German rights, territorial or other, which this country
could wish to see diminished. Therefore, so long as Germany's action does not
overstep the line of legitimate protection of existing rights she can always count
upon the sympathy and good-will, and even the moral support, of England.

G. P. Gooch and H. Temperley (eds), *British Documents on the Origins of the War
1898–1914, vol. 3: The Testing of the Entente (1904–6)*, London 1928, pp. 406–7,
416–17.

with alarm and suspicion. London began to see Germany as a rival and
potential enemy, who threatened to endanger Britain's supremacy at sea and
the colonial *status quo*, which was so much in Britain's favour.
Consequently, 'the mid-Victorian heritage of shared dynasties and mutually
admired cultures was dissolving fast. Instead, the two sides settled down to
a cold, hard fight to the finish.'[32]

The sociologist Max Weber gave the best-known contemporary evidence
of the swing in thinking on foreign policy in Germany and of her political
ambitions after 1890. In 1895, Weber, a representative of the educated
middle classes in Germany, gave eloquent expression to the nation's
bubbling vitality and missionary zeal. 'We must grasp', he urged, 'that the
unification of Germany was a youthful spree, indulged in by the nation in
its old age; it would have been better if it had never taken place, since it
would have been a costly extravagance, if it was the conclusion rather than
the starting-point for German power-politics on a global scale.'[33] Eleven
years earlier, in 1884, the famous historian Heinrich von Treitschke, a
nationalist through and through, had called the Reich a 'young giant' which
should use its might 'to render the name of Germany both fearsome and
dear to the world'.[34] Kaiser William II became the executor of exactly such
a policy. In 1900, attending the launch of a battleship for the rapidly growing German fleet, he declared: 'The ocean is indispensable for Germany's
greatness. But the ocean also demonstrates that at its distant shores, beyond
the waters, no important decision can be taken without the consent of
Germany and the German emperor.'[35]

The German politicians in charge thought along similar lines to William,
who had by now become an inexhaustible source of bombastic political

phrases. Bernhard von Bülow, Foreign Minister and later Imperial Chancellor, demanded in 1897 a 'place in the sun' for Germany, which she obviously did not yet have.[36] Bülow's demand became the catchword by which Germany's 'power-politics on a global scale' (as Max Weber had put it) were mocked. Undeterred, Bülow told the Imperial Diet in Berlin only two years later:

> We now have interests in all parts of the world. . . . The rapid increase in our population, the unprecedented boom in our industry, the efficiency of our merchants, in short, the enormous vitality of the German people have intertwined us with the world economy and drawn us into world politics. When the English speak of a Greater Britain, the French of a New France, when the Russians unlock Asia for themselves, then we, too, have a claim upon a Greater Germany, not in the sense of conquests, but rather in the sense of a peaceful expansion of our trade and its bases abroad.[37]

This sort of rhetoric, not unknown to politicians in other countries too, caused considerable anxiety, particularly in Britain and France, and poisoned the political climate in the years prior to the First World War. It sowed mistrust among the European nations, and fuelled tensions and aggression. When war broke out in August 1914 it was clear in the eyes of the Entente, right from the beginning, that there was a new German Question which demanded a new answer from the rest of Europe. As in 1814, 1848–51 and 1864–71, the German Question was once again firmly on the European agenda, first in the pre-war years, and then, with the greatest possible urgency, during the war and at the Paris Peace Conference of 1919. The answer was given in 1919 after a few months of deliberations, from which the Germans were excluded, but for the first time with the participation of a non-European power, the United States of America. The massive American intervention in the Great War had decided the outcome in favour of the European allies, led by Britain and France. Like Napoleonic France one hundred years earlier, Germany had challenged Europe, and in a joint response the European nations had crushed her, and now came together to decide her fate.

In retrospect, it is more than evident that in the past two centuries or so the Germans have, in fact, had only one chance to supply an answer to the German Question without the direct and open interference of their European neighbours. This chance came between 1864 and 1871, and makes the founding of the German Reich so unique in the history of the German Question. This is the only time that the Germans were free to decide more or less independently the shape and constitution of a state in which the largest part of the nation lived. At the Congress of Vienna in 1814–15 the Germans at least had a word to say in this matter, and likewise, perhaps even more so, in 1989–90 when the two German states of the post-war era were united.

However, in the years 1848–51 and again in 1919 their wishes and demands were not of much concern to the 'Concert of Europe'. Whether they liked it or not, the German Question was primarily seen as a European problem which had to be tackled according to the principle of what was best suited to the interests of Europe as a whole. At the beginning of both the nineteenth and the twentieth centuries the Germans resented the decisions made above their heads. In 1919 in particular they were quick to forget that they themselves had conjured up a peace settlement which they came to call the 'dictat of Versailles'. Severe as the Versailles Peace Treaty may have turned out to be in the eyes of the Germans in the inter-war years, it had been imposed by Europe as an act of self-defence after the experience of the years since 1890.

|5|

The German Question in war and peace

Fierce rivalry between the European great powers in Europe itself as well as overseas contributed considerably to the outbreak of war in August 1914, '*the* great seminal catastrophe of this century', as the distinguished American diplomat and historian George Kennan calls the First World War.[1] However, historical research in recent years has amply proved that it was mainly caused by the blind and irresponsible ambitions of the German Reich, its untempered quest for colonies overseas, a battle-fleet to match the jealously admired British one, and world-power status. German 'world politics' prior to the war brought about what Bismarck had always feared and tried to avoid at all costs: the 'cauchemar des coalitions' of the major European powers against the Reich. Seen from Berlin, this fateful development, which started in the early 1890s, was perceived as 'encirclement', but in reality it was more a sort of self-isolation and containment of the dynamic and seemingly aggressive Reich by the other powers. The military alliance between France and Russia, concluded as early as 1892–94, the Entente Cordiale of 1904 between France and Britain, and the Anglo-Russian agreement on colonial claims in Asia of 1907 – all these ominous agreements between Germany's neighbours represented logical steps in the common attempt to stabilise and strengthen the European balance of power. The mechanism was simple and well known, taken straight out of the diplomatic handbook. The German Reich tried everything to change the balance of power in its favour, and the other players in the game, led by Britain, strongly resisted this.

From Berlin's point of view the time for resolute action in Europe had finally come in July 1914. The assassination of the Austro-Hungarian heir to the throne in Sarajevo on 28 June 1914 was swiftly followed by allegations of Serbian complicity made by the government in Vienna. In the ensuing European crisis, only another in a long string of similar ones originating in the Balkans, the Berlin government supported its ally Austria-Hungary unconditionally and, at the same time, tried to profit from the general confusion by making political gains. The Reich was prepared to risk 'the leap into the dark', as the then Imperial Chancellor, Theobald von Bethmann Hollweg, characterised German foreign policy in the escalating crisis.[2] Barely concealed behind the 'leap' lingered the idea that Germany could now break up the restrictions imposed on her by the existing nation-state, gain political hegemony in Europe, and then rise to an internationally recognised world-power status. According to the German historian Fritz Fischer, who was the first to stipulate recognition of Germany's war guilt, the leaders in Berlin had been systematically preparing the Reich for the great conflict in Europe since the end of 1912. This coming conflict, pronounced to be 'inevitable', should be used by Germany for territorial gains, mainly at the expense of France and Russia. With these expansionist plans in mind, the German politicians responsible did not see any point in restraining their Austro-Hungarian ally in her policy towards Serbia, or in de-escalating the crisis that had sprung up after the assassination in Sarajevo. Consequently, the German Reich, in Fischer's view, has to bear 'the decisive part of the historical responsibility' for the ensuing world war.[3] Its leaders clearly saw the enormous risk in involving Germany deliberately in a European war which, in the event of defeat, would have dire consequences for her status as a member of the European pentarchy.

What is striking, however, and particularly shocking to later historians, is how unscrupulously and frivolously the existence of the 'belated' Reich of 1871 was put into jeopardy. Once the Great War had begun in August 1914 the eventual outcome could no longer be just a straightforward matter of victory or defeat, conquests or minor annexations. On both sides of the front, borders and territory naturally became an issue, especially the territorial and constitutional shape of the post-war German nation-state. In Germany, the nation-state within its existing frontiers was voluntarily called into question very soon after the outbreak of hostilities and initial German victories on the western front. Assuming that the war ended in a German victory, the men responsible in Berlin wanted to transform Germany into a greatly enlarged empire which would then have undisputed hegemony in Europe.

The best-known evidence for the absurd ideas and plans for the realisation of war aims in post-war Europe that were aired in Berlin in the early weeks of the war is a memorandum written by a close adviser to the Imperial Chancellor in early September 1914. The memorandum, the so-called 'September Programme', is entitled 'Provisional Note on the Guidelines of our Policy at Peace-Making' and was authorised by the Chancellor himself. It summed up, in unmistakable language, the proposals and ideas that were flourishing in Berlin government circles and the public at large during the first few weeks of the war, when everyone was elated by victory. In those early weeks German hegemony over Europe, despite some serious setbacks, particularly on the eastern front, seemed likely to become reality fairly soon. Consequently the 'September Programme' defined the general aim of the war as 'security for the German Reich in west and east for all imaginable time. For this purpose France must be so weakened as to make her revival as a great power impossible for all time. Russia must be thrust back as far as possible from Germany's eastern frontier and her domination over the now Russian vassal peoples broken.' The memorandum then turns to details and gives a long list of territories which must be yielded by France and Belgium. Luxemburg, a former member of the German Confederation, would be annexed by the Reich and the whole of Central Europe (including France, Denmark, Austria-Hungary, The Netherlands, and possibly even Italy) was to form a customs union under German leadership. As regards colonies, the 'September Programme' generously envisaged a later settlement: 'The question of colonial acquisitions, where the first aim is the creation of a continuous Central African colonial empire, will be considered later, as will that of the aims to be realised *vis-à-vis* Russia'.[4]

From today's perspective, all this planning appears rather ridiculous. But one has to see quite clearly that such ideas continued to circulate and to be elaborated upon throughout the course of the war. In the years to come, particularly during the Nazi dictatorship and the Second World War, they were to resurface in slightly modified form. They were certainly a disturbing part of the political discourse in twentieth-century Germany, obviously not devised on the spur of the moment and then quickly forgotten again. When, for instance, in the spring of 1915 the German army occupied wide tracts of tsarist Russia (Russian Poland, Lithuania, Latvia), Berlin planned to incorporate these territories into the Reich in some way or another, preferably by means of dynastic ties. The concept behind this thinking was still deeply rooted in the eighteenth and nineteenth centuries. The modern idea of national self-determination does not seem to have entered the minds of either politicians or generals.

What is striking about all these German plans for large-scale territorial annexations is the boundless urge to expand and the exaggerated thinking in terms of military and strategic security. This was, in many respects, the expression of a radical national egotism which aimed at perfect security by expanding German rule over almost all neighbouring states. National egotism, which had already thrived in the pre-war years as a powerful and disruptive force in state relations, became more acute due to the isolation the Reich was experiencing during the war. In the German debate on war aims virtually nothing remained, however remote, of the notion that a contented and peaceful Europe traditionally used to be constituted as a well-balanced system of great and small independent states. There were only vague reminders of this in the book *Mitteleuropa* by the liberal politician and writer Friedrich Naumann. It was first published in Berlin in 1915 and then, as in later years, attracted great publicity.[5] Naumann's idea of 'Central Europe' was that of a comprehensive economic union which would unite the people of Europe. Its core should be made up of the German Reich, Austria-Hungary and a resurrected Polish state. It went without saying that this prospective union should be led by Germany, but, in Naumann's view, the union should rely on cooperation between equals, not on subjection and ruthless domination. Nevertheless, the Central European economic union was still meant to be the economic basis for German world power.

All German plans to create a new order in Europe after the war, primarily designed to promote the interests of the Reich, and the German annexations in Eastern Europe which the Reich was able to force temporarily upon crumbling Russia, especially after the October Revolution of 1917, were to remain mere episodes. Concepts of a 'greater' Germany, in whatever territorial shape and political guise, receded in proportion to the degree to which the fortunes of war turned in favour of the Allies. The Imperial Chancellor Theobald von Bethmann Hollweg, who eventually stepped down in 1917, gradually began to realise that in the event of a German defeat the Reich's future existence would be in the hands of the victorious Allies. The war of attrition on the western front, the appalling number of casualties, and the American entry into the war had a sobering effect on politicians in Berlin. As early as October 1916 when the Imperial Chancellor met the representatives of the German states, his message had spread doom and gloom: 'If we can hold out against this overwhelming power of the Allies, and can end the war on the basis that we will be an equal partner in peace negotiations, then we will have won'.[6]

It is not known whether, at this point in time, the German government had any idea of what the Entente planned for the Reich in the event of an Allied victory. Since the beginning of the war the Allies had been debating possible options for Europe's post-war order and exchanging views on war aims, very much analogous to what had been happening in Germany at the same time. In essence the Allies' concepts and propositions were perhaps less radical than the German ones. But almost from the start of hostilities the Allies were adamantly determined that the aggressive Reich must be weakened decisively, and the idea of dividing it up into a number of independent states was soon on the agenda, if only as one possible option. An answer to the new German Question that envisaged a return to the *status quo ante*, that is, called the future existence of the German nation-state quite categorically into question, could thus not be ruled out. A report by Maurice Paléologue, the French Ambassador at the Tsar's court in St Petersburg, gives an unmistakable impression of how seriously this option was discussed in Allied circles. In his report, dated 12 September 1914, the Ambassador informs his government of a conversation he had had with the Russian Foreign Minister:

[The Minister] told us in broad outline how he understands the changes that have to be made on the map and in the constitution of Europe in order to meet the interests of the three Allies [Russia, France, Britain]. Firstly, the principal aim of the three Allies would be to break Germany's power and her claim to military and political pre-eminence. . . . Fourthly, France would regain Alsace and Lorraine and be free to add to them part of the Prussian Rhineland and the Palatinate. Fifthly, Belgium would be given significantly increased territory. Sixthly, Schleswig-Holstein would be given back to Denmark. Seventhly, the Kingdom of Hanover would be restored.[7]

The virtual dismemberment of Germany, or, for that matter, the decimation of the Reich of 1871, which is clearly referred to in this French report, was to be discussed again by the Allies towards the end of the war when Germany's defeat was imminent. A memorandum of October 1918 which was circulated at the Quai d'Orsay, the French foreign ministry, stipulated: 'To secure a permanent peace for Europe Bismarck's work has to be destroyed'.[8] But did the abdication of the vilified Kaiser in November 1918 and the proclamation of a democratic German republic not herald a change of heart on the part of the German people? No, said Marshal Ferdinand Foch, the supreme commander of the Allied forces on the western front. He warned the Allies in January 1919, a few days before the Paris Peace Conference was to begin its deliberations, that Germany, now transformed into a republic, would be the source of as many dangers and represent a similar threat to peace in Europe as the old imperial Germany which had annexed French territory in 1871 and started the war in 1914. Germany would remain a menace to civilisation, no matter who her rulers were. Therefore, in future, the western border of German territory must be the Rhine. 'Germany has to be denied any chance of starting an invasion again from the left bank of the Rhine, any military facilities, i.e. any sovereignty there, in one word, any opportunity to invade Belgium and Luxemburg swiftly, to march through to the coast of the North Sea and threaten England. . . . For the present and the immediate future this is an essential guarantee for the preservation of peace.'[9] The memorandum, addressed to the representatives of the victorious powers at the peace conference, was designed to make them prepared for French territorial gains at the expense of Germany. The British and the Americans chose, fairly tactfully, to disagree with their French ally. David Lloyd George in particular, British Prime Minister from 1916, objected to large-scale annexations of German soil whether by France, Belgium or the newly established Poland, nor was he keen on the long-term occupation of German territory by Allied forces.

The fact that, at the end of the day, the defeated German Reich was not divided up into a number of smaller states in 1918–19, thereby restoring the political situation in Central Europe prior to 1866, may seem little short of miraculous. However, on closer inspection this miracle can be explained. The German nation-state survived in 1918–19 because for the British, and indeed the Americans, the European balance of power had once again become the central issue in their policy-planning for the future of the continent. In their view, the European balance of power simply did not permit the dissolution of the Reich after the war, though it certainly needed to be weakened to a moderate extent. For the British and Americans the German

From David Lloyd George's notes of an interview between the French Prime Minister, Georges Clemenceau, the British Prime Minister, David Lloyd George and the representative of President Woodrow Wilson, Colonel House, in Paris on 7 March 1919

I informed him [Clemenceau] that the British Government were really more alarmed about Foch's proposal for an Army of Occupation to hold the Rhine from the Dutch to the Swiss frontier for an indefinite period. When I said it would mean an army of at least 300,000 Clemenceau said he did not think it would take more than 100,000 and that they would only hold two or three bridgeheads. I then informed him that I did not believe Great Britain could make a permanent contribution to this army. . . . I asked Colonel House whether America would contribute to a permanent Army of Occupation. He expressed great doubts but said he would put it to the President. . . . I informed him [Clemenceau] that the British Government did not like Marshal Foch's proposal for placing the Polish frontier on a line drawn from Danzig to Thorn; that this would mean incorporating the whole of Eastern Prussia, which was overwhelmingly German, in the Republic of Poland, and that we did not want any more Alsace-Lorraines in Europe, whether in the East or the West. Clemenceau answered neither did he. . . . We then went to look at the map and found that if Danzig were included in Poland Eastern Prussia presented a very serious geographical difficulty. Colonel House then said that Eastern Prussia might either be internationalised or converted into a separate republic. Clemenceau said that the more separate and independent republics were established in Germany the better he would be pleased.

David Lloyd George, *Memoirs of the Peace Conference*, vol. 1, New York 1972, pp. 188–9 (reprint of *The Truth about the Peace Treaties*, 2 vols, London 1938).

Question needed an answer in 1918–19 which effectively stabilised the balance of power in Europe on a new basis and took account of the new circumstances in post-war Europe. Feelings of revenge towards Germany and the quest for compensation for the destruction caused by the German armies on Allied territory could not be allowed to prevail over political rationality.[10] Moreover, what did victorious Britain have to fear from a Germany with very limited military forces, and without a navy or an airforce? As a counterweight to revolutionary Soviet Russia and an obstacle to world revolution spreading westwards, the now republican and democratic Germany seemed indispensable to the British and Americans.[11] A power vacuum in Central Europe would only fuel the fires of world revolution. This is probably the main reason why David Lloyd George fought against the Allied occupation of the Rhineland and the cessation of Upper Silesia to Poland.[12] Why should Britain discourage and make life difficult for a 'new' breed of German politicians who, as Social Democrats, Liberals and members of the Centre Party, had persistently been discriminated against by the autocratic regime of pre-war days?

The Germans failed to appreciate the moderating influence exerted by the British on the Allies' deliberations when they began in Paris in January 1919. The answer to the German Question that the Paris Peace Conference came up with may, objectively, have been an imposition, but it was certainly not a Carthaginian peace. Bearing in mind that Germany had willingly started the war and that, during the war, both sides in the conflict had voiced far-reaching plans for annexations, the Versailles Peace Treaty was, in fact, quite moderate. This is often overlooked in the face of the noisy complaints and condemnations made by its critics in later years, including, interestingly enough, Winston Churchill, for whom the Treaty of Versailles represented nothing less than 'the apotheosis of nationalism'.[13] All the propaganda against the Treaty, which, on the German side, already started before the actual signing on 28 June 1919, exactly five years after the assassinations in Sarajevo, was highly exaggerated. The Germans probably did not fully grasp how lightly they had escaped the consequences of war and defeat. Instead, the German delegation at Versailles declared that it accepted the imposed peace conditions, 'ceding to the overpowering force and without giving up its opinion on the unheard-of injustice of the conditions of peace'.[14] The influential writer Oswald Spengler derisorily called the Versailles Peace Treaty 'the continuation of war by other means',[15] alluding to a famous saying by the Prussian military thinker Karl von Clausewitz.

So, what did the Treaty of Versailles actually stipulate? Generally speaking, it punished the Reich for having started the war, yet without destroying it as either state or European great power. This was due to resolute British and American intervention. The British (and Americans) also made no territorial claims on the Reich, apart from the settlements concerning the former German colonies in Africa and the Pacific. Britain's primary war aim had been achieved easily enough, namely the neutralisation of the German battle fleet which she had considered an immediate menace. It was, of course, a foregone conclusion that the Treaty would sanction the return of Alsace and Lorraine to France. Belgium acquired the area around the towns of Eupen and Malmedy on her eastern border, inhabited by French- and German-speakers. In this case the principles of nationality and self-determination were interpreted in Belgium's favour. In a very similar way the north of Schleswig with its substantial Danish-speaking minority was handed over to Denmark. In the east the new Poland gained large sections of the Prussian province of Posen with its strong Polish minority, and parts of West Prussia, including the Baltic port of Gdingen. In the two decades between the world wars these areas made up the so-called 'Corridor' which separated East Prussia from Pomerania and Silesia. Danzig, an important port on the Baltic Sea, became a 'free city', henceforth administered by the

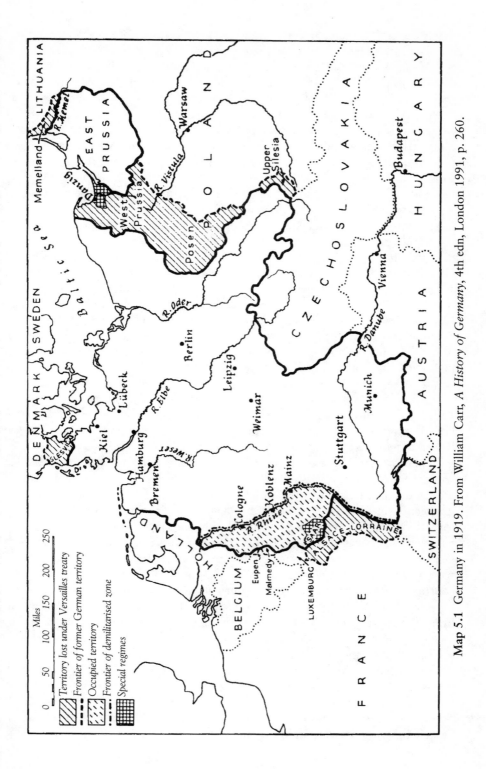

Map 5.1 Germany in 1919. From William Carr, *A History of Germany*, 4th edn, London 1991, p. 260.

newly formed League of Nations. Almost inevitably, both the 'Corridor' and Danzig, with its mainly German population, turned out to be the most dangerous troublespots in European politics in the turbulent years up to 1939. It was in Danzig that the first shot of the Second World War was fired.

Poland, conceived by the French as a buffer-state between Bolshevik Russia and Germany, also gained parts of Upper Silesia with their important coal and steel industries. The town and environs of Memel, another indisputably German territory, were placed under a French High Commissioner and then seized by the Lithuanians in 1923. On the other hand, the Treaty of Versailles forbade the political union of Germany and Austria, which the latter had wanted in 1918–19. The peacemakers of 1919 were not, of course, interested in strengthening Germany by finally realising the old dream of a 'greater' Germany, and they saw no reason to change this attitude in the 1920s and 1930s. When, in 1938, Germany, under Hitler, finally implemented the 'Anschluss' of Austria, the Western powers accepted it, albeit grudgingly. In the interests of preserving peace in Europe they succumbed to the aggressive and threatening diplomacy of the National Socialist regime. The Versailles Treaty put the Saar region under the administration of the League of Nations and accorded France the right to exploit its economic resources for fifteen years. In 1935, after a plebiscite, the Saar returned to the Reich. With regard to military matters, Germany was essentially disarmed and had to agree to far-reaching restrictions. The army's strength was limited to 100,000 men and the navy's to 15,000. The left bank of the Rhine became a demilitarised zone, and for a limited period Allied troops occupied strategically important cities in the Rhineland such as Cologne, Mainz and Koblenz.

Taken together, as regards severity and the way the defeated were dealt with, the terms of the Versailles Peace Treaty, which cannot all be enumerated in detail here, were not so different from those of earlier treaties in the nineteenth century, for example the Peace of Frankfurt (1871) which formally ended the Franco-Prussian War. In the history of peace-making, however, what was novel about the Treaty of Versailles, in contemporary German propaganda 'the peace of shame', was that the defeated countries were excluded from the negotiations. This had been decided – in sharp contrast to the Congress of Vienna, but with its history in mind – in order to deny the defeated powers any opportunity to interfere in the deliberations, thereby possibly dividing their opponents to their own advantage. In 1815 France had successfully applied these tactics, and the victors of 1918 took great care not to let this happen again.

On the other hand, there was nothing novel about parts of Germany being temporarily occupied by Allied troops. The same practice had been implemented in 1814 after the defeat of Napoleonic France and again in 1871 when German troops occupied parts of eastern France to ensure that French reparations were paid on time. However, there was another new element which undoubtedly influenced the participants at the Paris Peace Conference. This was the experience that, in an age of politically mobilised and excited masses, coolly calculating diplomats had to make concessions to the emotions and demands of the so-called public. The desire for revenge and to humiliate the defeated Germans ('Hang the Kaiser', 'Germany will pay all') could thus play a part in the peacemakers' deliberations. This may have been one of the reasons why the European order and the answer to the German Question devised in Paris in 1919 had such a short life-span. Unlike the Vienna order of 1815, which lasted for half a century, the Paris order of 1919 was in ruins within less than fifteen years. Not long afterwards another great war was to destroy Europe and bring unspeakable horrors to its people. There are many historians who regard the peace treaties of 1919–20 as one of its major causes.

If, in 1919, the Treaty of Versailles was Europe's answer to the German Question on an international level, then the Germans had already given their own answer some time earlier on the constitutional level. During the war the Reich had already undergone far-reaching constitutional changes. The Imperial Chancellor Bethmann Hollweg had foreseen this development when he spoke of the 'upheaval of all that exists',[16] caused by a war without parallel in European history. As an overall outcome of the ongoing military confrontation, the influence of the generals increased markedly at the expense of the politicians. From August 1916 onwards the German Supreme Command, with Field Marshal Paul von Hindenburg and General Erich Ludendorff at its head, had acquired almost dictatorial powers. For the political scientist Karl Dietrich Bracher it was abundantly clear by then that the Reich had turned into a military dictatorship. In his ground-breaking study on the dissolution of the Weimar Republic, Bracher wrote in 1955:

The appointment of Hindenburg and Ludendorff, under public pressure, meant that, although the constitution had not yet been changed, the Bismarckian system was, to all intents and purposes, at an end and revolution had set in. For, with their appointment, all authority at home and in the Reich's relations with the outside world was transferred from the Kaiser and his Chancellor to the military leaders. The high esteem in which Hindenburg and Ludendorff were held by the public had grown to such an extent that it would have been psychologically and politically impossible for the Kaiser to impose his will on them . . . or to dismiss them. With the establishment of this military dictatorship, the events surrounding the abdication of the Kaiser had already cast their shadow. For William II who, in contrast to his fateful activities in peace-time, had stepped back entirely from the political stage, did not think of putting up any resistance. By acting in this way he had handed over the power of the old order to a military dictatorship whose failure then left room for the democratic revolution.[17]

So, from 1916 the political influence of the Kaiser and the Imperial Chancellor was drastically reduced and they virtually disappeared from the scene. But not so the Imperial Diet, the *Reichstag*. While the power of the generals increased dramatically, the German political parties tried to counteract this development by demanding more legislative and controlling functions for the German parliament, which since 1871 had been elected by democratic suffrage granted to all men over twenty-five years of age. In these endeavours the parties of the centre and left were partially successful. With their 'Peace Resolution', passed by the *Reichstag* on 19 July 1917, the so-called 'majority parties' (Social Democrats, Centre Party, Liberals) publicly called for a negotiated peace with the Entente. They claimed political leadership in a most critical situation which had amply demonstrated the incompetence, indeed the bankruptcy of the existing regime with the Kaiser as its figurehead. This was the beginning of the transition to a parliamentary system in Germany which rapidly gained momentum with the Reich's worsening military situation. The centre of power in Germany had shifted again. When, on 3 October 1918, Prince Max von Baden, who was considered liberal and progressive, took over the office of Imperial Chancellor, the 'majority parties' provided the ministers. Thus, Germany's last Imperial Government cleared the way for a parliamentary system because it already had the character of a coalition, no longer responsible to the Kaiser but to parliament.

However, all this came about far too late. The old regime, devised by Bismarck and brought into disrepute by the backward-looking conservatism and poor diplomatic skills of its elites, had by then lost all credibility. The introduction of a parliamentary system in Germany, which the *Reichstag* decreed by law on 28 October 1918, took place against the background of military defeat and a mutiny on board the navy ships anchored in Kiel and Wilhelmshaven. These events started the German revolution of 1918–19. On 9 November 1918 Prince Max von Baden announced the Kaiser's abdication and handed over the office of Chancellor to the Social Democratic leader Friedrich Ebert, who formed a new government. On the very same day the Social Democrat Philipp Scheidemann proclaimed the 'German Republic'. Thus the great decisions on the German Question as a constitutional problem had been taken. From now on Germany was to be a parliamentary democracy and a 'social republic'. Under enormous pressure from inside and outside, her politicians had had to make an abrupt break with the past and lay the foundations for a new political order. This found expression in the new constitution of the Republic which had been drafted in Weimar. It was closely modelled on the constitution of 28 March 1849, the work of the Frankfurt National Assembly, but also adopted elements from Bismarck's constitution of 1867–71. The new constitution for the German Republic was signed in Weimar by the Reich's President, Friedrich Ebert, on 11 August 1919. Ebert had been elected the Republic's first President on 11 February 1919.

This is not the place to describe in great detail the characteristics of the Weimar constitution. Its fateful weaknesses are well-known: the over-strong position of the Reich's President who was often more like an 'Ersatzkaiser', especially during Hindenburg's long presidency (1925–34); the consequences of unrestricted proportional representation under which numerous small political parties thrived; and the notorious Article 48 of the constitution which gave the President special powers, including the right to declare a state of emergency. However, from the perspective of the historian considering the German Question, the failed attempt by the fathers of the constitution to reform the Reich's federal structure was highly significant. This attempt, further pursued in the following years, became known by the catchphrase 'reform of the Reich'.

In the Weimar constitutional system, in contrast to Bismarck's constitution of 1867–71, the sovereign power was no longer invested in the council of the allied German princes and free cities (the *Bundesrat*). The sovereign power now lay, at last, with the people, and consequently the *Reichstag* superseded the Bundesrat, now called the *Reichsrat*, in ranking within the political structure of the Reich. This relocation of the highest authority also had something to do with Prussia's slightly changed status within Germany. The fact is often overlooked that with the disappearance of the Hohenzollern dynasty Prussia had lost what was virtually her most important element of political cohesion. In the aftermath of the Kaiser's abdication the future of Prussia thus became a topic of debate. In 1918–19 it suddenly became glaringly obvious that other German states (now renamed *Länder*) such as Saxony, Württemberg, Baden or Bavaria could rely on a strong feeling of loyalty, even patriotism among their people. Not so Prussia, which was much larger and much more heterogeneous than the other states. When the dynasty was abolished and the last Prussian King (= Kaiser William II) had gone into exile, the dominant German state suddenly seemed like an orphan. Did Prussia, in fact, need to exist at all any more? Had she not, in reality, 'dissolved' into Germany long ago? Many historians would subscribe to this proposition and therefore date the dissolution of Prussia not to 1947, when the Allied Control Council abolished the state by decree, or to 1932, when the elected Prussian government was toppled by a *putsch*, but to 1871, when the Prussian state and dynasty created Germany as a nation-state.

The attitude of the constituent Prussian assembly may have been a symptom of this feeling that Prussia had done her job and was indeed no longer wanted. Elected at the same time as the National Assembly in Weimar (January 1919), the Prussian assembly hesitated for a remarkably long time before it started work on its main political task, namely the drafting of a new democratic and republican constitution for the Prussian state. Would it not be better for the whole of Germany to become a unitary state, now that the princes and dynasties had at last disappeared? As late as December 1919 – a year after the German revolution and four months after the

Weimar constitution had been signed – the Prussian assembly agreed on a resolution which advocated the unitary at the expense of the federal state with its constituent *Länder*. The resolution of December 1919 read: 'As the largest of the German states Prussia sees her duty already to start the attempt, as a first step, to create the German unitary state. With these considerations in mind the Prussian assembly asks the state government to contact the government of the Reich and make it start negotiations with the governments of all the German states on establishing a unitary state in Germany.'[18]

The resolution was carried by the Social Democrats, the Centre Party and the Liberals. They thought that the individual states (*Länder*) were reactionary bastions, still supporting the monarchical regimes which had just been toppled. To break up these alleged strongholds of the political right, Prussian politicians of the left and centre offered the voluntary disso-lution of Prussia, as a precedent for similar actions by the other states. But, in fact, the Prussian government stood alone in this. No other German state was prepared, at that moment, to follow her lead and almost all of them insisted (in a very similar way to today) on their identity and political autonomy within the framework of the Reich. Thus nothing came of the idea of creating a unitary state in Germany by abandoning the so-called federal traditions of German history. In view of some contemporary and later accusations directed against Prussia, her hegemony and militarism, there is a mild irony in the fact that Prussia had to accept her own contin-uing existence as a state (*Land*) within the Reich, very much against the explicit wish of her politicians of the day.

In many respects, however, the demand to abolish federalism marked, even in 1918–19, a radical and fairly transient position. It was simply too far-reaching in its consequences, almost revolutionary, to be generally adopted. Later attempts, too, which aimed at a weakening of the Reich's federal structure and dividing up Prussia into smaller administrative units, were only shortlived and failed to overcome traditional state patriotism in the long run. There were two attempts, in particular, which deserve to be mentioned here. The first was made by the National Socialists after 1933. They tried to supersede the traditional structure of the Reich by making the organisational unit of their party, the *Gau*, the administrative unit of the Reich that really mattered. In the National Socialist hierarchy the *Gauleiter* (chiefs of the *Gaue*) were directly subordinated to Hitler and his deputy respectively. There were thirty-nine such *Gaue* in 1939. The prime ministers of the states, if still in office at all after April 1933, were temporarily replaced by trusted party members, the *Reichsstatthalter* (special commis-sioners), placed under the Ministry of the Interior. On 30 January 1934 the National Socialist decree 'on the reconstruction of the Reich' formally sounded the death-knell of federalism in Germany by abolishing the autonomous states. This was part of the general process of coordination, or *Gleichschaltung*, which 'concentrated effective power in the hands of the Berlin government to a degree previously unknown'.[19]

The second attempt to end the German federal structure for good was made a few years after the Second World War, again by a totalitarian regime. In the Soviet zone of occupation, as in the western zones, the old states such as Brandenburg, Thuringia or Saxony had been swiftly restored after the demise of the National Socialist dictatorship. But not for long. As soon as the communist German Democratic Republic had, at least outwardly, consolidated its grip on power in eastern Germany, with the effective help of the Soviet Union, it dissolved the five restored states (*Länder*) and created districts (*Bezirke*), named after the major cities in the regions. In total the administrative 'reform' of 1952 led to fourteen *Bezirke* in the German Democratic Republic, plus East Berlin. The idea behind this hasty measure to remove completely any last vestiges of federal autonomy was 'to fuse Party and state into one and the same control machinery. The Party boss of the district was the most powerful local chief in all Party as well as administrative matters.'[20] Before German unification on 3 October 1990 the unloved districts were quickly abolished and the former *Länder* of the GDR resurrected.

When discussing German federalism one should, however, bear in mind that in some cases it was by no means as firmly rooted historically as the outside observer might assume. The West German *Saarland*, for instance, was only created after the Second World War on the orders of the French occupying power to suit its long-term political and economic purposes. Or, to give another example, all the new hyphenated *Länder*, such as North Rhine-Westphalia, Rhineland-Palatinate and Baden-Württemberg, were created by the Allies, partly on the territorial basis of former Prussian provinces. All these 'artificial' states, which were joined by Saxony-Anhalt and Mecklenburg-Western Pomerania in east Germany after unification in 1990, make considerable efforts to promote historical consciousness, a feeling of belonging together and a regional identity among their populations – not without success, all the more so if one considers the occasional arbitrariness apparent in the history of their creation.

In the tumultuous years 1918–19 the proposition that Germany should become a unitary state along Western European lines remained, in any case, a marginal option in the virulent constitutional debate, with little chance of being considered seriously. At the end of the day the participants in this debate showed a more realistic approach to Germany's federal problem. At the heart of the matter stood the question of whether the Prussian state should continue to dominate federal Germany or be divided up into a number of smaller successor states. The second option would certainly have created a more balanced federal system. For, after all, Prussia alone was larger, more populous, and economically more powerful than all the other German *Länder* put together. Therefore, to many observers both at home and abroad the Reich in 1871, as in 1918–19, was simply greater Prussia in disguise. Consequently it would have made sense in 1919 to dismember Prussia and form three or four medium-sized states which would have been in the same league as, for instance, Bavaria or Saxony. The first draft of the Weimar constitution did actually envisage such a partitioning of Prussia,[21] but in the end Prussia was not split up until after 1945, when the western part was taken to form the *Länder* North Rhine-Westphalia, Lower Saxony and Schleswig-Holstein in the new Federal Republic of Germany founded in 1949. The first Chancellor of the Federal Republic, Konrad Adenauer, very much favoured this solution to Germany's 'Prussian problem'. In 1919 he had already advocated the separation of the Rhineland from Prussia, not from the Reich. His political vision had turned full circle thirty years later.

It seems that in the few unsettled months immediately after the First World War the Prussian people would not have objected to Prussia dissolving into a unitary Germany, along with the other German states. But they were obviously not prepared for Prussia alone to be broken up and her provinces turned into autonomous states.[22] Thus, in the end, Prussia lived on. The only difference was that the royal government was replaced by a democratically elected republican one, led by the Social Democrats and the Centre Party. However, during the years of the Weimar Republic the structural reform of the Reich never ceased to be a topic of political debate.

> Prussia's dismemberment into provinces of equal size did not take place and the continuous conflict between federalism and unitarism was to become a further handicap to the democratic development, along with the problems of military, economic and social policy. The problem of reforming the Reich already turned out to be a severe trauma in the crises of the first five years, but especially during the agony of the Republic. It was a heavy burden for political and legal discussions on the constitution of the state, offered itself as a vehicle for the various tactical and propagandist excesses and was finally to contribute directly, in conjunction with Franz von Papen's putsch in Prussia, to the triggering off and escalation of the final crisis.[23]

|6|

The nemesis of dictatorship

The National Socialist dictatorship in Germany lasted a mere twelve years. It started with Hitler's so-called 'seizure of power', which was quickly followed by his monstrous abuse of power, by brutal aggression against Germany's neighbours, war and unspeakable crimes. The end, in May 1945, was marked by Germany's unconditional surrender to the Allied forces, by the devastation of many parts of Europe, human misery and degradation. Germany had become the outcast of the family of nations, and for many contemporaries there could be no doubt that the end of the Second World War also meant *finis Germaniae*.

How could a democratic regime, the Weimar Republic, so easily fall prey to an absurd ideology, be overturned and transformed into a totalitarian dictatorship? The events from 1930 onwards were undoubtedly an extraordinary sequence in German constitutional history, even taking account of the fact that the inter-war years witnessed an unmistakable trend towards establishing authoritarian and dictatorial regimes almost everywhere in Europe. Yet, on the other hand, there is no denying that in the larger democratic states such as Britain and France, but also Belgium, The Netherlands, or Scandinavia, authoritarian tendencies were successfully held in check and never had a chance to become a major political force. Only in the two large nations that had gained their nation-states belatedly was it possible to establish a dictatorship, in the one case of the Fascist variety, in the other National Socialist. This specific political development in Italy and Germany since the nineteenth century has led, quite naturally, to the question as to why, in these two countries, democracy succumbed so easily to the assault from the extreme right. Answers to this question are numerous and diverse.

Hitler and his National Socialist Party allegedly 'seized' power on 30 January 1933. 'Seizure of power' (*Machtergreifung*) is a National Socialist term and should be clearly understood as such. Moreover, the term does not correctly describe the fateful events of January 1933. First, Hitler did not 'seize' the office of German Chancellor; rather it was given to him by the ageing Reich President Paul von Hindenburg, the hero of the First World War. Hitler's appointment was not unavoidable, nor the only means of resolving the political crisis rampant in those weeks and months that presaged the death of the Republic. Second, a systematic and comprehensive consolidation of Hitler's power only started after 30 January, and took about eighteen months to achieve. By the end of this period the National

Socialists had established a totalitarian regime in Germany and crushed any public dissent as well as those centres of power that could have denied them unrestricted rule. The most important of these 'centres' were the elected President of the Reich, the army (*Reichswehr*), the organised left and the trades unions.

As they saw it, National Socialists therefore had four main priorities after Hitler's appointment as Chancellor. First, they had to secure the positions of power they had won in January 1933 by swiftly removing or weakening all direct or open opponents and those organisations that could put up resistance to their political progress. Second, the National Socialists had to extend their influence by ruthlessly pushing their own people into high offices or creating new organisations which would neutralise existing governmental structures or strongholds of their political opponents. Third, they had to establish a working relationship with two bodies which, in the Weimar Republic, had distanced themselves from close political affiliation: the army and big industry. In the long run, Hitler needed their unqualified cooperation. And, fourth, the National Socialists had to try to change the political climate in Germany. By using their well-developed propaganda machine, they had to fight the despondency and pessimism that had prevailed since the Great Slump of the late 1920s and create the impression of a new departure, of new activity and dynamism – in short, of a 'national awakening' (again, a National Socialist term), which would to a very large extent involve an aggressive turn against the outside world, the so-called system of Versailles.

Thus, the National Socialists made it quite clear right from the start that they would not only revolutionise Germany's constitutional order and rapidly transform democracy into dictatorship, but would also work for the complete destruction of the European order as devised at the Paris Peace Conference in 1919. The Conference had created the 'yoke' under which Germany had suffered for far too long. Germany's new rulers were therefore determined to destroy everything that was based on the fundamental decisions made in 1918–19, and this included both the political system within Germany and relations with her neighbours in Europe. It was not long before these neighbours realised that a new German Question had emerged. How did they react to the alarming developments in Germany?

Generally speaking, seen from abroad Hitler's appointment as Reich Chancellor on 30 January 1933 did not mark a major caesura in German politics. Germany had a new Chancellor whose rhetoric some observers found rather unpalatable and whose domestic policy they did not approve of at all, indeed very soon came to abhor. The democracies of Western Europe deplored the establishment of a dictatorial regime in Central Europe, but initially they saw no reason to worry about Europe's stability and peace. It was not until the mid-1930s, when all the menacing rhetoric about the alleged injustices of the Versailles Peace Treaty was suddenly turned into political action, that they started to perceive Germany once more as a threat. In the months immediately following Hitler's appointment, however, there was even sympathy and understanding for his political aims, at home and abroad. Nowadays, this is often overlooked, for very obvious reasons. Britain's attitude is a good example of the relatively late *volte-face* from sympathy for National Socialist Germany to rejection and eventually bitter enmity. Sir Horace Rumbold, the British Ambassador in Berlin from 1928, was a keen observer of the changes which Hitler's appointment brought about, and one of the few who did not indulge in illusions. A supporter of the former Reich Chancellor Heinrich Brüning, he was soon deeply shocked by Hitler's ruthless use of power and the criminal aspects of his rule. On 23 April 1933 Sir Horace urgently warned his superiors in London of Hitler's long-term intentions, which were manifestly obvious in his book *Mein Kampf*, published as early as 1925. His report was forwarded to Prime Minister Ramsay MacDonald and other members of the Cabinet, including Neville Chamberlain who was to become Prime Minister, as Stanley Baldwin's successor, on 28 May 1937.[1]

However, for the British public at large Hitler's appointment on 30 January 1933 was not, initially, anything sensational and did not seem to represent a break with the political system of the late Weimar Republic where cabinets relied entirely on the confidence of the Reich President, not on a majority in parliament. After all, the National Socialists had not come to power by means of an illegal *putsch* or *coup d'état*, and, at least on the surface, they were still moving within the framework of the existing, albeit distorted, constitution. Moreover, the old conservative Reich President Paul von Hindenburg was still seen as a guarantor of the established order, and in the sphere of foreign relations and Germany's diplomatic personnel no immediate or significant changes were discernible until well into 1934. Lord Rothermere, the influential press baron, visited Germany in the summer of 1933 and reported back in glowing terms: 'I write from a new country on the map of Europe. Its name is Naziland . . . I urge all British young men and women to study closely the progress of this Nazi regime in Germany. They must not be misled by the misrepresentations of its opponents. . . . The minor misdeeds of individual Nazis will be submerged by the immense benefits that the new regime is already bestowing upon Germany.'[2] Even the sober Anthony Eden wrote, after meeting Hitler in February 1934: 'Of one thing I am confident: the new Germany of Hitler and Goebbels is to be preferred to the old of Bülow'.[3]

But thanks to the Ambassador and other critical reports which became more frequent as time went on, the British government was soon no longer able to ignore the fact that quite extraordinary things were happening in Germany under her new rulers. By the mid-1930s British attention also had to focus more and more on Germany's new foreign policy which was becoming increasingly aggressive. In the same measure as the dictatorial regime consolidated its grip at home, it gained confidence in voicing its political aims abroad. National Socialist Germany maintained the revisionist positions in foreign policy adopted by the Weimar Republic, but now pursued them with dogged determination and unyielding rhetoric. Germany's neighbours in Europe now had to realise, whether they liked it or not, that they were again confronted with the German Question, though in a slightly different guise. They had to ask themselves whether Germany would continue to try to change the much-vilified 'system of Versailles' by peaceful means or whether her new rulers were planning to overturn the European order unilaterally, thus violating international law and, ultimately, peace in Europe. By mid-1936 the British Chiefs of Staff had already recognised Germany, along with Italy and Japan, as countries which were 'by their systems of government and by economic need, potential aggressors'.[4] They echoed Lord Cecil's warning, delivered a few weeks earlier, that 'Germany is preparing for war', and pleaded for a 'combination of all the forces of the members of the League [of Nations]' against her.[5] However, foreign policy planning in Britain was not yet totally dominated by the new German Question. In the years 1935–37 international crises such as Fascist Italy's intervention in Abyssinia, the Spanish Civil War and Japanese aggression against China demanded Whitehall's attention far more than developments in Germany. This was only to change with the dramatic escalation of events in Central Europe in 1938–39. Germany's territorial expansion now made it far more likely than in the early years of the National Socialist dictatorship that a new war, again triggered off by Germany, was looming on the horizon.

Nevertheless, until the Munich Conference in September 1938, which sanctioned the dismemberment of Czechoslovakia, Britain undeniably showed considerable understanding towards National Socialist Germany and her grievances and led the search for compromises. It does not seem to have mattered greatly that the German government was no longer in the hands of democratically elected politicians, but was now formed by a totalitarian movement which ignored civil rights and openly terrorised its opponents as well as certain minorities. This can partly be explained by the fact that many people in Britain felt Germany had suffered injustice at Versailles and that this should gradually be put right. Winston Churchill is a prominent example of the attitude which prevailed amongst the British political classes. Only later, in fact as late as the weeks before and after Munich, did he turn into the resolute enemy of Nazi Germany and Hitler that he is remembered as today. Earlier, in November 1935, Churchill had described the German dictator as 'a mystery'. At that point he did not rule out the possibility that Hitler might emerge as the Germans' saviour, 'as the man who restored honour and peace of mind to the great Germanic nation and brought them back serene, helpful and strong, to the European family circle'. Only the future would decide 'whether he will rank in Valhalla with Pericles, with Augustus, and with Washington, or whether in the inferno of human scorn with Attila and Tamerlane. It is enough to say that both possibilities are open at the present moment.'[6]

The attitude and policy which Europe, under British leadership, adopted towards Nazi Germany and her 'Führer' until late 1938 is generally described by the term 'appeasement' and is inextricably associated with the efforts of Neville Chamberlain's government to preserve peace with the dictators. But what did 'appeasement' or the 'policy of appeasement' mean at the time? According to Paul Kennedy, 'appeasement' is 'the policy of settling international (or, for that matter, domestic) quarrels by admitting and satisfying grievances through rational negotiation and compromise, thereby avoiding the resort to an armed conflict which would be expensive, bloody, and possibly very dangerous. It is in essence a *positive* policy, based upon certain optimistic assumptions about man's inherent reasonableness.'[7] Appeasement should, of course, be an ingredient of any sensible policy, especially so when the opposite side at the negotiating table is represented by an excitable, often irrational and aggressive dictator who has nothing but scorn for democratic procedures. 'Appeasement' towards Hitler's Germany was thus a policy which was prepared to make major concessions to the revisionist demands of her government, particularly with regard to a speedy removal of the remaining restrictions imposed on the Reich by the Versailles Peace Treaty. A modern historian has written:

> It is obvious that most, if not all, of the Western powers, the dominions included, were by and large in favour of a policy that would avert a major conflict with the fascist powers, if at all possible, even though this would mean partially abandoning the political system in Europe set up by the Paris Peace Conference in 1919–20. For diverse reasons they all favoured, at least for the time being, a policy of appeasing the dictators, rather than attempting to fight tooth and nail for a political order which in any case seemed to have become untenable.[8]

'Appeasement' was the basis of British policy towards Germany in the years leading up to 1938–39. The other Western powers followed a similar line. Only after the Munich Conference in September 1938, where the Sudetenland was ceded to Hitler's Germany by Czechoslovakia, did it become obvious that this policy had failed, and consequently the term 'appeasement' acquired the negative connotations it has had ever since, the epitome of how not to deal with dictators. The end of 'appeasement' is marked by the British and French declaration of war on Germany on 3 September 1939. The 'anti-appeasement' faction, which grew stronger after Munich and vigorously criticised Chamberlain's handling of the dictator, had been led by Winston Churchill.

On his return from the Munich Conference Chamberlain, to the delight of the cheering crowd, had pronounced: 'It is peace for our time'.[9] Churchill and his political allies, however, saw the outcome of the Conference in a quite different light. Churchill declared in the House of Commons:

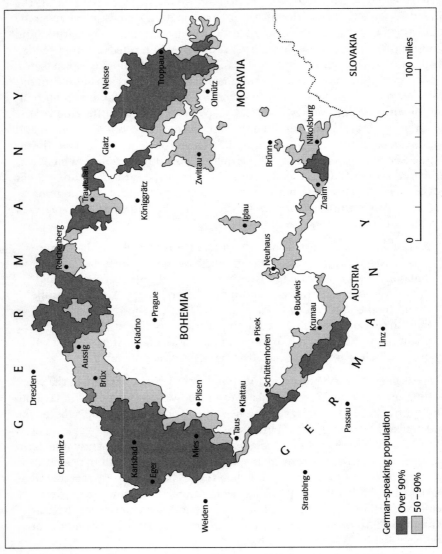

Map 6.1 The Sudetenland. From Hajo Holborn, *A History of Germany 1648–1890*, vol. 3, Princeton N.J. 1982, p. 781.

German-speaking population

■ Over 90%

□ 50 – 90%

0   100 miles

I do not grudge our loyal, brave people, who were ready to do their duty no matter what the cost, who never flinched under the strain of last week, the natural, spontaneous outburst of joy and relief when they learned that the hard ordeal would no longer be required of them at the moment; but they should know the truth. They should know that there has been gross neglect and deficiency in our defences; they should know that we have sustained a defeat without a war, the consequences of which will travel far with us along our road. They should know that we have passed an awful milestone in our history, when the whole equilibrium of Europe has been deranged, and that the terrible words have for the time being been pronounced against the Western democracies: 'Thou art weighed in the balance and found wanting'. And do not suppose that this is the end. This is only the beginning of the reckoning.[10]

On 10 May 1940, only a few hours after the German attack on Belgium and The Netherlands, Churchill replaced the unfortunate Neville Chamberlain as Prime Minister. The very man who had seen, only five years earlier, a chance for Hitler to enter Valhalla as a great statesman had now turned into his fiercest opponent. As one of the 'Big Three', Churchill was to play a decisive role when, in the later stages of the war, the question as to how defeated Germany should be treated by the Allies became ever more pressing. For him, as for President Roosevelt and Marshal Stalin, there could be scarcely any doubt that the German Question needed an answer which, contrary to the one produced in 1918–19, would put a stop, once and for all, to threats and aggression emanating from German soil. Thus no lengthy debates amongst the Allies of the anti-Hitler coalition were needed to define their supreme war aim. 'This time', the Foreign Office in London summed up previous inter-Allied discussions in March 1943, 'the victors, with the lessons of the inter-war period before them, intend and are planning to make a much more thorough and systematic job of disarming Germany and preventing her from ever again becoming a menace to the peace of Europe.'[11]

So, what were the concepts and plans developed by the Allies in the anti-Hitler coalition during the Second World War and its aftermath? Germany's post-war future, after the removal of the despicable Nazi regime, had been discussed by the Allies since about mid-1941 and then more intensively after the military turn-around in the east. After the surrender of the German army at Stalingrad (February 1943), the Allies created planning committees and inter-Allied commissions to work on schemes for the forthcoming resettlement of the German Question. Thus, Allied plans for Germany during the war, which are well documented by American and British sources, were formulated by the three wartime partners individually, but also, at the same time, in close consultation and cooperation. Experts in the respective foreign offices kept in close touch, supplemented by regular contacts

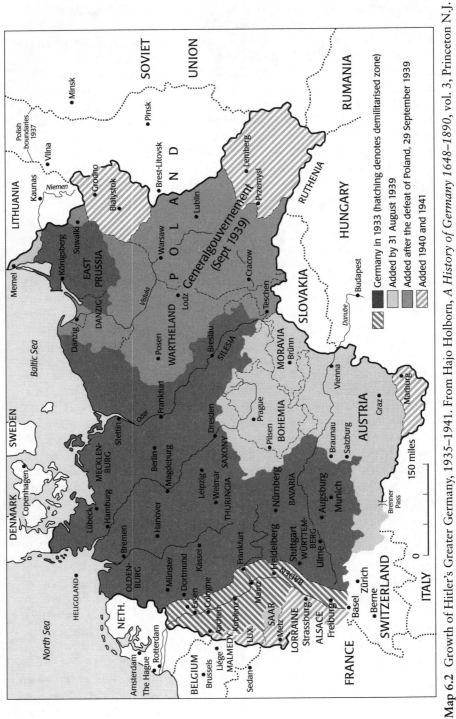

Map 6.2 Growth of Hitler's Greater Germany, 1935–1941. From Hajo Holborn, *A History of Germany 1648–1890*, vol. 3, Princeton N.J. 1982, p. 795.

between the ambassadors and foreign ministers. The major decisions were discussed and finalised at the numerous conferences of the 'Big Two' and later 'Big Three'. The 'Big Two' conferences, i.e. meetings between Churchill and Roosevelt, began early in the war, on the British initiative, even before the United States had officially entered it (11 December 1941). The first of these bilateral conferences, which soon became institutionalised on a fairly regular basis, took place off the Canadian Atlantic coast in August 1941. Its outcome was the proclamation of the Atlantic Charter on 14 August 1941, a document which broadly outlined the guiding principles for reshaping the world after the war.

'Big Three' conferences were not instigated until much later. For quite some time Stalin resisted the pressure from the other two powers for a meeting of heads of government. Naturally, there has been considerable speculation about the motives for this attitude. The most plausible explanation put forward so far is probably the assumption that Stalin tried to avoid a meeting with Roosevelt and Churchill until the military and strategic situation on the eastern front had turned decisively in the Soviet Union's favour. Once this had happened, in early 1943, the Soviet Union was undoubtedly in a much stronger position at the negotiating table and her views could not be ignored when the 'Big Three' were deciding on the future of Germany and Europe as a whole.

The 'Big Three' only met twice during the war, first in Tehran between 28 November and 1 December 1943, and thereafter in Yalta, on the Crimean Peninsular, between 4 and 11 February 1945. Pushed by Roosevelt and Churchill, the cunning Soviet leader had finally agreed to meet them in the Iranian capital of Tehran, a venue not too far from Russia's southern border, but on the other hand rather complicated to reach for Roosevelt and Churchill. At both conferences, in Tehran and Yalta, the German Question figured prominently on the agenda, although other questions such as military and strategic aspects of the war and Europe's post-war order were also discussed, sometimes in great detail and with considerable controversy. Whatever the ideas put forward on Germany by Roosevelt, Stalin and Churchill at Tehran, subsequent negotiations among the three Allies about the steps to be taken after the war did not suggest anything but one central authority in Germany which would carry out the instrument of surrender. The assumption that the Allies would have to deal with a single German state was important for two reasons: first, it was a necessary prerequisite for any sensible and coordinated planning for the period after hostilities; and, second, policing and administering an undivided and potentially dangerous Germany was the sole *raison d'être* for maintaining the Alliance after the war.

In the context of this book there is little point in following at length what was discussed and subsequently rejected at the numerous meetings of Allied experts, foreign ministers and heads of government during the war. On all these occasions Germany, by her very nature as the main opponent, was

Anthony Eden's visit to Moscow

Record of an interview between the Foreign Secretary and M. Stalin, December 16, 1941, at 7 p.m.

Present:

Mr. Eden
Sir S. Cripps

M. Stalin
M. Molotov
M. Maisky (who acted as interpreter throughout the talks)

M. Stalin suggested that there should be two treaties between the two countries, both for publication.

The first an alliance including mutual military assistance, as to which he thought there would be no objections.

Secondly, a mutual agreement of a general nature as to post-war reconstruction of Europe and the content of the Peace Treaties.

He then handed M. Maisky two drafts in Russian, which M. Maisky translated. He added that there should be to the second treaty a secret protocol concerning the map of Europe after the war, and he suggested the following contents:

1. The boundary of Poland should be extended at the expense of Germany so as to get rid of the Corridor by the transfer of East Prussia to Poland. The portion of Germany containing Tilsit and to the north of the Niemen River should be added to the Lithuanian Republic of the U.S.S.R.
2. Czechoslovakia should be restored to her old frontiers, including Sudetenland. This latter could, under no circumstances, be transferred to Germany . . .
9. As to Germany, I think it is absolutely necessary in order to weaken Germany to detach the Rhineland from Prussia, especially the industrial district. What should be done with it could be discussed afterwards; whether it was made an independent State or a protectorate, &c. I think this is the only guarantee which will ensure that Germany would be permanently weakened.

    Austria should be restored as an Independent State and possibly Bavaria also might be constituted as an independent country . . .

M. Stalin: There are two other questions I should like to ask as to post-war matters. First, what is your view as to reparations for the damage done by Germany and her satellites to Great Britain, the Soviet Union and other countries; and, second, as to the maintenance of peace and order in reconstituted Europe? It will be necessary to have some military force for this purpose and I think it is desirable that there should be a military alliance between the democratic countries which would be organised under a council of some sort and it will have an international military force at its disposal. If certain of the countries of Europe wish to federate, then the Soviet Union will have no objection to such a course.

Mr Eden: As to post-war Europe, I am very grateful to you for disclosing your mind so fully and personally. I am in agreement with much that you have said. When I spoke of France just now I meant to indicate that the responsibility for post-war Europe would fall on our two countries, together with the United States of America, so far as that country was prepared to co-operate, and it is in that sense that we are now tackling the problem.

As regards the future of Germany, you may be quite sure that the British people are determined that every possible measure should be taken in a military sense to prevent Germany again breaking the peace.

Exactly how this is to be done will require careful consideration. I should have thought that there was no doubt that some sort of military control would be necessary over Germany and that Great Britain, the Soviet Union and the United States of America, if they would help, would have to be the people to undertake it. As regards the partition of Germany no decision has been taken either way by His Majesty's Government. There is no objection to it in principle. It is a question of which is the best way of keeping Germany under control. If we could bring about a dismemberment of Germany by action from within we should, I think, gain a great deal; and we have not closed our minds to the consideration of a separate Bavaria or Rhineland and we are certainly definitely in favour of a separate Austria. I must confess that we have not gone so far as to examine this in detail as you have here, and I could not commit my colleagues on such a question without first consulting them . . .

M. Stalin: I quite understand. My desire is to establish that the war aims of our two countries are identical, as then our alliance will be all the stronger. If our war aims were different then there would be no alliance.

Mr. Eden: I agree. I see no reason why our war aims should be different, but these frontier questions I must discuss with my colleagues. My object will be to seek to reconcile the war aims of the two countries. There may be some points on which there are differences . . .

Mr. Eden: Did you say anything about this to the Poles?

M. Stalin: No, but you can tell them it will be necessary. Up as far as the River Oder should be given to Poland and then the rest left for a Berlin State.

Public Record Office, London (CAB 66/22, W. P., 42, 8).

---

bound to be high on the agenda, and decisions regarding her fate were, at times, not without their contradictions and confusions. In retrospect, however, at least four enduring characteristics are discernible in Allied planning for Germany.

First, during the war the Allies in the anti-Hitler coalition neither succeeded in designing a consistent joint policy for Germany, nor were they able to agree fully on what they ultimately wanted to achieve in Germany and Europe. There were a number of reasons for this failure. One was the uneasy alliance between Britain, the Soviet Union and the United States, primarily held together by their enmity towards Hitler and his dictatorial regime. Moreover, virtually right up to the end of the war, the 'Big Three' concentrated mainly on how it was to be conducted in the various theatres, tending to postpone crucial decisions on post-war matters and leave them to special committees manned by experts from the foreign service. It was not until January 1944 that, following a British initiative, a joint Allied planning committee was established in London: the European Advisory Commission, which France also joined in November 1944. But even then the Allies' planning for Germany often lacked consistency. This can partly be explained by the ever-changing course of the war, the repercussions on national interests, and the general assessment of the international situation by the respective governments.

Second, Britain was the country where planning for post-war Germany and Europe had begun early and continued to be most intense. Why Britain? The answer is comparatively easy to find. First of all, Britain had been in the war since 1939. In view of her diminishing importance as a world power, as well as the ongoing strain of the war effort, the officials and diplomats of the Foreign Office in London hoped to stabilise Britain's role in Europe and to influence political decision-making on post-war Europe by concluding binding treaties and written agreements with her two powerful Allies as early as possible. However, both the United States and the Soviet Union seem to have seen through this strategy and only reluctantly familiarised themselves with British proposals, designed to settle the future of Europe at an early stage. The uncommitted and sometimes even evasive attitude of Britain's Allies made all British planning for Germany somewhat unreal and tentative. As a consequence, Britain's policy on the German Question once the war was over also lacked real cohesion. No clear line had been agreed upon. All British efforts to settle legal claims and decide upon spheres of political influence before the war came to an end resulted on only one thing: the joint resolution by the Allies to divide Germany into zones of occupation. The zonal division of Germany was clearly a British idea and subsequently the brainchild of the first meeting of the tripartite European Advisory Commission in London in mid-January 1944. The occupation of Germany by the Allies was the compromise arrived at from a wide spectrum of demands and political concepts. These ranged, for example, from the proposed Carthaginian peace as advocated by the American Morgenthau Plan of 1944, whereby Germany would be deindustrialised, to the Russian insistence that substantial reparations be exacted from defeated Germany.

Third, with respect to Germany and her treatment at the end of the war the Allies had reached a minimal consensus. This consisted of three elements. a) The anti-Hitler coalition demanded, contrary to what had happened at the end of the First World War, the unconditional political and military surrender of Germany. This had been proclaimed by Roosevelt and Churchill at their conference in Casablanca in January 1943. Stalin also agreed to this a little later.[12] b) As early as 1944 the Allies had decided that the whole of Germany was to be occupied by their forces. Military occupation was considered an essential instrument for securing total German disarmament and denying her any chance to launch another war. Moreover, occupation of all German territory should also serve to demonstrate to the German people the extent of their defeat. From the Allies' point of view only then was there any hope of a fundamental 'change of heart' on the part of the Germans – a term which surfaced again and again in British deliberations during the final phase of the war. How occupation was to be achieved became clearer in the months before the war ended. It had not initially been decided whether Allied troops should jointly occupy the entire country or whether Germany should be divided into separate zones of occupation. The Soviets were in favour of 'mixed' occupation; the British advocated separate zones. c) The Allies were unanimously agreed that none of them should enter into a separate peace treaty with Germany. This is the reason why all secret peace initiatives launched by the German resistance movement during the war were doomed. Obviously, the Allies were not even prepared to consider concluding a peace agreement with Hitler's opponents, i.e. with a German government formed after the successful overthrow of the National Socialist regime. In the British view in particular this would simply have offered the nationalistic and conservative elites who had supported Hitler another opportunity to escape their joint responsibility for the war and the crimes against humanity committed during its course. Thus the failure of the assassination attempt against Hitler on 20 July 1944 was recorded in London with relief rather than disappointment. Had it succeeded, the Allies would have been forced to decide whether to seek a swift peace with the new German government or stick to demanding unconditional surrender first and talking about peace afterwards.

Finally, the fourth characteristic of all Allied planning for Germany during the war was the recurrent question of whether Germany should be dismembered. 'Dismemberment' meant the dissolution of the German nation-state within its boundaries of 1937, i.e. not including Austria and the Sudetenland which had both been annexed in 1938. The debate on dismemberment reached its peak at the Tehran Conference of the 'Big Three' in 1943. At the Conference the Allies were clearly in favour of dismemberment. Roosevelt and Churchill even produced plans as to how the partitioning of Germany should be implemented. Churchill's proposal was that Prussia should be isolated and southern Germany united with Austria, perhaps even Hungary, to form a Danubian Confederation. 'I thought', Churchill later wrote in his memoirs, 'Prussia should be dealt with more sternly than the other parts of the Reich, which might thus be influenced against throwing in their lot with her.'[13] For, Churchill concluded his account of the Tehran Conference, 'we all deeply feared the might of a united Germany. Prussia had a great history of her own. It would be possible, I thought, to make a stern but honourable peace with her, and at the same time to recreate in modern form what had been in general outline the

Winston Churchill: a talk with Stalin about Germany, Tehran, 28 November 1943

After dinner on this first evening, when we were strolling about the room, I led Stalin to a sofa and suggested that we talk for a little on what was to happen after the war was won. He assented, and we sat down. Eden joined us. 'Let us', said the Marshal, 'first consider the worst that might happen.' He thought that Germany had every possibility of recovering from this war, and might start on a new one within a comparatively short time. He feared the revival of German nationalism . . .

Stalin thought we should consider restraints on Germany's manufacturing capacity. The Germans were an able people, very industrious and resourceful, and they would recover quickly. I replied that there would have to be certain measures of control. I would forbid them all aviation, civil and military, and I would forbid the General Staff system. 'Would you', asked Stalin, 'also forbid the existence of watchmakers' and furniture factories for making parts of shells? The Germans produced toy rifles which were used for teaching hundreds of men how to shoot'.

'Nothing', I said, 'is final. The world rolls on. We have now learnt something. Our duty is to make the world safe for at least fifty years by German disarmament, by preventing re-armament, by supervision of German factories, by forbidding all aviation, and by territorial changes of a far-reaching character . . .

I suggested that we should discuss the Polish question . . .

Mr. Eden here remarked that he had been much struck by Stalin's statement that afternoon that the Poles could go as far west as the Oder. He saw hope in that and was much encouraged. Stalin asked whether we thought he was going to swallow Poland up. Eden said he did not know how much the Russians were going to eat. How much would they leave undigested? Stalin said the Russians did not want anything belonging to other people, although they might have a bite at Germany. Eden said that what Poland lost in the east she might gain in the west. Stalin replied that possibly she might, but he did not know. I then demonstrated with the help of three matches my idea of Poland moving westwards. This pleased Stalin, and on this note our group parted for the moment.

Winston S. Churchill, *The Second World War*, vol. 5: *Closing the Ring*, 4th edn, London 1968 (1952), pp. 317–20.

Austro-Hungarian Empire, of which it has been well said, "If it did not exist it would have to be invented".'[14] A sort of restored Habsburg monarchy was certainly not what Stalin wanted to emerge from the war. He did not object to a federation of the south German states, including Austria, but, according to Churchill, strongly opposed the inclusion of Hungary.[15]

In Tehran, Roosevelt presented the most far-reaching plan for the dismemberment of Germany. He suggested that the Reich should be partitioned into five separate states. Prussia should be reduced in size to consist of a territory vaguely similar to the German Democratic Republic that emerged after 1949. The Saar region, the Kiel Canal, Hamburg and the Ruhr area should come under the control of the future United Nations. Stalin indicated at Tehran that he favoured Roosevelt's scheme. However, the 'Big Three' did not vote on the two plans, preferring instead to refer the problem to the European Advisory Commission for further deliberations. Nevertheless, they were united in their resolution that in future the River Oder should constitute Poland's western border. Both Churchill and Roosevelt, in particular, separately and arbitrarily proposed that Poland should move westwards. The territory gained by the Poles from Germany in the west would supposedly compensate them for that which they ceded to Russia in the east. Again, this important issue was not debated in any detail at Tehran and was not formally acknowledged by a joint ruling or declaration. It was only later that conflicting views were expressed regarding the course of the southern part of the new German–Polish border. The matter was eventually settled at the Yalta and Potsdam Conferences in February and early August 1945. Almost half a century later, the reunited Germany finally recognised the Rivers Oder and western Neisse as the border between Germany and Poland.

It is quite obvious from what we know about the official and unofficial talks in Tehran in late 1943 that the 'Big Three' were in favour of a drastic solution. However, the experts in Whitehall and at the State Department in Washington rejected the idea of dismembering the Reich and denounced it as repressive and retrograde. A modern historian has quite rightly argued that 'too much attention has been focused on the deliberations of the "Big Three" who enjoy, as it were, the limelight of history and too little on the officials who briefed them and were later to make sense of their decisions'.[16] As a footnote to all this it should be borne in mind that Stalin was quick to announce the territorial gains he sought from Germany and this had major consequences. As early as December 1941, when meeting the British Foreign Secretary Anthony Eden in Moscow, Stalin had already indicated the Soviet wish to acquire the Memel area with the town of Tilsit (Klaipeda). Now, at Tehran, he demanded the northern half of East Prussia including the town of Königsberg for the Soviet Union, arguing that his country needed an ice-free port on the Baltic Sea. In this matter, too, Roosevelt and Churchill did not explicitly object. When the 'Big Three' met for the last time at Potsdam in the summer of 1945, the Soviet annexation was virtually sanctioned; divided East Prussia was put under Polish and Soviet 'administration'. After the collapse of the Soviet Union in 1991, post-communist Russia retained her part of East Prussia, now forming an enclave without any direct territorial link to Russia proper.

Although there was never any dispute among the Allies that, in Churchill's words, Poland 'should receive substantial accessions of German territory', the British Prime Minister had, at least occasionally, the foreboding that 'for the future peace of Europe here was a wrong beside which Alsace-Lorraine and the Danzig Corridor were trifles'.[17] He considered it would be 'a great pity to stuff the Polish goose so full of German food that it died of indigestion'.[18] But Germany was not to be dismembered after all. Towards the end of the war none of the Allies wished to compromise the idea of joint occupation any further or to incur the wrath of the German people by openly advocating dismemberment. Stalin made this quite clear when, on 9 May 1945, he declared that the Soviet Union, while celebrating victory, 'does not intend either to dismember or to destroy Germany'.[19] There was only one major dissenting voice. When the American and British joint Chiefs of Staff were asked to state their views in September 1944, they opted, much to the surprise and dismay of the Foreign Office, for the division of Germany along zonal boundaries. They preferred a western, manageable part of Germany to the unmanageable whole, especially as 'an insurance against the possibility of an eventually hostile Soviet Union'.[20] Their advice was ignored.

The French, who, to the consternation of General de Gaulle, had not been invited to participate in the Allied wartime conferences, were the only ones to persist in their demands for the dismemberment or division of Germany well beyond the end of the war. It was not until 1947 that they modified their attitude, when the Cold War between East and West was fast becoming a reality. When the Allied foreign ministers met in London in September 1945, the French government produced a memorandum advocating the secession of the Rhineland and Westphalia from the Reich.[21] If implemented, the French proposal of 13 September 1945 would have represented a further major amputation of the Reich's territory. The French initiative ran aground because the British, in particular, opposed it. But a few days after the London conference General de Gaulle made another effort, clearly aimed at taking advantage of the still unsettled situation in Central Europe. Addressing military and civilian personnel at the headquarters of the French Military Government in Baden-Baden, he answered the question 'What is going to happen with Germany?' as follows:

> We will do everything to establish France here. By doing this we follow a certain historical vocation of our country which has been interrupted several times in the past and which we will now try to realise for a last time and under the best possible circumstances. To establish France here means, first of all, securing France's hold over a territory which, by its nature, is connected with her. This applies to the regions on the left bank of the Rhine . . . and the Saar. These regions which are all interconnected must also be connected with France. . . . Does this mean annexation? No, but let us not fight about words. The aim is an economic and psychological union, a French presence, unlimited control.[22]

As the time of this speech de Gaulle was head of the French government. Four months later Foreign Minister Georges Bidault took up the subject, but expressed himself much more cautiously on Germany's future than his Prime Minister. Speaking in Paris on 17 January 1946 Bidault indicated that France was particularly interested in reaching international agreement regarding the heart of Germany, the Ruhr area:

> The security of both Europe and the world requires that Germany, once and for all, loses her potential for making war which consists of the resources and raw materials of the Rhenish-Westphalian region. . . . With regard to the Ruhr area, Europe's gigantic treasury with its coal-mines and coal-dependent factories which normally employ five million workers, the French Government holds the opinion that it should be regarded, in unison with the general interests of mankind, as a political entity which is independent of Germany and must be subordinated, politically and economically, to international control. The Rhineland should belong to neither Germany nor France. The problem we have to confront is not how to keep Germany miserable on purpose. On the contrary, the challenge is how to improve her lot without conjuring up a new catastrophe for the world and peace.[23]

The idea of internationalising the Ruhr met with Stalin's full support.

It is only fair to point out, however, that the spectrum of French views on the future of Germany was much broader in 1945 and 1946 than represented by de Gaulle and Bidault. Their attitude in those early post-war years mirrored the traditional thinking of the political class in France. Yet there were others whose thinking incorporated totally new elements and ideas which eventually proved extremely fruitful in shaping post-war Europe. Among them were leading members of the French resistance movement during the years of German occupation. The Résistance rejected the concept of dismemberment and French annexations of German territory as no longer acceptable if a policy of reconstruction and reconciliation were to be pursued. The editor of the underground newspaper *Combat*, Claude Bourdet, had written in March 1944:

> On the part of the Résistance there cannot be an absolutely unanimous view on the future fate of Germany. . . . It has to be said that the revolutionary spirit of the Résistance turns unanimously to the Europe of the future and this Europe cannot be built without Germany. . . . It has to be said that we will not profit from resurrecting, in the middle of the twentieth century, a small-state system in Central Europe on the model of the Westphalian Peace.[24]

Instead, Bourdet pleaded for Germany to be put under Allied tutelage for a limited period. Then, at the invitation of her neighbours, democratic Germany should join the process of European integration, which was considered to be an unavoidable consequence of Europe's destruction by

Fig. 6.1 Defeated Germany, 16 July 1945. The British Prime Minister Winston Churchill, attending the Potsdam Conference, visits the ruins of Hitler's new Reich Chancellory near the Brandenburg Gate in Berlin. Reproduced with permission of the Imperial War Museum, London.

nationalism, hatred and war. This was a policy which, vigorously implemented by the governments of Western Europe with the dedicated assistance of the United States of America, did indeed give Europe a new
foundation in the second half of the twentieth century and initiated an era
of cooperation and peace with Germany as an equal and trusted partner.

|7|

Germany in the Cold War

For more than four decades after 1945 the German Question meant the division of Germany into two states which belonged to two different ideological and military blocs. From the point of view of the West Germans and the Federal Government in Bonn, however, from 1949 onwards the term 'German Question' did not merely stand for the problem of partition, but also for the quest to reunite the divided country.

For the rest of Europe the German Question circumscribed the problem of guaranteeing its security against Germany. Not for the first time in its long history since the Congress of Vienna the German Question had two very diverse meanings which were difficult to reconcile, even bound to clash. For Europe a united Germany seemed to be too strong and potentially dangerous. Even if domesticated by the two superpowers in East and West, the Soviet Union and the United States of America, she would have been a cause for anxiety given the experiences of the two world wars and the Nazi dictatorship with all its accompanying horrors. On the other hand, historical experience showed that a plurality of states in Central Europe, while promising a weak centre, could easily fall prey to outside interests. Moreover, Germany divided up into a multiplicity of states could rekindle a feeling among the German people that, as a 'belated nation', they had missed out on the successful development of other nations and make them once again prone to a collective and aggressive inferiority complex. This, too, was a familiar aspect of Europe's experience with the German Question.

The partitioning of Germany after 1945, however, was not a foregone conclusion nor a sort of punishment for Germany's repeated 'misbehaviour' in the first half of the twentieth century. It was, as must be stressed once again, the outcome neither of joint Allied planning for Germany during the war nor of decisions made at Tehran and Yalta. The division of Germany, which became apparent in 1949 when both the Federal Republic of Germany and the German Democratic Republic were founded, was not even decided by the Potsdam Conference in July/August 1945. On the contrary, the Potsdam Agreement of 2 August 1945 repeatedly refers to 'Germany as a whole'.

Partitioned Germany was, in fact, rather the unforeseen outcome of the Cold War – the political and ideological rift that rapidly developed between the Western Allies and the Soviet Union after the end of hostilities and Germany's unconditional surrender. Partition resulted from the dissolution of a great coalition against the 'Third Reich'. In other words, the policy of dismembering Germany, so prominent at the Tehran Conference, was consciously and deliberately thrown out through the front door while the division of Germany slipped in through the back, purely as a consequence of technical arrangements and zonal boundaries. Of course, certain events and developments after the war, such as the collapse of a central authority for the occupied country or the French veto against its resurrection, accelerated the pace towards two Germanies. The outcome was virtually inevitable once Germany had been divided into separate zones of Western and Soviet influence, unless one takes the view that the Cold War could easily have been avoided. Not for the first time in history all the political planning for the future eventually proved to be utterly useless. It was overtaken by reality and replaced by unforeseen developments.

While the dismemberment of Germany remained on the agenda at Allied conferences until it became an obsolete issue, the total occupation of Germany was unavoidable once unconditional surrender had been achieved. It was to have decisive long-term significance. In the Berlin 'Declaration Regarding the Defeat of Germany and the Assumption of Supreme Authority with Respect to Germany' of 5 June 1945, the Allies explicitly took over supreme authority in Germany. The Declaration obviously assumed that Germany would continue to exist within her borders of 1937 because the victorious powers stated that they 'will hereafter determine the boundaries of Germany or any part thereof and the status of Germany or of any area at present being part of German territory'.[1] Another declaration, issued at the same time, established four zones of occupation. The response to the National Socialist challenge by Europe and almost the whole world was thus to make the Germans submit absolutely to the victorious powers, to deny them their sovereign statehood and to subject them to Allied military government. The purpose behind all this was to establish political conditions in Central Europe that would effectively remove the danger of a new war emanating once again from German soil.

The concept of occupation and all the details connected with it had been worked out by the London-based European Advisory Commission (EAC) during 1944. The EAC had been established at the end of 1943 as an inter-Allied board of experts to make proposals for the future European order. France had joined it in November 1944. The scheme for the occupation of Germany had been supplemented by an agreement on the Allied control system in Germany, dated 14 November 1944. This agreement stipulated that the supreme power in Germany should rest with the Allied Military Governor in each of the four zones. In all matters affecting Germany as a whole, responsibility lay with the Allied Control Council consisting of the four Military Governors and based in Berlin. The Control Council should also supervise the German 'central administration' which was supposed to

Declaration Regarding the Defeat of Germany and the Assumption of Supreme Authority with Respect to Germany by the governments of the United States of America, the Union of Soviet Socialist Republics and the United Kingdom, and the provisional government of the French Republic, signed at Berlin, on 5 June 1945

The German armed forces on land, at sea and in the air have been completely defeated and have surrendered unconditionally and Germany, which bears responsibility for the war, is no longer capable of resisting the will of the victorious Powers. The unconditional surrender of Germany has thereby been effected, and Germany has become subject to such requirements as may now or hereafter be imposed upon her.

There is no central Government or authority in Germany capable of accepting responsibility for the maintenance of order, the administration of the country and compliance with the requirements of the victorious Powers.

It is in these circumstances necessary, without prejudice to any subsequent decisions that may be taken respecting Germany, to make provision for the cessation of any further hostilities on the part of the German armed forces, for the maintenance of order in Germany and for the administration of the country, and to announce the immediate requirements with which Germany must comply.

The Representatives of the Supreme Commands of the United States of America, the Union of Soviet Socialist Republics, the United Kingdom and the French Republic, hereinafter called the 'Allied Representatives', acting by authority of their respective Governments and in the interests of the United Nations, accordingly make the following Declaration:

The Governments of the United States of America, the Union of Soviet Socialist Republics and the United Kingdom, and the Provisional Government of the French Republic, hereby assume supreme authority with respect to Germany, including all the powers possessed by the German Government, the High Command and any state, municipal, or local government or authority. The assumption, for the purposes stated above, of the said authority and powers does not effect the annexation of Germany.

The Governments of the United States of America, the Union of Soviet Socialist Republics and the United Kingdom, and the Provisional Government of the French Republic, will hereafter determine the boundaries of Germany or any part thereof and the status of Germany or of any area at present being part of German territory . . .

Ingo von Münch (ed.), *Dokumente des geteilten Deutschland*, Stuttgart 1968, pp. 19–20.

exist in the immediate post-war years. The Yalta Conference of February 1945 sanctioned the provisions devised by the EAC.

It was only in their initial state of shock that the Germans believed the Allied military regime to represent nothing less than *finis Germaniae*. The Potsdam Agreement of 2 August 1945 already made it clear that the Allies assumed the German state would continue to exist, even if they had widely differing views as to its future shape. In the years that followed, the former Allies, in their separate ways, tried to influence the shape of the two German states according to their own political ideas, and to restore sovereignty along lines which each side had determined more or less individually and which suited their own purposes. That the period of occupation had to be limited was obvious and was already acknowledged by all the Allies in the moment of victory. Nor was there any doubt that occupation and administering the country by military government was only a temporary answer to the German Question. The Western powers, in particular, initially feared that the political division of Germany would increasingly jeopardise Europe's stability. They understood the German Question, once the immediate post-war years were over, as an open, potentially dangerous question, and they reacted by producing plans and ideas to bring it close to a solution.

All these Western plans had two things in common. First, they shared the conviction that the German Question needed an answer which would grant the Germans the right to self-determination, in order to give Europe a sound basis for future democratic and economic development. In February 1966 General de Gaulle, now President of France, expressed the principles which had been guiding and still guided Western policy towards Germany as follows:

> Quite naturally, the Germans are increasingly pre-occupied with reunification. In the long run we believe that this reunification is desirable, but, it goes without saying, on condition that it is achieved peacefully and is the result of an agreement by all who are concerned. That means it has to be founded on an understanding between East and West. Moreover, it can only take place on condition that the present borders, especially those with Poland as well as those with Czechoslovakia, are honoured.[2]

Second, common to all Western plans for Germany, at least from 1949 onwards, was that, in the long run, they aimed at restoring German unity. As far as the Western powers were concerned, a united Germany should certainly be a country closely modelled on Western concepts for ordering state, society and the economy. After the founding of the Federal Republic, Western plans for Germany were, as a rule, in tune with the Bonn government. To what extent these plans contained elements of propaganda or were designed to appeal to the German people by agreeable political rhetoric cannot be discussed here. The Cold War was, after all, primarily a

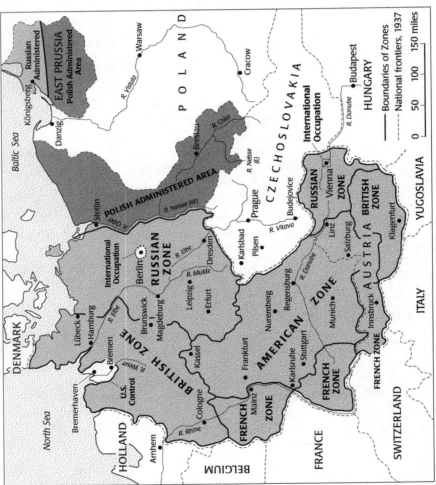

Map 7.1 Occupation zones in Germany and Austria, July 1945. From W. S. Churchill, *The Second World War, vol. 6: Triumph and Tragedy*, London 1954, facing p. 566.

propaganda war on both sides. The Soviet Union, in particular, very often tried to neutralise Western plans for a settlement of the German Question by putting forward arguments that were taken from the arsenal of communist propaganda. These were clearly meant to nip serious negotiations about Germany in the bud since they had no chance whatsoever of being considered in earnest by the Western powers or by the West German government.

Consequently, the former wartime Allies' post-war policy towards Germany was generally characterised by stagnation and fruitless rhetoric. This applies particularly to the years from 1945 to 1961 when the fateful Wall in Berlin was built. It was a period which saw no progress towards German reunification, which, at least until then, politicians in West and East had declared to be a top priority in international politics. If anything, the opposite occurred. The Western powers and the Soviet Union made every effort to consolidate the part of Germany that had fallen within their respective spheres of influence after 1945 and to integrate it into their alliance system, politically as well as economically and militarily. Cynics soon realised that all plans that aimed at reuniting Germany were, under the prevailing circumstances, utopian and merely designed to gain advantage in the ongoing and ever-intensifying ideological conflict between East and West. When published, these plans dominated the headlines and leaders for a few weeks – then crawled away to take their place in the archives. Between 1945 and 1961 this was the fate of the four better-known Western plans for Germany as well as the Soviet counter-proposals for resolving the German Question. Nevertheless, the various plans show how the powers of the former anti-Hitler coalition, whose relationship had turned sour, conceived the future of Germany at the height of the Cold War.

The first plan to be mentioned in this context is the proposal for a treaty put forward by the American Secretary of State (1945–47) James F. Byrnes on 29 April 1946. Byrnes gave a rough outline of its main features again when he delivered his famous speech in Stuttgart on 6 September 1946. His plan, which had been coordinated with the British and French governments, suggested a demilitarised and neutralised Germany, the creation of a central administration in Germany as stipulated by the Potsdam Agreement, and finally political unity. The plan was remarkable because it not only took the resolutions of the Potsdam Conference as its guidelines, but also introduced into the debate the concept of a neutralised Germany, an idea which was to re-emerge sporadically in later years. Reacting to his American colleague's proposal, the Soviet Foreign Minister Vyacheslav Molotov, in office since 1939, proposed that Germany be demilitarised for forty years and democratised following the model of the Soviet occupation zone. In the West the term 'democratisation', whose interpretation by the Soviets was well known, and the allusion to events in the Soviet Zone, were immediately assessed, with good reason, as a signal that the Soviets were not really interested in serious negotiations on Germany and her future position in Europe.

Fig. 7.1 Prime Minister Attlee feeds his valuable dollars to the cuckoo, 1947. From the *Daily Mail*, 6 August 1947.

At that moment the Soviets were apparently playing for time and speculating on an American withdrawal from Europe sooner rather than later. Since the Yalta Conference there had been numerous hints that the United States was planning just that.

In spite of the Soviet attitude, a new plan for dealing with the German Question was circulated at another conference of the foreign ministers of the four former Allies in March/April 1947. This plan is frequently called the Bevin Plan, named after the then British Foreign Secretary (1945–51), Ernest Bevin. It was now Britain's turn to launch an initiative on Germany. From the summer of 1946 onwards the British firmly advocated the creation of a West German state and the end of cooperation with the Soviets in the German Question. 'Apart from food, the remedy for the present difficulties of Germany lies in the successful fusion first of the British and American zones, and then of the other two zones, as soon as they are ready,' declared Bevin in the House of Commons on 15 May 1947. 'The

The Conservative politician Harold Macmillan, British Prime Minister (1957–63), on Germany

Through all these critical years [after the war], there remained the problem of Germany, obscure to many of us but charged with dire foreboding. Even as early as the debate in February 1946, which was mainly devoted to the growing concern about Russian policy, Germany had been much in my mind. I had always felt that since the rise of Bismarck Germany, not France or even Russia, had been, and remained, the key of Europe. I had therefore declared, less than a year after the defeat of Hitler and his forces, that apart from the countries which we were then discussing there was another great nation, with a large population, great agricultural and mineral resources, great in industrial capacity, with great intellectual and organising power, and with great past achievements. For the moment it was wrapped in mystery and darkness. We had practically no information of what was happening; there was a statistical and international blackout. Yet that country lay at the centre of Europe and at the centre of the European problem. Her name was Germany.

[From Macmillan's speech in the House of Commons on 20 February 1946]:

What is our policy towards Germany? Unless an accommodation can be found, and a formula established between the Eastern and Western hemispheres, you can have no sound policy regarding Germany. If that accommodation is reached Germany, so often the scourge of Europe, can in due course be transformed into a healthy and valuable member of the European family. Only so, can the soul of the German people be saved. But if not, if there is dispute and acrimony and intense feeling between the East and the West, she will once more become a menace to peace. Nothing can prevent the inevitable and logical development of this situation. Germany, now cast down, despised, shunned like an unclean thing, will once more be courted by each of the two groups, and from a starving outcast she will become the pampered courtesan of Europe, selling her favours to the highest bidder. She will once more have lost the war and won the peace, and Hitler's dream and mad prophecies will have come true. Therefore, before it is too late let us act.

Harold Macmillan, *Tides of Fortune, 1945–1955*, London 1969, pp. 120–1.

fusion agreement as I have stated so often is open for the others to join. Ultimately, I hope and believe it will lead to the creation of a unified Germany.'[3] With the benefit of hindsight the joint Anglo-American initiative proves to have been a decisive turning-point in world politics. 'The two faces of British policy gradually emerged', writes Anne Deighton in her study on the Cold War, 'the one maintaining the appearance of unity and co-operation between the Allies, the other laying the ground for a programme of gradual preparation for a division of Germany, should genuine co-operation with the Soviet Union on Western terms, and in a way that would preserve British interests in Europe, become impossible.'[4] The political and economic reconstruction of Western Europe and its military security had, in the British view, gained absolute priority. The three zones of Germany occupied by the Western powers had to be part of this joint effort to overcome the short-term and long-term effects of the disastrous war.

The Bevin Plan, too, spoke of a German government, a comprehensive democratisation of the country, a constitution and a gradual transfer of power from the Allied Control Council to the nascent German government. Ultimately, this British plan was frustrated by the French, who thought that all moves towards installing an all-German government to deal with political and economic matters and reconstruction were premature so soon after the war. Nor did the Soviet government do much in 1947 that could be interpreted as supporting the Bevin Plan. The French attitude did not change until a year later when the American Senate, with the Vandenberg resolution of 11 June 1948, opened the way for the participation of the United States in a peacetime alliance. Only after the subsequent signing of the North Atlantic Treaty on 4 April 1949, which founded NATO as a defence alliance between the United States, Canada and ten West European countries, did the French come round to the idea of a West German state. They eventually agreed to allow their zone of occupation, as a preliminary step, to become part of the so-called tri-zone. The Federal Republic of Germany, founded shortly afterwards, was thus not created by the action of a sovereign German nation, but resulted from the desire of the United States, Britain and France to merge their occupation zones into a functioning entity. In other words, they granted the population in the Western zones the right to establish a state under Allied tutelage.

After the failure of the short-lived Bevin Plan, seven years passed before another Western plan for settling the German Question was launched. This was the so-called Eden Plan of January 1954, named after Sir Anthony Eden, the then British Foreign Secretary and soon to become Churchill's successor as Prime Minister. In many ways Eden's initiative represented the West's reaction to Stalin's much-discussed note of 10 March 1952, which suggested negotiations about the possibility of reuniting Germany and concluding a peace treaty with her. It also proposed that a reunited Germany should have her own armed forces but should stay neutral between the emerging political and military blocs in East and West. The Western powers, with the full support of the West German Chancellor Konrad Adenauer, had flatly rejected the Soviet offer, calling it a tactical move launched in the midst of the heated debate in the West on proposals for a European Defence Community aimed at tying a rearmed Federal Republic into Western defence. Stalin's intervention was considered a last attempt at luring West Germany into neutrality and splitting her from the West.

According to the Eden Plan of 1954, German reunification should be the long-term result of a cautious process of rapprochement between East and West in the German Question, of progressing step by step rather than taking hasty action overnight. The process should be set in motion by free and democratic elections in both German states, followed by the convening of the elected national assembly. The assembly would draft a constitution and prepare a peace treaty. The formation of a German government would be the next step, and finally the signing of the peace treaty between Germany and her former enemies. However, this plan also fell through, this time due to Moscow's blunt rejection of any proposal to hold democratic elections in the whole of Germany. The Soviet Union feared that a reunited Germany would be firmly anchored in the Western camp. The results of parliamentary elections in West Germany had clearly demonstrated since 1949 that the Communists did not have the remotest chance of winning a majority or even of emerging as the strongest party. In free elections in the Soviet Zone, since 1949 the so-called German Democratic Republic, the Soviets expected similar, from their point of view most unwelcome, results. Attitudes hardened on both sides of the 'iron curtain', as Churchill had called the dividing line between East and West in Europe. Was it possible that the ideal solution to the German Question had been found: two separate German states? Each ideological bloc had got hold of as much of Germany as it could use and digest. Western Europe, under the American military and political umbrella, had gained the biggest slice, the increasingly prosperous Federal Republic. Eastern Europe, dominated by the dictatorial Soviet Union, had acquired a much smaller slice, the rather unattractive German Democratic Republic, led by an unimaginative class of communist bureaucrats. The appeal of the *status quo* in Central Europe after 1949 was, of course, that no one could really be blamed for this unforeseen and unplanned solution to the German Question and thus held responsible for it by the Germans. After all, they had not been asked whether they wanted the 'iron curtain' dividing East and West (and their country). Partition had been caused by the so-called Cold War between the former Allies, and this seemingly simple explanation almost gave it the appearance of a natural phenomenon, not the product of political calculations and mismanagement.

There was hardly any change in the political *status quo* in Central Europe in the years following the establishment of the two German states. The German Question remained, at least for the Germans, *the* big unsolved issue in Europe and the Federal Republic the only Western state that sought a fundamental overturn of the post-war order by demanding German reunification on Western terms. Consolidation, stagnation and a minimisation of mutual contacts characterised inter-German and international politics in the 1950s and 1960s. By contrast, the political rhetoric of the time tried to convey a dynamic impression. In the West politicians talked about a 'roll-back' of communist rule in Eastern Europe and continued to demand free elections to trigger German unification. The Western insistence on free democratic elections meant that the Western powers could only conceive of a united Germany as part of the Western bloc. For the Soviet Union free elections in Germany implied, more or less automatically, the renunciation of war booty and the sacrifice of the communist system in East Germany, with unpredictable consequences for the rest of her empire in Eastern Europe and elsewhere.[5] Even in the unsettled years after Stalin's death in March 1953, the Soviet Union was not prepared to take this step. The greatest concession to which the Soviets seem to have given serious consideration as a political option had been contained in a proposal announced by Moscow in January 1959. According to this, the two German states should continue to subsist and form a confederation which would act as a sovereign subject in international law. Confederated Germany should not adhere to any military alliance that was aimed against one of the victors of the Second World War. Both states should withdraw from NATO and the Warsaw Pact respectively, to which they had belonged since 1955–56. Moreover, Germany, demilitarised and practically neutral, should publicly and formally renounce claims on former German territory beyond the Rivers Oder and Neisse, now incorporated into Poland and the Soviet Union.

Predictably, what Moscow suggested as a way out of the entanglements of the German Question was not acceptable to the West. The Soviet initiative of 1959 would have involved greater concessions from the Western powers than from the Soviet Union: the release of the Federal Republic, economically and politically so successful only ten years after its foundation, from their sphere of influence. The West German people, too, were overwhelmingly against such a policy, whose outcome, it seemed, was highly risky. The West's response to Moscow's move was the Herter Plan, made public during the Geneva Conference of foreign ministers of the victorious powers in May 1959. Like the earlier Byrnes, Bevin and Eden Plans, this plan was also named after a foreign minister in office, in this case the American Secretary of State (1959–61), Christian Herter. For the first time since the end of the war a plan was put forward that built on the close connection between German reunification and European security. In other words, Germany was to be reunited in a prolonged process, while at the same time becoming an integral part of a European security system. This was intended to assuage Soviet fears of a Western-orientated united Germany. The firm incorporation of the reunified and democratic country, which encompassed a much smaller territory than the Germany of 1919, into a European framework clearly represented a relatively new idea in Western plans for Germany. It was to play a major role in the future. In his Zurich speech of 19 September 1946 Winston Churchill had already vaguely referred to it when he spoke of 'a structure under which [the European family] can dwell in peace, in safety, and in freedom'.[6]

However, even the Herter Plan of 1959 still contained too much talk of free elections for Moscow's taste. On both sides of the 'iron curtain', moreover, there seems to have been a growing perception that the German Question could not be answered by designing grand plans which, in the mid to long term, aimed at reuniting a divided Germany. In the foreign ministries of the former Allies, therefore, the experts' will to devise new plans for Germany definitely started to wane. The time for such plans seemed to have passed now that German partition was firmly cemented. This found its shocking, as well as symbolic expression in the erection of the Berlin Wall in August 1961 and the subsequent months. Following this fateful event, which caused indescribable human misery and hardship in the years to come, the Western Allies and the Soviet Union restricted themselves to consolidating the *status quo* in Germany. They now tried, starting tentatively in the mid-1960s, to lift the German Question on to a higher level by making it part of the policy of *détente* between the superpowers and the ideological blocs.

Fig. 7.2 The Berlin Wall in 1961 (building began on 13 August). View from the *Reichstag* building towards the Brandenburg Gate and Pariser Platz in East Berlin. Reproduced with permission of AKG London/Gert Schütz.

This involved a gradual 'normalisation' of political relations between the two German states, and between them and the four victorious powers, however reluctantly this was initially inaugurated by the Federal Republic.

In the course of this new departure in world and German politics the solution to the German Question was increasingly seen by all parties involved in a long-term perspective. As early as 1956, when he received the Charlemagne Prize in Aachen, Churchill had warned the Germans not to be too hasty in their desire for reunification.[7] Allied and West German politicians never tired of stressing that German reunification in a free and liberal state would come one day – but not in the foreseeable future. In the West the conviction grew that the 'key to the German Question', as it was put, lay in the Kremlin. But, as late as in October 1988, the then leader of the Soviet Union, Mikhail Gorbachev, told the visiting German Chancellor Helmut Kohl in Moscow, in no uncertain terms, that the division of Germany had to be seen as 'the result of history', and that any attempt to change the situation would be 'unpredictable and even dangerous'.[8] The German Question was pigeonholed, and only occasionally revived for Sunday speeches. 'While the two Germanies had been radically ripped apart in the 1950s', it has rightly been observed, 'and energetically pointed in different directions, there had yet been a lingering sense of impermanence; but in the 1960s, with division sealed, the two societies witnessed changes of generation and internal divergences as they more gradually, but no less fundamentally, proceeded to grow apart.'[9]

However, there is no end to history, nor to politics. At the beginning of the 1980s the German Question re-emerged as a topic of political debate and serious international deliberations on the future of Central Europe in a climate of *détente* between the superpowers. Could the 'iron curtain' which hung across Germany remain so unrelentingly iron when there were numerous substantial moves towards rapprochement and cooperation on vital issues between East and West? Moreover, from the late 1970s onwards the Germans in the Federal Republic had embarked upon an energetic and quite public search for their national identity which had obviously become blurred, even lost, in the post-war era. Had they, after all, turned into a nation separate from the self-styled 'socialist nation' in the East? And was the Federal Republic not, to all intents and purposes, now a democratic, liberal and prosperous nation-state among similar nation-states in Western Europe? In spite of *détente*, unification of the two Germanies still seemed a very remote prospect indeed.

During the 1970s and 1980s statesmen as varied in their views as the Italian Prime Minister (1976–79) Giulio Andreotti, the French President (1981–95) François Mitterand and the British Prime Minister (1979–90) Margaret Thatcher 'all directly or indirectly expressed a wish that West Germany should retain its separate existence and not aspire to recreating a single German nation. That . . . showed that there was a fear that reunification might undo all that had been achieved.'[10] Readily confirmed by their

Western European neighbours, the Germans themselves, at least those in the Federal Republic, were increasingly convinced that post-war developments in world politics had settled the German Question and that their political future lay in ever-closer integration within a unifying Europe. The stipulation in the Preamble to the Basic Law of 1949 that the whole German people continues to be summoned to bring about Germany's unity and freedom by free self-determination appeared to have been surpassed by subsequent developments. France, the Benelux countries and Britain, in particular, accompanied this prolonged process of adjustment and re-orientation with more than just a watchful eye. Britain, along with the United States, had been one of the midwives at the birth of the Federal Republic in 1949 and since then had always given public support to its ultimate political objective – the reunification of the country's two divided halves.

Nevertheless, British politicians carefully asserted the Germans' legitimate wish for national unity against the backdrop of the First and Second World Wars. The lasting security and peace of Germany's neighbours were never far from their minds. From the British point of view these could best be guaranteed by integrating Germany firmly into the Western camp, politically as well as militarily. Foreign Secretary Ernest Bevin felt that the Western powers would have to secure Western Germany and Western Europe with American backing. Britain's role, indeed her duty, was to lead this new policy to restore a healthy balance in Europe. Speaking at the newly founded Council of Europe in Strasbourg on 17 August 1949, Churchill, as Harold Macmillan recalls, 'in a dramatic outburst, looking round the hall, . . . demanded almost fiercely, "Where are the Germans?" He pressed for an immediate invitation to the West German Government to join our ranks . . . "We cannot part at the end of this month on the basis that we do nothing more to bring Germany into our circle until a year has passed".'[11] At the end of 1949 Churchill declared in the House of Commons that West Germany's future lay 'in ever-closer association with the Western World'.[12] She was to become part of a new balance of power in Europe.

Moreover, as early as 19 September 1946 Churchill had appealed for 'a kind of United States of Europe'. In his view, the 'first step in the re-creation of the European family' had to be 'a partnership between France and Germany. In this way only can France recover the moral leadership of Europe. There can be no revival of Europe without a spiritually great France and a spiritually great Germany.'[13] Britain would stand apart, defining her role as that of the superior enabler and sponsor, at the centre of three interlocking circles: the British Commonwealth, the United States of America and the future European Union. Britain was to act as 'the vital link between them all'.[14]

Churchill's stirring call for continental Europe to unite was given a 'challenging turn', the London *Times* commented, 'by the inclusion of Germany within the unity he postulates'.[15] Was not Germany the enemy who had just threatened the very existence of Britain and European civilisation? When Chancellor Konrad Adenauer visited Britain in December 1951 Churchill explained his stance to him: 'It is said that I have fought against Germany all my life. In reality it was only five years. All my life I have felt a strong sympathy for France. How wonderful it would be if Germany were included in this, if a great bond of mutual loyalty would link Britain, France and Germany and lead our people in a broad stream towards a resplendent future.'[16]

But was France, after all one of the victorious and occupying powers, ready for a partnership with Germany so soon after the war? After Germany's surrender in May 1945 the Provisional French Government under General de Gaulle considered the revival of a new sovereign German state in the foreseeable future to be highly unlikely. Foreign Minister Georges Bidault had passionately rejected the idea of creating a new central government for Germany in early 1946. Now, after the Zurich speech, when Churchill's son-in-law Duncan-Sandys visited the General at home in the village of Colombey-les-deux-Eglises in December 1946, he reported back to Churchill:

> He [de Gaulle] said that the reference . . . to a Franco-German partnership had been badly received in France. Germany, as a state, no longer existed. All Frenchmen were violently opposed to recreating any kind of unified, centralised Reich. . . . Unless steps were taken to prevent a resuscitation of German power, there was the danger that a United Europe would become nothing else than an enlarged Germany. . . . De Gaulle further thought that France should make her support for the policy of European federation conditional upon the settlement of outstanding differences between herself and Britain. A permanent allocation of coal from the Ruhr; consent to the continuance of French military occupation in Germany over a long period and possibly the incorporation of the Northern Rhineland in the French Zone; the establishment of a regime of international control of the Ruhr industries satisfactory to France.[17]

Even when France finally had to acknowledge that her Anglo-Saxon partners were determined to form a West German state by linking together the three western zones of occupation, she insisted on exercising continuing political and economic control in some form or another. 'A federal Germany and a Ruhr area under effective control are the basic conditions for French security', declared Georges Bidault in the French National Assembly on 13 February 1948. 'Integral part of this are also the occupation of the Rhenish provinces for an unlimited period of time and the restraint or complete suppression of certain industries.'[18] In a slightly modified way the United States and Britain pursued this policy too. Churchill once said in the House of Commons that 'Britain and France should in the main act together so as to be able to deal on even terms with Germany, which is so much stronger than France alone'.[19] So, after creating the Federal Republic on the basis of the three western zones, the Western Allies retained quite substantial powers in and over Germany. 'On the face of it, all that had occurred was a transfer from Military Government to a limited form of self-government.'[20] In the first three years of its existence the Federal Republic could not conduct its own foreign policy, and, when relating to the outside world, had to use the services of the Allied High Commissioners, the representatives of the victorious powers. Coal and steel production in the Ruhr, West Germany's industrial heartland, was controlled by the International Ruhr Commission. This body had been created in 1949 especially to meet French anxieties that Germany would quickly recover her economic strength and again become a threat to her neighbours. It went without saying that West Germany was not allowed her own armed forces. For the time being the new republic remained under the tutelage of the three Western Allies.

Yet the Cold War created a political and psychological climate which facilitated West Germany's joining the Western club with amazing speed. In May 1950 the great French Foreign Minister Robert Schuman admitted that 'le rassemblement des nations européennes exige que l'opposition séculaire de la France et l'Allemagne soit éliminée'.[21] Especially after the outbreak of the Korean War in 1950 things began to change rapidly. First, the formation of the European Coal and Steel Community in 1951, under French leadership, ended discrimination against Germany through Allied control of the Ruhr area and assured Germany's neighbours in the West that her industrial resources would be used in close cooperation with them. The path was opened that finally led to the founding of the European Economic Community by 'The Six': France, Italy, the Benelux countries and West Germany in 1957. The same far-sighted policy, namely integrating the West Germans as equal partners into the community of Western nations, was applied on the military level. After the failed attempt to form a joint Western European army in August 1954, the Federal Republic was invited to join NATO as its fifteenth member in 1955. At this point it finally gained complete sovereignty, only restricted by the Allies' right to station large numbers of troops on German soil, though they were no longer considered as occupying forces, and to considerable emergency powers. Obviously, the speed of the process that transformed West Germany from an occupied country into a partner within the Western framework had much to do with the common fear of Soviet subversion and aggression so prevalent at that time.

The Cold War had affected Germany and her people more than any other country in Europe. The 'iron curtain' hung right across her territory. After the building of the Berlin Wall in 1961, the 'most conspicuous monument of the Cold War and of the failure of socialism',[22] the two states were separated almost hermetically. From then on, travelling between the two parts of Germany became virtually impossible, communicating extremely difficult. However, West Germany also profited from the Cold War. Without the rising tensions between East and West and a Soviet Union perceived as a threat to freedom and democracy by the Western powers, the economic recovery of the Western zones of occupation and then the Federal Republic would not have been feasible so shortly after unconditional surrender and the destruction of the country. The speedy re-creation of a German state in the West, its acceptance as a partner and its rearmament would have been unthinkable.

Only ten years after the Second World War the Germans in West and East had turned into their neighbours' allies and partners. Apprehensions and distrust towards them abated much more quickly than contemporaries in war-torn Europe would ever have expected in their wildest dreams in May 1945. But the Germans had to pay a price for all this. Political rehabilitation and economic recovery were based *de facto* on their accepting the partitioning of the country. After 1945 the German Question had been temporarily solved by the victors, not as a consequence of their deliberate planning for Germany, but by their mounting disagreements about the future shape of Europe and the ideological orientation of its nations. Certainly, the demand for German reunification remained on the political agenda, albeit more and more rhetorically. In the West a unified Germany could only be perceived as part of the Western world. As early as 1947 the British sensed how the division of Germany would one day be overcome. On 1 February 1947 Patrick Dean, head of the German department at the Foreign Office, commented: 'We want to keep the Iron Curtain down (unless we get satisfaction on all our conditions) and build up Western Germany behind it . . . so that when a reasonable standard of living and prosperity has been restored there is more chance of drawing Eastern Germany towards the West than vice versa'.[23] With a powerful Soviet Union blocking such a turn of events, unification was widely considered to be highly unlikely.

For forty years, from 1949 until 1989, the German Question had found a rather unexpected answer which Germany's neighbours in Europe could live with and the Germans themselves had learned to accept as the inevitable outcome of the war and their responsibility for starting it. This acceptance was, however, only gradual and accompanied by much agonising and soul-searching. In the late 1980s, reunification of the country seemed to be a lost cause which Europe no longer had to worry about. Only after the amazing events of 1989–90 did it become apparent that recognising post-war developments in Europe had made *détente* possible, and *détente* did turn out to favour the Germans and their national aspirations.

8

The German Question 1989–90: a dream come true?

In the 1980s the reunification of Germany as an answer to the German Question was increasingly perceived as an option that could only be realised in a very distant future. No detailed plans existed anywhere as to how unification of the two German states that had arisen from the rubble of the 'Third Reich' should and could be achieved. The Final Act of the Conference on Security and Cooperation in Europe (CSCE), signed in Helsinki on 1 August 1975, guaranteed the inviolability of existing borders and thus, in practical terms, the permanence of Moscow's post-war territorial gains and influence in Central and Eastern Europe.

Then, with the suddenness of a thunderstorm and to everybody's surprise, the German Question became an issue once again in the summer of 1989. 'Europe is changing,' marvelled the President of Finland a few months later. 'This change is so swift and fundamental that hardly anyone could have predicted such a chain of events only a year ago. All those who regard themselves as experts on international politics feel incompetent.'[1] The Irish journalist Paul Gillespie wrote at about the same time: 'German politics have in this year of 1990 been on the fastest of fast tracks, so much so that even the most experienced and sober observers have been left dumbfounded and breathless by the sheer pace of events'.[2]

Within a few months of these statements, on 3 October 1990, the two German states that had been the unforeseen result of the Cold War and were now often seen as 'a guarantee against the revival of nationalism'[3] in Germany were united, or, as some people still prefer to say, reunited. Even a key player in the process like Mikhail Gorbachev was taken aback by the speed of political change in 1989–90. With the benefit of hindsight he later admitted: 'I should be less than sincere if I said that I had foreseen the course of events and the problems the German question would eventually create for Soviet foreign policy. As a matter of fact, I doubt whether any of today's politicians (in either East or West) could have predicted the outcome only a year or two beforehand.'[4] For the second time in the history of the German Question since the late eighteenth century Europe witnessed the birth of a German nation-state. The first time was in 1870–71 under Prussian leadership. At that time German unification was not necessarily welcomed by Europe, but was silently tolerated by the great powers Britain and Russia. Only their determined intervention could have prevented the founding of the German Reich, and this was not forthcoming. In other words, Europe tolerated the founding of the Reich in the middle of an unfinished war. Indeed the imperial proclamation in the Hall of Mirrors at the palace of Versailles was deliberately staged as an act of triumph on the territory of the defeated opponent. All this was completely different in 1990. This time responsibility for the German Question was shared jointly by the Germans and their European neighbours, with the crucial support of the USA, which since 1945 had guaranteed the military security and survival of Western Europe in the face of the Soviet threat. Many observers were convinced that in 1990, after so many attempts, the German Question had finally been answered since the new unification of Germany was not based on conflict and violence, but on reason and consensus.

How, then, did German unification come about so swiftly, relatively uncontroversially and, as it now seems with the benefit of hindsight, to the obvious satisfaction of almost all of Germany's fellow-Europeans? The starting-point of the unification process was the fall of the Berlin Wall in early November 1989. The factual disappearance of this infamous symbol of dictatorial oppression and blatant inhumanity was the direct consequence of the imminent collapse of the communist regime in East Germany *vis-à-vis* growing public protests in Leipzig, Berlin and other East German towns and cities. Not only had it lost the support of the population, if indeed it had ever had it, but also that of its protecting power, the Soviet Union, which had created the German Democratic Republic in the territory of its zone of occupation in 1949. From the summer of 1989 onwards the GDR population had demonstrated against their self-appointed rulers, openly denied their legitimacy, and finally demanded unification with the Federal Republic ('We are one people'). The opening of the Berlin Wall on the evening of 9 November 1989 may have resulted from a misunderstanding amongst the leadership in East Berlin, or possibly from an attempt by the unsettled communist government to quell the obvious dissatisfaction and revolutionary mood amongst the population. This can no longer be precisely reconstructed. What is certain is that the spectacular fall of the Wall gave the political map of Europe completely new contours within a few months.

Looking back at the dramatic events of 1989 and 1990 what is striking is that after November 1989 many foreign politicians became aware of the inevitability of German unification far earlier than the Germans themselves. Something which for centuries had been discussed, disputed and negotiated, in vain, was suddenly tangibly close to realisation. It took the Germans some time to grasp this and to adjust their political activity accordingly. However, immediately after the fall of the Wall the victorious powers of the Second World War began to set up the international framework within which the unification of the two states, now expected sooner or later, should take place. The very able American Secretary of State, James Baker, declared early on that the Germans in East and West should be the ones to decide about unification. In December 1989 he talked of 'a new architecture' in 'a new era' in which 'there must be an opportunity to overcome through peace and freedom the division of Berlin and of Germany'. But he also warned that 'hopes for a Europe whole and free are tinged with concern by some that a Europe undivided may not necessarily be a Europe peaceful and prosperous'.[5] America's primary concern was that, come what may, a united Germany must remain a member of NATO and of the European Community. In the following months, full of drama and surprising developments, the Americans never wavered from this clear-cut position.

But what about the Europeans? In general, they found it more difficult than the Americans to adjust to the new situation in Europe. The French President François Mitterand paid a much-criticised state-visit to East Berlin as late as December 1989. It was interpreted as an attempt to bolster up the failing communist regime. The Soviet and French Presidents met in the Ukrainian capital of Kiev in early April 1990. Both warned against allowing the two German states to go it alone in their future relations with one another. The balance of power and the political situation in Europe as it had evolved since 1945 must be taken into consideration when dealing with the German Question. The Soviet Union, for its part, would not hear of a united Germany being integrated politically and militarily into the West. Initially it insisted that a united Germany should be neutral. This was the position it had already adopted in the 1950s.[6] As the Soviet Foreign Minister Eduard Shevardnadze declared in February 1990, at this stage of the unfolding scenario NATO membership for united Germany, with more than 80 million people, definitely did not fit into Soviet conceptions of Europe's future security and stability.[7] A few days earlier, however, the reformist Soviet President Mikhail Gorbachev, who had been appointed General Secretary of the Communist Party of the Soviet Union in March 1985, had already conceded that the Germans had a right to unity.[8] But, he added cautiously,

the unification of Germany concerns not only the Germans. With all respect for their national right to take this step, the prevailing situation makes it impossible to imagine that the Germans will come to terms and then let all others merely endorse the decisions made by them. . . . It should likewise be made clear right from the start that neither the process of rapprochement between the FRG and the GDR nor a united Germany should represent a threat to or harm the national interests of their neighbours or anybody else for that matter. And, of course, any encroachment upon the borders of other states should be ruled out.[9]

The last sentence of Gorbachev's statement specifically addressed virulent Polish fears. Backed by the Western powers, too, the Poles had insisted since the end of the Second World War on formal and binding recognition of the future Polish–German border along the Rivers Oder and Neisse by the West German government in Bonn. These rivers, according to the 'Big Three' at the Potsdam Conference of July/August 1945, constituted the line separating the Soviet zone of occupation and the German territory put under Polish and Soviet administration until the conclusion of a peace treaty with Germany. Now, in 1990, the Poles wanted definitive recognition of this border. So in general terms, the overall framework for the subsequent negotiations on German unification was already in place at the beginning of 1990.

However, as it turned out, the complicated process of unification ran anything but smoothly, due, amongst other things, to an unexpected stumbling block on the path towards the desired goal. This block had been built in London. Of all the Federal Republic's allies, Britain opposed the idea of a new unified German state for longer than any other. That the regime in the GDR had the population firmly in its grip; that the Soviet Union wanted to prevent German unification at all costs; that German unity could only be brought about gradually, at the end of a long process and in the context of European unification – all this had been repeated for so long and with such conviction by many leading politicians in Britain that any contrary evidence was generally ignored or rejected. In September 1989, when fundamental assumptions about the *status quo* began to erode rapidly, one of the greatest experts on German affairs wrote: 'The future period during which German unity could be regarded as feasible has shrunken from a matter of decades to perhaps only 10 or 15 years'.[10] The then Prime Minister, Margaret Thatcher, made no secret of the fact that she did not favour rapid German unification. In her view, if unification were inevitable, then it should be dragged out for as long as possible. When asked by an Italian newspaper in February 1990 whether she thought an Entente Cordiale between France, Britain and perhaps Italy would be possible as a counter-weight to a united Germany, Mrs Thatcher stated that this was an interesting question.[11] In more official statements she gave unqualified support to German unification, though always reminding the Germans of the European dimension to this process. 'Just as the conditions for German unification were created by the efforts and resolve of many different countries', she warned her audience at the Anglo-German Königswinter Conference in Cambridge in March 1990, 'so the *consequences* of that unification also affect us all. We are all entitled to express our view on the implications for NATO, for the European Community, for Four Power rights and responsibilities and for Germany's neighbours and their borders.'[12]

In her memoirs Margaret Thatcher is more open about her reservations and fears regarding German unification. Here she envisages a unified Germany moving towards neutrality, dominating Europe and again becoming 'a destabilising rather than a stabilising force in Europe'.[13] Reflecting on the dramatic events since the late 1980s, she writes:

The Europe that has emerged from behind the Iron Curtain has many of the features of the Europes of 1914 and 1939: ethnic strife, contested borders, political extremism, nationalist passions and economic backwardness. And there is another familiar bogey from the past – the German Question. If there is one instance in which a foreign policy I pursued met with unambiguous failure, it was my policy on German reunification. This policy was to encourage democracy in East Germany while slowing down the country's reunification with West Germany.[14]

In private conversation the 'iron lady' in Downing Street seems to have been even more blunt. One of her advisers reported her strong views on Germany in December 1989: 'The Prime Minister is extremely reluctant to see Germany assume a role other than that of a divided country, still controlled by the post-war arrangements. . . . There is no question that if the Germans were reunited they would, once again, dominate the whole of Europe.' For Margaret Thatcher Germany was 'historically a dangerous power'.[15] Her fears were echoed by Nicholas Ridley, then Secretary of State for Industry, who painted a picture of Germany aiming 'to take over the whole of Europe'.[16]

There has been much speculation about the sceptical attitude of the British political class to a unified Germany, and attempts made to explain it. The answer which always emerges is Britain's traditional concern for the balance of power, which now, in a sort of knee-jerk reaction, again came to the fore. The historical experience of two world wars in which Germany had been the aggressor and threatened Britain's existence also played a role. However, in 1990 Whitehall was unable to develop an obstructive policy based on fear of the Germans since most of the British population, albeit with decreasing enthusiasm, welcomed German unification.[17] An openly anti-German stance would have meant Britain's international isolation.

During a visit to Germany in February 1990 British Foreign Secretary Douglas Hurd made far more positive noises than his troubled Prime Minister. He declared that it was 'unimaginable' to deny the Germans the right to self-determination. In his view, which echoed that of his American colleague James Baker, 'at the end of an orderly transition, German unity and a new stable architecture in Europe could be completed together'.[18] Other leading Conservatives also spoke in favour of German unification, for example the former Prime Minister (1970–74), Edward Heath. 'I warmly and unreservedly welcomed the unification of Germany', he later wrote. However, Heath appreciated the fears of other Europeans:

> It was understandable that the idea of a united Germany struck fear into the hearts of many European countries. There still remained a residue of anxiety that, despite the passage of time, the new Germany might behave like its forebears and become militarily aggressive again or at least seek to exert political and economic power over its neighbours.

Fig. 8.1 'A spectre is haunting Europe', by Horst Haitzinger in *Tageszeitung*, 29 November 1989. Reproduced with permission from Karin Herrmann *et al.*, eds, *Coping with the Relations. Anglo-German Cartoons from the Fifties to the Nineties*, Osnabrück 1993, p. 33. On the ghost's chest: German reunification. The caption alludes ironically to the opening line of the *Communist Manifesto* of 1848 which reads 'A spectre is haunting Europe – the spectre of communism'. The three leaders, left to right, are Thatcher, Bush and Mitterrand.

This fear was intensified after the remarkable break-up of the Soviet Union in 1991. I was appalled by the rabid, bigoted, xenophobic attacks on Germany within the UK during this momentous period. Support for German unity had been a consistent feature of British foreign policy since the late 1940s. By abandoning it, Mrs Thatcher undermined at a stroke the trust which a whole generation of German politicians had reposed in us. West Germany had acted as a model member of the European Community and a united Germany had no designs on 'taking over Europe'.[19]

The official British attitude, which was tempered by warm congratulatory messages from the Queen and both Houses of Parliament, undoubtedly led to certain tensions in Britain's relationship with the Federal Republic and with the other victorious powers in 1989 and the early months of 1990. But ultimately Britain followed the political line of the USA, the Soviet Union and France and accepted a rapid reunification of Germany. With the fall of the Berlin Wall on 9 November 1989 the unification process had already been set in motion and it was concluded barely a year later, on 3 October 1990. This was amazing by any standards, but particularly in view of the complex and problematic nature of the German Question hitherto. It had seemed a virtually insoluble problem, a question to which the superpowers in East and West had diametrically opposed answers. How the stalemate was overcome in such a short space of time, and the political and technical manoeuvres that eventually offered a way out of this long-standing deadlock, deserve closer scrutiny.

Two different levels must be clearly distinguished in the events leading up to German unification: the national and the international; in other words, a level on which the two German states dealt with one another and a level on which the German states negotiated with the former Allies, and for a time also with Poland, over the external aspects of German unification. These two levels were closely related: developments and agreements on the inner-German level had to be integrated into the international framework and approved by the Allies. Unification could thus not be achieved unconditionally. In this context, all the Allies were anxious to settle the external aspects of German unification in advance, not to leave them to be sorted out in later negotiations. Margaret Thatcher expressed this attitude very clearly in an interview: 'You cannot just ignore the history of this century as if it did not happen and say: "We are going to unify and everything else will have to be worked out afterwards." That is not the way.'[20] These external aspects were certainly of vital importance: for example, what financial costs would unification involve? How should the problem of the German–Polish border be resolved once and for all? How would the rights of the victorious powers in Berlin and the whole of Germany be abolished? What repercussions would German unification have for the European Community, for NATO and the security of Europe?

On the level of inner-German negotiations three steps were of crucial significance. The first was when free elections were held in the German Democratic Republic in March 1990, the first of their kind since the founding of the state, and a shortlived democratic government formed under the Christian-Democratic Prime Minister Lothar de Maizière in early April. On 1 July 1990 monetary, economic and social union came into force. The final step was the signing of the 900-page unification treaty in East Berlin on 31 August, which paved the way, under the terms of Article 23 of the West German Basic Law, for the accession of the newly recreated East German *Länder* (states) to the Federal Republic. West Germany's Basic Law, the provisional constitution of 1949, was extended, after some debates, to cover the united country. From a legal point of view both treaties, the one on economic and monetary union and the one on unification, were international treaties that liquidated a European state like a bankrupt company. They were concluded between two countries, each of which, at the time, was a sovereign state subject to international law. The unification treaty represents, both actually and symbolically – like the breaching of the Berlin Wall a year earlier – the abolition of the division of Germany. When the treaty was signed, the German weekly *Die Zeit* called it 'a unique event in world history. Never before have two states with systems so antithetical been unified with one another virtually without transition.'[21] This audacious procedure accounts for many of the difficulties that were to follow in the process of integrating the new *Länder* with the established *Länder* of the Federal Republic.

The external conditions of German unification were determined by the so-called 'Two-Plus-Four' Treaty, which was negotiated and signed in parallel with the German–German unification treaty. What was this treaty all about, and where did it get its name? First, the name: why were the parties to it called 'Two-Plus-Four'? The then West German Foreign Minister, Hans-Dietrich Genscher, wrote in his memoirs about the diplomatic background to the treaty and the talks which preceded it: 'Negotiations between the two German states under the direction of the four powers . . . was appropriate in the fifties, but not in the nineties. So we had to find a way by which we, the two German states, could conduct these discussions *with* the four powers, on the same level, with equal rights.'[22] This was apparently the thinking behind the 'Two-Plus-Four' formula, invented and sanctioned during Genscher's visit to Washington on 2 February 1990. The German Foreign Minister seems to have been the one who thought it up and carried it through. 'It was important to me that the two German states, the ones involved in unification, should talk to the Four [victorious powers] about the international aspects, and not the other way round. We had to avoid giving any impression that the Four were negotiating *about* Germany. This is how the word-order in the title of the conference came about: Two plus Four, not Four plus Two.'[23] Here Genscher was apparently referring to the British Foreign Secretary Douglas Hurd, who was reported to have preferred a 'Zero-Plus-Four' formula.[24]

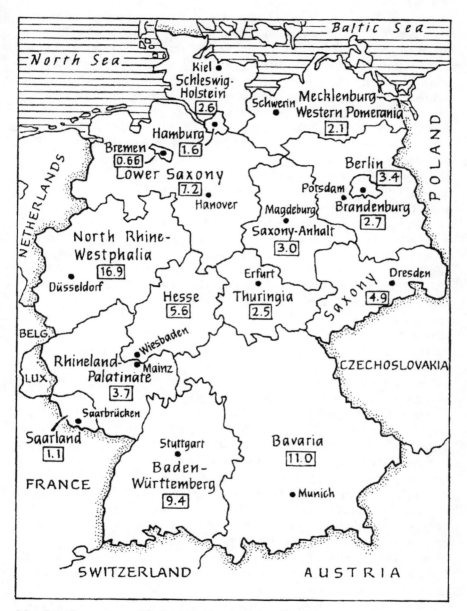

Map 8.1 Germany reunified, 1990. Numbers shown in boxes refer to population in millions. From Mary Fulbrook (ed.), *German History since 1800*, London 1997, p. 469.

According to his own account, Genscher's American colleague James Baker already concurred with him at the February meeting in Washington that the basis of the forthcoming negotiations with the victorious powers should be that Germany would not enter into any discussions about her membership of NATO or the European Community. Germany's continued membership of both organisations should be considered a Western *and* German *sine qua non* in the forthcoming talks with the Soviet Union. If necessary the Western Allies should be prepared to take account of Soviet sensitivities and to find a special status for the area of the GDR once it joined the Federal Republic as part of NATO. The idea was that only German troops should be stationed in this area, not troops of the NATO allies. One of Gorbachev's most influential advisers had hoped that at least the equivalent of France's status could be achieved for Germany: political, but not military inclusion in the Western alliance.[25] But all Soviet initiatives in this direction came to nothing.

A few days after Genscher's visit to Washington the 'Two-Plus-Four' talks were agreed upon, at a joint conference of NATO and Warsaw Pact states in the Canadian capital Ottawa. A diplomatic forum had been constituted that was to be so successful that many people claimed it as their brainchild. With some justification Margaret Thatcher declared that it was her doing that the international aspects of German unification were resolved so quickly and effectively.[26] In Ottawa it was decided to hold a series of conferences in order, as it said in the official communiqué, to discuss the external aspects of establishing German unity, including all questions which concerned the security of the Germans' European neighbours.[27] Today, a plaque in the Ottawa Conference Centre commemorates this momentous departure in European post-war diplomacy.

The series of 'Two-Plus-Four' talks began in Bonn on 5 May 1990 and ended in Moscow on 12 September with the signing of the 'Treaty on the Final Settlement with Respect to Germany'. In it the six signatories expressed their conviction 'that the unification of Germany as a state with definite borders is a significant contribution to peace and stability in Europe'.[28] Four meetings took place altogether. Given the importance of the questions and problems to be dealt with this seems an amazingly small number. But it must be borne in mind that between the talks many meetings of experts and advisers were held. Here the details of the important decisions were worked out so that they only had to be confirmed by the foreign ministers. The significance and intensity of this work by the experts is revealed in the memoirs of Foreign Minister Genscher. And finally, one further meeting of experts should not be forgotten: the well-prepared special summit of the European Community which took place on 28 April 1990 in Dublin. This was vital to the success of the 'Two-Plus-Four' talks because it gave the green light for the incorporation of the territory of the GDR into the Community. In this way Germany's European partners gave their seal of approval to the course of events and to the German people's desire for political unity. In Dublin they expressed the hope that this had created 'the opportunity of overcoming the division of our continent and building a new system of relations between the States of Europe'.[29]

The first of the 'Two-Plus-Four' meetings convened in Bonn on 5 May 1990. The plan was that the capitals of the six nations involved should each host a conference in turn. As it happened, London's turn never came, but as Genscher reported, the British did not take offence at this. At the Bonn meeting in May 1990 the participants agreed that the process of German unification should be set in motion quickly, with no delay. They also agreed that the Germans had the right to decide independently about what form unification should take and how it should be achieved. Furthermore, there was general consensus that the united Germany must recognise Poland's western border in its existing form, and that this should be binding under international law. For this reason Poland was to be included in the discussions when the question of the German–Polish border was on the agenda. The debate as to which political alliance united Germany should belong to was left open in Bonn. Clearly, at the first meeting of the six powers general principles were formulated and there were reservations and objections which it took some weeks to overcome. These included, for example, the Soviet demand that the rights of the four victorious powers should remain in force for some time after German unification, and Moscow's insistence that united Germany should not be accepted as a member of NATO.

Between the first and second 'Two-Plus-Four' meetings another round of bi- and multilateral consultations took place. The second meeting was held in East Berlin on 22 June. No really fundamental decisions were taken at this session either. The Soviet Union once again tried to tie the sovereignty of the future united Germany to certain injunctions. The problem of Germany's membership of NATO was discussed again. No solution to this tricky problem was found in East Berlin; in fact it was not until the famous meeting between the heads of the Russian and German governments in the Caucasus on 16 July 1990 that the matter was resolved. This meeting was so vital to the unification process, indeed sensational, because it was here that the Soviet Union not only agreed to the full sovereignty of united Germany without any restrictions, but also granted united Germany the right to decide which alliance system it would belong to. Chancellor Kohl's notable haste in the summer of 1990, writes the British historian Jonathan Osmond,

> must be understood in its international setting. He knew that the Americans would not tolerate a Germany outside NATO, nor did he wish any such thing himself. On the other hand, he had to have the agreement of the Soviet Union, and if negotiations took too long there was no guarantee that the relatively accommodating Gorbachev would still be in place. It therefore came to him as an immense and astonishing relief when at the meeting of the Chancellor and the

Soviet President in the Caucasus in mid-July 1990 the latter agreed to
all-German NATO membership. This was not the last hurdle in the
way of German unification, but it was the most important one and the
subsequent negotiations . . . could proceed with energy.[30]

As a concession to the Soviet Union the Western Allies agreed to accord
special status to the territory of the former GDR until 1994, and even afterwards neither armed forces of Germany's NATO allies nor nuclear weapons
were to be stationed there.

Just a day after this sensational breakthrough in the 'question of questions' (Hans-Dieter Genscher), that is, united Germany's NATO membership, the third round of 'Two-Plus-Four' talks was convened. The Polish
Foreign Minister took part in the meeting in Paris on 17 July because the
German–Polish border was now on the agenda. In reality there was, of
course, very little left to negotiate concerning the German–Polish border, a
border which had been such a burden to the German–Polish relationship
over the years. For decades the Western powers and the member states of
the Conference on Security and Cooperation in Europe (CSCE) had made
it quite clear that Poland's western border along the Rivers Oder and Neisse
was an integral part of the post-war European order. Leading West German
politicians had also said much the same thing. On a state visit to Poland in
May 1990 Federal President Richard von Weizsäcker had declared that the
question of the Oder–Neisse border had, in essence, been 'irreversibly
settled'.[31] The main purpose of the 'Two-Plus-Four' talks was therefore to
decide the form in which this could be made as binding as possible under
international law. In the course of the talks in Paris the two German states
declared that a treaty on the German–Polish border should be signed as
soon as possible after unification, and indeed the ceremony took place in
Warsaw on 14 November 1990.

Once the question of united Germany's borders had been settled, the path
was clear for the conclusion of the 'Two-Plus-Four' talks. The basic issues
that played a role in the external aspects of German unification had been
settled with the wartime Allies. The Paris summit in July had unanimously
agreed on five principles that circumscribed the future shape of Germany.
'The united Germany will comprise the territory of the Federal Republic of
Germany, the German Democratic Republic and all of Berlin' – this was the
key statement regarding principle one. The third principle confirmed that 'the
united Germany has no territorial claims against other states and will also not
raise any in the future'.[32] The 'Two-Plus-Four' talks ended on 12 September
in Moscow with the signing of the 'Treaty on the Final Settlement with
Respect to Germany'. This rather dry title was something of an understate-
ment, given its significance for German and European post-war history. Under
the terms of the treaty the victorious powers of the Second World War gave
up their 'responsibilities relating to Berlin and to Germany as a whole. As a
result, the corresponding quadripartite agreements, decisions and practices

are terminated and all related Four-Power institutions are dissolved. The united Germany shall have accordingly full sovereignty over its internal and external affairs' (Article 7).[33]

With hindsight the English historian Timothy Garton Ash has criticised the Moscow treaty. In his much-acclaimed book *In Europe's Name*, Garton Ash complains about the lack of balance between the six participants in the 'Two-Plus-Four' talks. He writes:

> The formula agreed in mid-February for negotiating the external aspects of unification was '2 + 4'. But of the two German states, the Eastern one was always a fraction of the Western one, and a rapidly disappearing fraction at that. France and Britain were a somewhat larger and more constant fraction of the American one. But the most important negotiations were between Bonn, Moscow and Washington – the Big Three at the end of the Cold War. Genscher would subsequently characterise the true mathematics of '2 + 4' to the author as 'perhaps two and a half', meaning that the central deal was between Bonn and Moscow, but with Washington playing a very important supporting role. Co-ordination between Bonn and Washington was exceptionally close and successful in this period, as was policy co-ordination inside the American government.[34]

A few pages later Garton Ash's assessment reveals even more resentments, which mirror once again the peculiar, and often ambivalent role which Britain played in the process of German unification:

> Indeed, in some ways the whole negotiation of German unification recalled the meeting that had been held in another scenic Soviet location, in the Crimea, forty-five years before. Here, so to speak, a Yalta to undo Yalta. It was, to be sure, diplomacy in peace not war. It was diplomacy transformed by the new technologies of communication. But it was still élite, great-power diplomacy, the few deciding about the many. While thousands of diplomats, officials and experts were involved in the whole process, Stephen Szabo, who has made a close study of the diplomacy of unification, concludes that the most important decisions and deals were made by eleven men in three capitals. And even President Bush and James Baker were apparently surprised and just a little piqued by the German–Soviet deal in the Caucasus. The Federal Republic's closest and most important West European allies, France and Britain, were neither present nor intimately involved in the crucial negotiations. In this sense Britain now experienced what France had always most bitterly resented about Yalta – not being there.[35]

From a perspective of this sort, as represented by Garton Ash, there can, of course, be no question of German unification being 'anchored in Europe', nor indeed of 'agreement' between Germany's European neighbours. On the contrary, it focuses on rivalries and resentments which do not bode well for Europe's future. A more impartial assessment of the 'Two-Plus-Four' process than the one offered by Garton Ash would probably conclude that the Treaty on the Final Settlement with Respect to Germany was negotiated in a climate of goodwill, with a surprising degree of political harmony and parallel interests on the part of all the powers. At the end of the Paris summit in July 1990 the French Foreign Minister, Roland Dumas, spoke of 'the satisfaction of all concerned', and his British counterpart Douglas Hurd, among others, was quick to agree.[36] By 1989–90 the last vestiges of the Cold War and the confrontation between the world powers had disappeared. Ultimately, this was the basic prerequisite for a solution to the German Question. In 1989–90 the interests of the great powers were running in more or less the same direction, though it was undoubtedly the Soviet Union which had to make the most drastic adjustments to its position. All in all the wide-ranging agreements and treaties negotiated during the *annus mirabilis* between the fall of the Berlin Wall in November 1989 and German unification in October 1990 can rightly be described as 'one of the greatest triumphs of diplomacy in the twentieth century'.[37]

To all intents and purposes, the 'Two-Plus-Four' talks represented the supervisory board with whose gentle guidance the German states worked out their unification. The victorious powers of the Second World War had formulated conditions during the discussions which the German states fulfilled. What is more, the 'Two-Plus-Four' talks were a symbolic demonstration to the whole world that German unification had taken place with European and international approval. Compared with 1870–71 this was a dazzling success: German unity had been brought about with the consent of all the powers concerned. There is therefore every reason to hope that the answer to the German Question arrived at in 1990 will be an enduring one. The two aspects of the German Question mentioned at the beginning of this book[38] were resolved in conjunction with Germany's European neighbours. On the one hand, Germany's territorial shape, so long uncertain and disputed, was defined once and for all and secured by international agreements. On the other hand, the political constitution of Germany as a parliamentary democracy made the united country part of a community governed by the principles of freedom, constitutionality, rule of law and social equality. Scepticism is often expressed about the fact that the second German democracy has not yet had to weather a real storm and still has to stand the acid test, but this has not really done much to shake the general confidence in its strength in years to come.

Occasionally, however, the solution to the German Question reached in 1990 does give rise to certain anxieties. Would a united Germany with more than 80 million people again seek hegemony in Europe as, for example, Margaret Thatcher feared? Would Germany, as the strongest economic power on the continent, seek to impose her will on the other nations of Europe? Would she remain in NATO or, in the long run, choose a 'third

Speech by the French President François Mitterand at the Spring Session of the North Atlantic Treaty Organisation Assembly, Paris, 1 May 1990

I don't need to explain the new situation in which Europe finds itself. You know what it is and most of you are experiencing it first hand. We are seeing the central and eastern European countries once more exercising their full sovereignty and evolving, admittedly at different speeds, towards democracy; all are seeking to become reintegrated in our continent's life at every level, on the economic plane most certainly and on many others. Germany has begun the process that will lead her to unification, a major event and a natural one if you consider the logic of history and reality of a people. Let us, as I have done already, wish her good luck.

An order is disappearing in Europe. It must give way to a new balance. There is to be greater military stability thanks particularly to the disarmament measures currently being negotiated in Vienna with a view to reducing the asymmetries so as to achieve a balance of power at the lowest possible level . . .

People are talking about Germany's new situation. We agree that unified Germany, the whole of the new Germany, is naturally destined to belong to the Atlantic Alliance. There's no going back on that otherwise we would end up with preposterous arrangements. Simply, sensible measures must be taken. That does not mean that it will be necessary to move the military capabilities further East. No posture capable of arousing the Soviet Union's fear or suspicion must be adopted. Simply, as we have always said, there must be balance, symmetry, a joint, concomitant and comparable démarche and, once we have those, we shall see what changes are going to take place within the Warsaw Pact, what the balance of forces will be and in what terms we shall be able to envisage security in future years. We are making sure, as we ask the others opposite us to do, that we don't undertake any unnecessary action that might be imprudent.

Adam Daniel Rotfeld and Walther Stützle (eds), *Germany and Europe in Transition*, Oxford 1991, pp. 117–18.

way' of non-alignment after all? At the beginning of the twenty-first century such apprehensions and fears seem unfounded, despite the occasional ambivalent speech by second-rate German politicians, outbursts of xenophobia and racism, traces of anti-Semitism and demonstrations by members of the extreme right. The far-fetched and misleading concept of a 'Fourth Reich', however, as Germany's allegedly unavoidable long-term destiny and likely path into the future, is, at best, the stuff of sensational journalism.[39] Conjuring up such images, closely connected with old spectres, is a blatant distortion of reality and of the new Germany's intentions and political goals.

United Germany is certainly well aware of the political limitations imposed by her hegemonic and annexationist aspirations of the past, and of the sensitivities of her neighbours in Europe. Virtually all politicians of the major parties have, since the 1960s, been pledged to unwavering support for the North Atlantic Alliance and for the great and novel project of the European Union. United Germany no longer wants, and, more to the point, is no longer able, to pose a military threat to her neighbours. Without external support her fighting forces are capable neither of attack nor defence. In a symbolic act of profound significance, the Preamble and the same Article 23 of the West German Basic Law under which German unification had been achieved was amended so that Germany is now committed to 'the realisation of a united Europe'. Germany is uniquely and irreversibly bound up in the European and world economy. She is so far removed from those ambitions of the past which troubled Europe for so long and brought it to the brink of the abyss, that there can be no going back. The extent of the mental and political changes in Germany since 1945 can hardly be overstated. Thus a British historian has reached the conclusion that Germany 'must never return to old patterns of dominance or domination. The current reinvention of Germany, which began in 1990, must continue to uphold the values of the reinvention that preceded it.'[40]

The mood of the Germans *vis-à-vis* their unexpected unification and new future was put into words in 1990 by the much-respected journalist Peter Bender. They are still valid today:

> Germany is big and lies in the middle of the continent; she is unavoidable simply in terms of geography. So it is all the more imperative not to make an ideology either out of her position, or her history: the Germans have no 'function' as a bridge, nor a 'duty' as a mediator, nor a 'role' as an angel of peace; they are a European nation like any other. If they feel and behave like one, and if the others regard them as one, then an age-old problem will have been solved: an answer found to the German Question that suits both the Germans and their European neighbours.[41]

There is every reason to believe that this attitude will guarantee Germany's future role in Europe.

Notes

1 The German Question and Europe

1 Wilhelm Röpke, *The German Question*, London 1946, p. 152 (German edition: Erlenbach/Zurich 1945).
2 Quoted by Röpke, ibid.
3 Julius Heyderhoff and Paul Wentzcke, *Deutscher Liberalismus im Zeitalter Bismarcks. Eine politische Briefsammlung*, vol. 1 (1925), reprint Osnabrück 1970, p. 494.
4 Bismarck on 9 Nov. 1876. Quoted in Theodor Schieder, 'Bismarck und Europa. Ein Beitrag zum Bismarck-Problem', in idem, *Begegnungen mit der Geschichte*, Göttingen 1962, pp. 253–4.
5 Gordon A. Craig, *Europe since 1815*, New York 1962, pp. 10–11.
6 Quoted by Ralf Dahrendorf, *Society and Democracy in Germany*, London 1968, p. 5.
7 See below Chapter 6.
8 See below Chapter 8.
9 Quoted by Wolf D. Gruner, *Die deutsche Frage in Europa 1800–1990*, Munich/Zurich 1993, p. 15.
10 Ibid.
11 Anselm Doering-Manteuffel, *Die deutsche Frage und das europäische Staatensystem*, Munich 1993, p. ix.
12 Röpke, *German Question*, p. 21.
13 Ibid., p. 15.
14 Walther Hubatsch (ed.), *The German Question*, New York 1967, p. 5. The first German edition was published in 1960.
15 Gerhard Ritter, *Das Deutsche Problem. Grundfragen deutschen Staatslebens gestern und heute*, 2nd edn, Munich 1966, p. 11. An earlier version of the book was published under the title *Europa und die deutsche Frage. Betrachtungen über die geschichtliche Eigenart des deutschen Staatsdenkens*, Munich 1948.
16 Dahrendorf, *Society and Democracy in Germany*, p. 14.
17 Theodor Schieder, 'Die deutsche Frage', in *Meyers Enzyklopädisches Lexikon*, vol. 6, Mannheim 1972, p. 521.
18 See David Calleo, *The German Problem Reconsidered. Germany and the World Order, 1870 to the Present*, Cambridge/New York 1978. The American edition of Gerhard Ritter's book bears the title *The German Problem: Basic Questions of German Political Life, Past and Present*, Columbus Ohio 1965.

19 Jean-Baptiste Duroselle, 'Vom historischen Erbfeind zum europäischen Partner', in Walther Hofer (ed.), *Europa und die deutsche Einheit. Eine Bilanz nach 100 Jahren*, Cologne 1970, p. 64.
20 A. J. P. Taylor, *The Course of German History. A Survey of the Development of German History since 1815*, London 1976 (reprint), p. ix.
21 Ibid., p. x. From the Preface, written in 1961.
22 Ibid., p. 1.
23 Foreign Minister Bernhard von Bülow on 6 Dec. 1897 in the Reichstag (*Stenographische Berichte über die Verhandlungen des Deutschen Reichstags*, 9th Legislaturperiode, 5th Session, vol. 1, Berlin 1898, p. 60).
24 Quoted by Klaus Hildebrand, *Reich – Großmacht – Nation. Betrachtungen zur Geschichte der deutschen Außenpolitik 1871–1945*, Munich 1995, p. 14.

2 Vienna 1815: the quest for stability

1 Imanuel Geiss, *The Question of German Unification, 1806–1996*, London/New York 1997, p. 31.
2 Quoted in Hilde Spiel (ed.), *Der Wiener Kongress in Augenzeugenberichten*, 3rd edn, Düsseldorf 1965, p. 44.
3 Quoted in Eberhard Kolb (ed.), *Europa und die Reichsgründung. Preußen-Deutschland in der Sicht der großen europäischen Mächte 1860–1880*, Munich 1980, p. 279.
4 Quoted in Spiel (ed.), *Wiener Kongress*, p. 12.
5 See Henry A. Kissinger, *A World Restored*, London 1977, pp. 7–28.
6 Quoted in Spiel (ed.), *Wiener Kongress*, p. 259.
7 Spiel, 'Einleitung', in ibid., p. 13.
8 Letter of 4 May 1820 to the Minister of Baden in Vienna, in K. L. Graf von Metternich, *Schriften und Briefe*, Vienna 1911, p. 85.
9 Quoted by Geiss, *Question of German Unification*, p. 37.
10 Anselm Doering-Manteuffel, *Die deutsche Frage und das europäische Staaten-system*, Munich 1993, p. 6.
11 Geiss, *Question of German Unification*, p. 36.
12 Christopher Clark, 'Germany 1815–1848: Restoration or Pre-March?', in Mary Fulbrook (ed.), *German History since 1800*, London 1997, p. 44.
13 Quoted in E. R. Huber, *Deutsche Verfassungsgeschichte seit 1789*, vol. 1, 2nd edn, Munich 1975, p. 563.
14 A. H. L. Heeren, *Der Deutsche Bund in seinen Verhältnissen zu dem europäi-schen Staatensystem*, Göttingen 1816, p. 11.
15 Heinrich von Treitschke, *Deutsche Geschichte im 19. Jahrhundert*, vol. 2, 7th edn, Leipzig 1912, p. 142.

3 Economic progress and political failure

1 Henrik Steffens, *Über die Idee der Universitäten*, ed. Eduard Spranger, Leipzig 1910, p. 101.
2 Harold James, *A German Identity 1770–1990*, London 1989, p. 59.
3 Heinrich von Treitschke, *Die Anfänge des deutschen Zollvereins*, Berlin 1872, p. 5.
4 Quoted by Thomas Nipperdey, *Germany from Napoleon to Bismarck, 1800–1866*,

Dublin 1996, p. 319. H. W. Koch, *A Constitutional History of Germany in the Nineteenth and Twentieth Centuries*, London/New York 1984, p. 24.

5 James, *German Identity*, p. 58.

6 Nipperdey, *Germany*, pp. 316–19.

7 See William Carr, *Schleswig-Holstein 1815–48. A Study in National Conflict*, Manchester 1963. Keith A. P. Sandiford, *Great Britain and the Schleswig-Holstein Question, 1848–64: A Study in Diplomacy, Politics and Public Opinion*, Toronto 1975.

8 Quoted in Walter Bussmann (ed.), *Europa von der Französischen Revolution zu den nationalstaatlichen Bewegungen des 19. Jahrhunderts*, Stuttgart 1981, p. 499.

9 Deputy Georg Beseler on 3 July 1848, in Franz Wigard (ed.), *Stenographischer Bericht über die Verhandlungen der deutschen constituierenden Nationalversammlung zu Frankfurt am Main*, vol. 1, Frankfurt 1848/49 (reprint 1976), p. 700.

10 Koch, *Constitutional History*, p. 67.

11 Harm-Hinrich Brandt, 'The Revolution of 1848 and the Problem of Central European Nationalities', in Hagen Schulze (ed.), *Nation-Building in Central Europe*, Leamington Spa 1987, pp. 107–34. Frank Eyck, *The Frankfurt Parliament, 1848–1849*, London/New York 1968.

12 Quoted in Norman Davies, *Europe. A History*, Oxford/New York 1996, p. 931.

13 Lewis Namier, *1848: The Revolution of the Intellectuals*, 6th edn, Oxford 1971, p. 33.

14 See, for example, Günter Wollstein, *Das 'Großdeutschland' der Paulskirche. Nationale Ziele in der bürgerlichen Revolution 1848/49*, Düsseldorf 1979.

15 E. du Guichen, *Les grandes questions Européennes et la diplomatie des puissances sous la Seconde République Française*, vol. 1, Paris 1925, p. 166.

16 See Peter Alter, *Nationalism*, 2nd edn, London 1994, p. 76.

17 František Palacký, *Gedenkblätter. Auswahl von Denkschriften, Aufsätzen und Briefen*, Prague 1874, pp. 149–51.

18 Lawrence D. Orton, *The Prague Slav Congress of 1848*, New York 1978.

19 Andreas Hillgruber, 'Die Deutsche Frage im 19. und 20. Jahrhundert – Zur Einführung in die nationale und internationale Problematik', in Josef Becker and Andreas Hillgruber (eds), *Die deutsche Frage im 19. und 20. Jahrhundert*, Munich 1983, p. 15.

20 Alexis de Tocqueville, *Recollections*, Garden City/New York 1970, p. 247.

21 John Clarke, *British Diplomacy and Foreign Policy 1782–1865. The National Interest*, London 1989, p. 226.

22 See Alan Sked, *The Decline and Fall of the Habsburg Empire 1815–1918*, London/New York 1989.

23 Quoted in Bussmann (ed.), *Europa*, p. 515.

4 German unity: first attempt 1870–71

1 See, for example, Ernst Engelberg, *Bismarck. Urpreuße und Reichsgründer*, Berlin 1985. Otto Pflanze, *Bismarck and the Development of Germany, vol. 1: The Period of Unification, 1815–1871*, Princeton N.J. 1963 (German edition with the title *Bismarck. Der Reichsgründer*, Munich 1997). Fritz Stern, *Gold and Iron. Bismarck, Bleichröder and the Building of the German Empire*, London 1977.

2 Anselm Doering-Manteuffel, *Die deutsche Frage und das europäische Staatensystem 1815–1871*, Munich 1993, p. 39.

3 See Klaus Hildebrand, *Das vergangene Reich. Deutsche Außenpolitik von Bismarck bis Hitler 1871–1945*, Stuttgart 1995, p. 16.
4 Klaus von Beyme, 'Shifting National Identities. The Case of German History', *National Identities* 1 (1999), p. 40.
5 Richard Millman, *British Foreign Policy and the Coming of the Franco-Prussian War*, Oxford 1965, p. 218.
6 Quoted in William F. Monypenny and George E. Buckle, *The Life of Benjamin Disraeli, Earl of Beaconsfield, vol. 2: 1860–1881*, London 1929, pp. 473–4.
7 Muriel E. Chamberlain, *'Pax Britannica'? British Foreign Policy 1789–1914*, London/New York 1988, p. 124.
8 Werner E. Mosse, *The European Powers and the German Question, 1848–71, with Special Reference to England and Russia*, Cambridge 1958, p. 359.
9 William E. Gladstone, 'Germany, France, and England', *Edinburgh Review* 132 (1870), reprinted in William E. Gladstone, *Gleanings of Past Years, 1843–1878*, vol. 4, London 1879, p. 241.
10 Gordon S. Haight (ed.), *The George Eliot Letters*, vol. 5, Oxford 1955, p. 159.
11 Quoted in F. Hardie, *The Political Influence of Queen Victoria, 1861–1901*, 2nd edn, London 1938, p. 153.
12 Quoted in John Morley, *The Life of William Ewart Gladstone*, vol. 2, London 1903, p. 357.
13 Quoted in W. N. Medlicott, *Bismarck, Gladstone, and the Concert of Europe*, London 1956, reprint, New York 1969, p. 36.
14 John Clarke, *British Diplomacy and Foreign Policy 1782–1865. The National Interest*, London 1989, pp. 224–5.
15 James Garvin, 'The Imprisoned Empire', *The Outlook*, 10 March 1906, p. 327.
16 Alfred Francis Pribram, *England and the International Policy of the European Great Powers 1871–1914*, Oxford 1931, p. 10.
17 *The Times*, 7 Sept. 1876. Quoted in Klaus Hildebrand, 'Von der Reichseinigung zur "Krieg-in-Sicht"-Krise. Preußen-Deutschland als Faktor der britischen Außenpolitik 1866–1875', in Michael Stürmer (ed.), *Das kaiserliche Deutschland. Politik und Gesellschaft 1870–1918*, Düsseldorf 1970, p. 227.
18 Helmut Altrichter, ' ". . . und ganz unter dem Schweif stehen Lessing und Kant . . .". Das Deutsche Reich aus russischer und sowjetischer Sicht', in Klaus Hildebrand (ed.), *Das Deutsche Reich im Urteil der Großen Mächte und europäischen Nachbarn (1871–1945)*, Munich 1995, p. 184.
19 Quoted in Jean-Baptiste Duroselle, 'Die europäischen Staaten und die Gründung des Deutschen Reiches', in Theodor Schieder and Ernst Deuerlein (eds), *Reichsgründung 1870/71. Tatsachen, Kontroversen, Interpretationen*, Stuttgart 1970, pp. 406–7. See also Mosse, *European Powers*, pp. 389–94.
20 Mosse, *European Powers*, pp. 95–8 and 284–90.
21 Quoted in Dietrich Beyrau, 'Der deutsche Komplex: Rußland zur Zeit der Reichsgründung', in Eberhard Kolb (ed.), *Europa und die Reichsgründung*, Munich 1980, p. 85.
22 Dietrich Beyrau, 'Russische Interessenzonen und europäisches Gleichgewicht 1860–1870', in Eberhard Kolb (ed.), *Europa vor dem Krieg von 1870. Mächtekonstellation, Konfliktfelder, Kriegsausbruch*, Munich 1987, p. 75.
23 Paul Matter, *Bismarck et son temps*, vol. 3, Paris 1908, p. 231.
24 *Documents Diplomatiques Français (1871–1914)*, 1st series, vol. 1, Paris 1929, p. 41.
25 Hildebrand, *Das vergangene Reich*, p. 20.
26 Sebastian Haffner, *Von Bismarck bis Hitler. Ein Rückblick*, Munich 1987, p. 15.
27 February 1878. Otto von Bismarck, *Die gesammelten Werke*, vol. 2, Berlin 1929, p. 526.
28 William L. Langer, *European Alliances and Alignments 1871–1890*, reprint

Westport Conn. 1977. Otto Pflanze, *Bismarck and the Development of Germany*, vol. 2: *The Period of Consolidation, 1871–1880*, and vol. 3: *The Period of Fortification, 1880–1898*, Princeton N.J. 1990.

29 Quoted from Bismarck's 'Kissinger Diktat', June 1877 (*Die Große Politik der Europäischen Kabinette 1871–1914*, vol. 2, Berlin 1927, p. 154).

30 Modris Eksteins, *Rites of Spring. The Great War and the Birth of the Modern Age*, London 1990, pp. 129–30.

31 Memorandum by Eyre Crowe on the 'Present State of British Relations with France and Germany', 1 January 1907 (*British Documents on the Origins of the War 1898–1914*, vol. 3: *The Testing of the Entente, 1904–06*, ed. G. P. Gooch and Harold Temperley, London 1928, p. 403).

32 Paul M. Kennedy, *The Rise of the Anglo-German Antagonism 1860–1914*, London 1980, p. 463.

33 Max Weber, *Selections in Translation*, ed. W. G. Runciman and E. Matthews, Cambridge 1978, p. 266.

34 Heinrich von Treitschke, 'Die ersten Versuche deutscher Kolonialpolitik', in idem, *Deutsche Kämpfe. Schriften zur Tagespolitik*, Leipzig 1896, p. 335.

35 Ernst Johann (ed.), *Reden des Kaisers*, Munich 1966, p. 89.

36 *Stenographische Berichte über die Verhandlungen des Deutschen Reichstags*, 9th Legislaturperiode, 5th session, vol. 1, Berlin 1898, p. 60.

37 Johannes Penzler (ed.), *Fürst Bülows Reden nebst urkundlichen Beiträgen zu seiner Politik*, vol. 1: *1897–1903*, Berlin 1907, p. 92 (11 Dec. 1899).

5 The German Question in war and peace

1 George F. Kennan, *The Decline of Bismarck's European Order. Franco-Russian Relations, 1875–1890*, Princeton N.J. 1979, p. 3.

2 Quoted in Andreas Hillgruber, *Deutschlands Rolle in der Vorgeschichte der beiden Weltkriege*, Göttingen 1967, p. 54.

3 Fritz Fischer, *Griff nach der Weltmacht*, abridged edn, Düsseldorf 1967, p. 82.

4 The 'September Programme' is printed in Fritz Fischer, *Germany's Aims in the First World War*, 2nd impression, London 1977, pp. 103–5.

5 Friedrich Naumann, *Central Europe*, London 1916. In the Introduction to this translation Naumann is called 'probably the most widely read political writer in Germany' (p. v).

6 Quoted in Klaus Hildebrand, *Reich – Großmacht – Nation. Betrachtungen zur Geschichte der deutschen Außenpolitik 1871–1945*, Munich 1995, p. 16.

7 Quoted in Otto Hoetzsch (ed.), *Die Internationalen Beziehungen im Zeitalter des Imperialismus*, vol. 6/1, Berlin 1934, pp. 102–3.

8 Quoted in Hildebrand, *Reich – Großmacht – Nation*, p. 18.

9 Marshal Foch's memorandum of 10 January 1919 is printed in *Die französischen Dokumente zur Sicherheitsfrage 1919–1923. Amtliches Gelbbuch des französischen Ministeriums der Auswärtigen Angelegenheiten. Urkunden über die Verhandlungen betr. die Sicherheitsbürgschaften gegen einen deutschen Angriff (10.1.1919–7.12.1923)*, Berlin 1924, pp. 3–6.

10 See Douglas Newton, *British Policy and the Weimar Republic 1918–1919*, Oxford 1997.

11 Michael L. Dockrill and J. Douglas Goold, *Peace without Promise. Britain and the Peace Conferences 1919–1923*, London 1981. Arno J. Mayer, *Politics and Diplomacy of Peacemaking. Containment and Counterrevolution at Versailles 1918–1919*, New York 1967. L. S. Jaffé, *The Decision to Disarm Germany: British Policy towards Post-war German Disarmament 1914–1919*, London 1985.

12 See Donald C. Watt, 'Deutschland im Zwiespalt britischer Politik', in Walther Hofer (ed.), *Europa und die Einheit Deutschlands. Eine Bilanz nach 100 Jahren*, Cologne 1970, p. 138.

13 W. S. Churchill, 'The United States of Europe', *Saturday Evening Post*, 15 February 1930, reprinted in Michael Wolff (ed.), *The Collected Essays of Sir Winston Churchill*, vol. 2, London 1976, p. 179.

14 Memorandum of the German government to the Allied and Associated Powers, 23 June 1919, in H. Michaelis and E. Schraepler (eds), *Ursachen und Folgen. Vom deutschen Zusammenbruch 1918 und 1945 bis zur staatlichen Neuordnung Deutschlands in der Gegenwart*, vol. 3, Berlin 1958, p. 388.

15 Oswald Spengler, *Preußentum und Sozialismus (1919)*, 2nd edn, Munich 1921, p. 19.

16 Quoted by Hillgruber, *Deutschlands Rolle*, p. 45.

17 Karl Dietrich Bracher, *Die Auflösung der Weimarer Republik. Eine Studie zum Problem des Machtverfalls in der Demokratie*, 5th edn, Villingen 1971, p. 11.

18 Sebastian Haffner, *Preußen ohne Legende*, 2nd edn, Munich 1981, p. 476.

19 William Carr, *A History of Germany 1815–1990*, 4th edn, London 1991, p. 288.

20 Lothar Kettenacker, *Germany since 1945*, Oxford/New York 1997, p. 50.

21 Carr, *History of Germany*, pp. 253–55.

22 Haffner, *Preußen ohne Legende*, p. 482.

23 Bracher, *Auflösung der Weimarer Republik*, p. 22.

6 The nemesis of dictatorship

1 Martin Gilbert, *Sir Horace Rumbold. Portrait of a Diplomat 1869–1943*, London 1973, pp. 367–78. Francis L. Carsten, *Britain and the Weimar Republic: The British Documents*, London 1984.

2 *Daily Mail*, July 1933. Angela Schwarz, 'British Visitors to National Socialist Germany: In a Familiar or in a Foreign Country?', *Journal of Contemporary History* 28 (1993), pp. 487–509.

3 Quoted in Gottfried Niedhart, 'Zwischen negativem Deutschlandbild und Primat des Friedens: Großbritannien und der Beginn der nationalsozialistischen Herrschaft in Deutschland', in Wolfgang Michalka (ed.), *Die nationalsozialistische Machtergreifung*, Paderborn 1984, p. 278.

4 Quoted in Roy Douglas, 'Chamberlain and Appeasement', in Wolfgang J. Mommsen and Lothar Kettenacker (eds), *The Fascist Challenge and the Policy of Appeasement*, London 1983, p. 79.

5 Quoted in: R. A. C. Parker, 'The Failure of Collective Security in British Appeasement', in Mommsen and Kettenacker (eds), *Fascist Challenge*, p. 23.

6 Winston Churchill, 'The Truth about Hitler', *Strand Magazine* 90 (Nov. 1935), pp. 10–11.

7 Paul M. Kennedy, 'The Tradition of Appeasement in British Foreign Policy, 1865–1939', in idem, *Strategy and Diplomacy 1870–1945. Eight Studies*, London 1983, p. 16.

8 Wolfgang J. Mommsen, Foreword, in Mommsen and Kettenacker (eds), *Fascist Challenge*, p. x.

9 *Daily Herald*, 1 Oct. 1983 (front page).

10 *The Collected Works of Sir Winston Churchill, vol. 22/1: The Second World War: The Gathering Storm*, London 1975, pp. 206–7.

11 Quoted in Lothar Kettenacker, *Krieg zur Friedenssicherung. Die Deutschlandplanung der britischen Regierung während des Zweiten Weltkrieges*, Göttingen/Zurich 1989, p. 206.

12 Note Churchill's interpretation of unconditional surrender: 'By "unconditional surrender" I mean that the Germans have no *rights* to any particular form of treatment. For instance, the Atlantic Charter would not apply to them as *a matter of right*. On the other hand, the victorious nations owe it to themselves to observe the obligations of humanity and civilisation' (W. S. Churchill, *The Second World War, vol. 5: Closing the Ring*, London 1952, p. 617).
13 Ibid., p. 318.
14 Ibid., pp. 359–60.
15 W. S. Churchill, *The Second World War, vol. 6: Triumph and Tragedy*, London 1954, p. 210.
16 Lothar Kettenacker, *Postwar Planning for Germany during the War: Assumptions and Realities*, Foreign and Commonwealth Office, Historical Branch, Occasional Papers, No. 3, London 1989, p. 7.
17 Churchill, *Triumph and Tragedy*, pp. 560–1.
18 Ibid., p. 327.
19 Quoted in Herbert Feis, *Churchill – Roosevelt – Stalin. The War They Waged and the Peace They Sought*, Princeton N.J. 1957, p. 620.
20 Military Aspects of the Proposal that Germany should be dismembered, COS (44) 822, 9 September 1944, FO 371/39080/C 12806, Public Record Office, London. See also Victor Rothwell, *Britain and the Cold War, 1941–1947*, London 1982, pp. 114–23.
21 John W. Young, *Britain, France and the Unity of Europe 1945–1951*, Leicester 1984, pp. 28–30. Bernd Ebersold, *Machtverfall und Machtbewußsein. Britische Friedens- und Konfliktlösungsstrategien 1918–1956*, Munich 1992, p. 138.
22 Quoted in Franz Knipping and Ernst Weisenfeld (eds), *Eine ungewöhnliche Geschichte. Deutschland-Frankreich seit 1870*, Bonn 1988, p. 142.
23 Quoted in *Geschichte in Quellen. Die Welt seit 1945*, Munich 1980, pp. 101–2.
24 Quoted in Gilbert Ziebura, *Die deutsch-französischen Beziehungen seit 1945*, Pfullingen 1970, pp. 29–30.

7 Germany in the Cold War

1 The Declaration of 5 June 1945 is printed in English in Ingo von Münch (ed.), *Dokumente des geteilten Deutschland*, Stuttgart 1968, pp. 19–24, quote p. 20.
2 Quoted in Wilfried Pabst, *Das Jahrhundert der deutsch-französischen Konfrontation*, Hannover 1983, p. 119.
3 Quoted in Harold Macmillan, *Tides of Fortune, 1945–1955*, London 1969, pp. 112–13.
4 Anne Deighton, *The Impossible Peace. Britain, the Division of Germany and the Origins of the Cold War*, Oxford 1990, p. 35.
5 Terry McNeill, 'The Soviet Union's Policy Towards West Germany, 1945–90', in Klaus Larres and Panikos Panayi (eds), *The Federal Republic of Germany since 1949. Politics, Society and Economy before and after Unification*, London/New York 1996, p. 255.
6 Winston S. Churchill, 'The Tragedy of Europe', in Robert Rhodes James (ed.), *Winston S. Churchill. His Complete Speeches, 1897–1963, vol. 7: 1943–1949*, New York/London 1974, p. 7380.
7 See Martin Gilbert, *Winston S. Churchill*, vol. 8, London 1988, p. 1197.
8 Quoted by Philip Zelikow and Condoleezza Rice, *Germany Unified and Europe Transformed*, Cambridge Mass./London 1995, p. 33. In his memoirs Mikhail Gorbachev insists that the 'Soviet leaders were genuinely convinced that our security could be guaranteed only by perpetuating the division of Germany at

all costs. I must admit that my views on the question were rather similar' (*Memoirs*, London 1996, p. 517).

9 Mary Fulbrook, *Germany 1918–1990. The Divided Nation*, London 1991, p. 177.

10 Mark Roseman, 'Division and Stability: The Federal Republic of Germany, 1949–1989', in Mary Fulbrook (ed.), *German History since 1800*, London 1997, p. 382.

11 Macmillan, *Tides of Fortune*, p. 176.

12 Quoted in Gilbert, *Churchill*, vol. 8, p. 448.

13 Churchill, 'Tragedy of Europe', pp. 7380–1.

14 Quoted in Gilbert, *Churchill*, vol. 8, pp. 265–6.

15 Quoted in ibid., p. 266.

16 Churchill's meeting with Adenauer and their conversation is described in Herbert Blankenhorn, *Verständnis und Verständigung. Blätter eines politischen Tagebuchs 1949–1979*, Frankfurt am Main 1980, pp. 129–30.

17 Quoted in Gilbert, *Churchill*, vol. 8, pp. 286–7.

18 Quoted in *Archiv der Gegenwart* 18/19 (1948/49), p. 1382.

19 Speech made on 26 June 1950 (Gilbert, *Churchill*, vol. 8, p. 536).

20 Lothar Kettenacker, *Germany since 1945*, Oxford/New York 1997, p. 53.

21 See Beate Gödde-Baumanns, 'Frankreich und die deutsche Einheit: 1870/71–1989/90', in: Klaus Schwabe and Francesca Schinzinger (eds), *Deutschland und der Westen im 19. und 20. Jahrhundert*, Stuttgart 1994, p. 109.

22 Kettenacker, *Germany*, p. 63.

23 Lothar Kettenacker, 'Britain's Policy Towards Germany', in Gerhard Krebs and Christian Oberländer (eds), *1945 in Europe and Asia. Reconsidering the End of World War II and the Change of the World Order*, Munich 1997, pp. 77–8.

8 The German Question 1989–90: a dream come true?

1 Speech by Mauno Koivisto, President of the Republic of Finland, at the Parliamentary Assembly of the Council of Europe, Strasbourg, 9 May 1990, in Adam Daniel Rotfeld and Walther Stützle (eds), *Germany and Europe in Transition*, Oxford 1991, p. 144.

2 Paul Gillespie, 'German Unification and the Future of Europe', in Dermot Keogh (ed.), *Beyond the Cold War: Europe and the Superpowers in the 1990s*, Cork/Dublin 1990, p. 68.

3 Gian Enrico Rusconi, 'Listiger Beifall. Italien und die deutsche Einigung', *Frankfurter Allgemeine Zeitung*, 25 July 1990. Jens Petersen, 'Die Einigung Deutschlands 1989/90 aus der Sicht Italiens', in Josef Becker (ed.), *Wiedervereinigung in Mitteleuropa. Außen- und Innenansichten zur staatlichen Einheit Deutschlands*, Munich 1992, pp. 55–90.

4 Mikhail Gorbachev, *Memoirs*, London 1996, p. 516.

5 Address by James A. Baker to the Berlin Press Club on 12 December 1989, in Rotfeld and Stützle (eds), *Germany and Europe*, p. 96.

6 See pp. 120 and 122.

7 See Rotfeld and Stützle (eds), *Germany and Europe*, p. 104.

8 Gorbachev reports of a meeting with his closest advisers in January 1990 at which 'we agreed ... that German reunification should be regarded as inevitable' and decided that 'we should more closely co-ordinate our policy on the "German question" with Paris and London' (Gorbachev, *Memoirs*, p. 528).

9 Interview given by President Gorbachev to *Pravda*, February 1990, quoted in Rotfeld and Stützle (eds), *Germany and Europe*, pp. 101–2.

10 David Marsh, in *Financial Times*, 30 Sept. 1989.

11 Quoted in Günter Trautmann (ed.), *Die häßlichen Deutschen? Die Deutschen im Spiegel der westlichen und östlichen Nachbarn*, Darmstadt 1991, p. 19.

12 Quoted in Rotfeld and Stützle (eds), *Germany and Europe*, p. 110.

13 Margaret Thatcher, *The Downing Street Years*, London 1993, pp. 769 and 783.

14 Ibid., p. 813.

15 Quoted from the diary of George R. Urban (*The Times*, 23 Sept. 1996, p. 16). See George R. Urban, *Diplomacy and Disillusion at the Court of Margaret Thatcher. An Insider's View*, London 1996, pp. 83, 104–5, 124.

16 Interview with *The Spectator*, 14 July 1990, p. 8.

17 See the figures in Richard Davy, 'British Views on the German Question', *Europa-Archiv* 45 (1990), p. 140.

18 Quoted in Julian Bullard, 'Die britische Haltung zur deutschen Wiedervereinigung', in Becker (ed.), *Wiedervereinigung in Mitteleuropa*, p. 40.

19 Edward Heath, *The Course of My Life. My Autobiography*, London 1998, pp. 712–13.

20 *Sunday Times*, 25 Feb. 1990.

21 *Die Zeit*, 7 Sept. 1990.

22 Hans-Dietrich Genscher, *Erinnerungen*, Berlin 1995, p. 709.

23 Ibid., pp. 716–17.

24 Lothar Kettenacker, *Germany since 1945*, Oxford/New York 1997, p. 197.

25 Valentin Falin, *Politische Erinnerungen*, Munich 1993, pp. 480–92.

26 Interview with *Der Spiegel*, 26 March 1990.

27 Printed in Rotfeld and Stützle (eds), *Germany and Europe*, p. 168.

28 The text of the treaty is printed in ibid., pp. 183–6.

29 Printed in ibid., p. 159.

30 Jonathan Osmond, 'The End of the GDR: Revolution and Voluntary Annexation', in Mary Fulbrook (ed.), *German History since 1800*, London 1997, pp. 466–7.

31 Quoted in Trautmann (ed.), *Die häßlichen Deutschen?*, p. 7.

32 Printed in Rotfeld and Stützle (eds), *Germany and Europe*, p. 182.

33 Printed in ibid., p. 185.

34 Timothy Garton Ash, *In Europe's Name. Germany and the Divided Continent*, London 1993, p. 348.

35 Ibid., p. 353.

36 Transcript of the press conference on 17 July 1990, printed in Rotfeld and Stützle (eds), *Germany and Europe*, pp. 172 and 175–6.

37 Kettenacker, *Germany since 1945*, p. 198.

38 See p. 6.

39 See, among others, Conor Cruise O'Brien, 'Beware! The Reich is Reviving', *The Times*, 31 Oct. 1989.

40 Anthony Glees, *Reinventing Germany. German Political Development since 1945*, Oxford 1996, p. 279.

41 Peter Bender, 'Über der Nation steht Europa: Die Lösung der deutschen Frage', *Merkur* 1990, p. 375.

Chronology

1806	Confederation of the Rhine (12 July)
	Dissolution of the Holy Roman Empire (6 Aug.)
	Defeat of Prussia at Jena and Auerstedt: collapse of Old Prussia (14 Oct.)
1807	Peace of Tilsit: territorially diminished Prussia preserved as vassal state of Napoleon (7 July)
1808	Reforms in Prussia as response to French Revolution and military defeat
1813–15	Wars of Liberation
	Napoleon defeated at 'Battle of the Nations' near Leipzig (16–19 Oct. 1813)
	Defeat of France by European Grand Coalition at Waterloo (18 June 1815)
1815	Congress of Vienna (Sept. 1814–June 1815): Rhineland and Westphalia to Prussia; German Confederation (8 June)
1830	July Revolution in France (27–29 July)
	Unrest in Germany
1834	German Customs Union under Prussian leadership, Austria excluded (1 Jan.)
1848	Revolution in Europe
	First German–Danish War (9 April–26 Aug.)
	Paulskirche Assembly in Frankfurt am Main (18 May)
1849	Paulskirche Constitution: King of Prussia as Emperor of a new German Reich that excludes Austria ('Lesser Germany'); rejected by Prussia (28 April)
1850	The Prussian King Frederick William IV summons German Parliament to Erfurt (20 March)
	Punctuation of Olmütz (29 Nov.): restoration of the German Confederation
	Dresden Conferences (23 Dec. 1850–May 1851)
	Prince Schwarzenberg suggests an 'Empire of 70 millions' (23 Dec.)
	Industrial take-off in Central Europe

1851	German Confederation formally restored (15 May)
1853–56	Crimean War: Britain and Russia withdraw from Central Europe
1858	Prince William appointed Prince Regent in Prussia (26 Oct.): Prussia aims for 'moral conquests' in Germany
1859–60	Victory of Italian 'risorgimento' influences German national movement
1862	Otto von Bismarck appointed Prussian Prime Minister in the midst of a constitutional conflict (23 Sept.)
1864	Second German–Danish War: Austria and Prussia defeat Denmark (1 Feb.–30 Oct.): Denmark cedes Schleswig and Holstein to Austria and Prussia
1866	German War: victory of Prussia over Austria at Königgrätz/ Sadowa (3 July): Prussia annexes Schleswig-Holstein, Hanover, Hesse-Cassel and Frankfurt End of German Confederation (24 Aug.)
1867	North German Federation: unification of Northern Germany under Prussian leadership (1 Jan.) *Ausgleich* (Compromise): Dual Monarchy Austria-Hungary (12 June)
1870	Candidacy of south German Hohenzollern for Spanish throne (6 July) Franco-Prussian War: defeat of French armies at Sedan (2 Sept.)
1871	Foundation of the Second German Reich under Prussian leadership at Versailles (18 Jan.) Berlin new German capital Treaty of Frankfurt: France cedes Alsace and Lorraine (10 May)
1878	Congress of Berlin: Imperial Chancellor Bismarck as Europe's arbitrator (13 June–13 July)
1879	Dual Alliance of Germany with Austria-Hungary (7 Oct.)
1882–84	Period of active colonial policy by Bismarck
1887	Reinsurance Treaty with Russia (18 June)
1888	Year of the Three Emperors: death of William I (9 March) and Frederick III (15 June), Emperor William II succeeds (to 1918)
1890	Dismissal of Bismarck as Imperial Chancellor and Prussian Prime Minister (20 March)
1894	Formation of Franco-Russian alliance (4 Jan.)
1896	William II congratulates President Kruger of the Boer Republic on repelling the Jameson Raid (3 Jan.)
1898	Construction of German battle fleet begins
1900	Bernhard von Bülow becomes Chancellor (17 Oct.): German *Weltpolitik* to gain 'a place in the sun' for Germany
1904	Formation of the 'Entente Cordiale' between Britain and France (8 April)

1912	Lord Haldane's mission to Berlin fails to end naval race (Feb.–March)
1914	Assassination of Archduke Franz Ferdinand of Austria in Sarajevo (28 June) First World War begins (28 July)
1918	Military defeat of Germany (9 Nov.) Monarchy overthrown by November Revolution Request by Austrians and Sudeten Germans for *Anschluss* (12 Nov.) rejected by Allies
1919	Peace Treaty of Versailles imposes territorial losses and reparations on Germany (28 June) German National Assembly in Weimar: democratic, liberal and republican constitution for Germany (11 Aug.) Austria independent state against her will
1923	Inflation peaks Occupation of the Ruhr by French and Belgian troops (11 Jan.) Hitler's and Ludendorff's *putsch* in Munich (8/9 Nov.)
1925	Conference of Locarno (5–16 Oct.): Germany recognises its new western, but not eastern borders
1926	Germany enters the League of Nations (8 Sept.)
1929	The 'Great Slump': devastating repercussions on Germany (25 Oct.)
1930	Crisis of the Weimar Republic: first authoritarian presidential cabinet under Heinrich Brüning (29 March)
1933	Adolf Hitler appointed Chancellor of the Reich (30 Jan.): end of Weimar Republic and establishment of totalitarian dictatorship Reichstag in Berlin burns (27 Feb.); state of emergency declared
1934	Death of President Paul von Hindenburg; Hitler becomes 'Führer' and Reich President (2 Aug.)
1936	German troops march into demilitarised Rhineland (7 March)
1938	*Anschluss* of Austria: Greater German Reich (13 March) Munich Agreement: annexation of Sudetenland (29 Sept.) Pogrom against Jews (*Reichskristallnacht*, 9 Nov.)
1939	Occupation of remaining Czech lands: Bohemia and Moravia 'Protectorate' of the Reich (15 March) Germany invades Poland (1 Sept.) Britain and France declare war on Germany (3 Sept.)
1940	Occupation of Denmark and Norway (9 April) German invasion of Belgium, The Netherlands, Luxemburg and France (10 May–22 June)
1941	German attack on Soviet Union (22 June)
1943	Casablanca Conference: Roosevelt and Churchill demand unconditional surrender of Germany (23 Jan.)

	Tehran Conference (28 Nov.–1 Dec.)
1944	Allied troops land in north-western France (6 June)
	Failure of 'July Plot' to assassinate Hitler (20 July)
1945	Allied armies occupy Germany (Jan.–April)
	Yalta Conference (4–11 Feb.)
	Hitler commits suicide (30 April)
	Unconditional surrender of the 'Third Reich' (8 May)
	Potsdam Conference (17 July–2 Aug.)
	Four occupation zones, four sectors in Berlin, Austria under separate Allied occupation (5 June)
	Nuremberg International Military Tribunal opens (20 Nov.)
1946	Speech by Winston Churchill in Zurich: calls for 'a kind of United States of Europe' (19 Sept.)
1947	British and American zones fused into 'Bizone' (1 Jan.)
	State of Prussia officially dissolved by Allied Control Council (25 Feb.)
	Marshall Plan announced (5 June)
1948	Currency reform in the Western zones (21 June)
	Berlin Blockade and Allied airlift (24 July 1948–12 May 1949)
	Parliamentary Council meets in Bonn to discuss draft constitution (5 Sept.)
	London Six Power Conference: treaty for International Ruhr Authority signed (28 Dec.)
1949	Basic Law promulgated (23 May)
	Federal Republic and German Democratic Republic (to 1990)
	North Atlantic Treaty Organisation (NATO) founded (4 April)
	Conference of Foreign Ministers in Paris; no solution to German Question (23 May–20 June)
	Konrad Adenauer Federal Chancellor (15 Sept.)
1950	French Foreign Minister Robert Schuman proposes Western European authority to administer coal and steel production (9 May)
	GDR recognises the Oder–Neisse border (6 July)
1951	Treaty of European Coal and Steel Community signed in Paris (18 April)
1952	GDR *Länder* dissolved and replaced by fourteen districts (23 July)
	The Soviet Union offers reunification to a neutral Germany (10 March)
1953	Uprising in GDR (17 June)
1954	Four Power Conference in Berlin: no agreement on agenda for German unification (25 Jan.–18 Feb.)
1955	Paris Treaties: Federal Republic becomes sovereign state (5 May)

Federal Republic in NATO (9 May), GDR in Warsaw Pact
(27 Jan. 1956)

State Treaty for Austria: four powers guarantee sovereignty
and neutrality (15 May)

1957   Treaty of Rome sets up European Economic Community
(25 March)

1959   Bonn rejects Soviet proposal for 'free city of West Berlin',
recognition of GDR and confederation of the two German
states (10 Jan.)

1961   Building of Berlin Wall (since 13 Aug.) to halt mass exodus
from GDR via Berlin

1963   Konrad Adenauer and Charles de Gaulle sign Elysée Treaty
(22 Jan.)

1964   Last all-German team at Olympic Games in Tokyo (10–24 Oct.)

1965   The Federal Republic and Israel resume diplomatic relations
(13 May)

1966   Bonn offers non-aggression treaties to all Eastern European
countries (25 May)

1969   Socialist-Liberal coalition (Chancellor: Willy Brandt) in Bonn
inaugurates *Ostpolitik* and supports *détente* between East and
West (21 Oct.)

1970   Moscow (13 Aug.) and Warsaw (7 Dec.) Treaties: Federal
Republic establishes *modus vivendi* with communist countries
Chancellor Willy Brandt honours the victims of the Warsaw
Ghetto (7 Dec.)

1971   Four Power Agreement on Berlin confirms Western rights and
links between the Federal Republic and West Berlin (3 Sept.)

1972   GDR recognised by Federal Republic and Western powers
(21 Dec.)

1973   The two Germanies join the UN (18 Sept.)
Prague Treaty between Federal Republic and Czechoslovakia:
Munich Agreement of 1938 declared null and void (11 Dec.)

1982   Helmut Kohl forms coalition of Christian Democratic Union
(CDU)/Christian Social Union (CSU) and Free Democratic
Party (FDP) (1 Oct.)

1985   Mikhail Gorbachev becomes General Secretary of Soviet
Communist Party (11 March): attempted reforms through
perestroika and *glasnost*

1987   American President Ronald Reagan visits West Berlin and asks
Gorbachev to pull down the Wall (12 June)

1989   Exodus of East German citizens via Poland, Czechoslovakia
and Hungary takes on dramatic dimensions (Aug.)
Gorbachev attends GDR fortieth anniversary celebrations
(7 Oct.): thousands of East Germans demonstrate against the
communist dictatorship

Opening of Berlin Wall (9 Nov.)

1990 'Open-skies' conference between NATO and Warsaw Pact states in Ottawa (13 Feb.)

American President George Bush assures full US support for unification (25 Feb.)

European Community heads of state and government welcome German unification at special summit in Dublin (28 April)

Currency, economic and social union between Federal Republic and GDR (1 July)

NATO summit in London declares that a united Germany within the Alliance will be stability factor (5–6 July)

Gorbachev and Chancellor Kohl meet in Caucasus (15–16 July)

GDR parliament decides to join the Federal Republic (23 Aug.)

Unification Treaty (31 Aug.)

'Two-Plus-Four' Treaty signed in Moscow (12 Sept.)

Unification of the two German states (3 Oct.)

First all-German elections to Bundestag (2 Dec.)

Select bibliography

Addison, Paul, *The Road to 1945. British Politics and the Second World War*, London 1975

Adomeit, Hannes, *Imperial Overstretch. Germany in Soviet Policy from Stalin to Gorbachev. An Analysis Based on New Archival Evidence, Memoirs, and Interviews*, Baden-Baden 1998

Ardagh, John, *Germany and the Germans*, 3rd edn, London 1987

Armstrong, Anne, *Unconditional Surrender. The Impact of the Casablanca Policy upon World War II*, New Brunswick N.J. (n.d.)

Attali, Jacques, *Verbatim, vol. 3: Chronique des années 1988–1991*, Paris 1995

Austensen, R. A., 'Austria and the "Struggle for Supremacy in Germany", 1848–1964', *Journal of Modern History* 52 (1980), pp. 195–225

Backer, John H., *The Decision to Divide Germany. American Foreign Policy in Transition*, Durham N.C. 1978

Baker, James A., *The Politics of Diplomacy, Revolution, War and Peace, 1989–1992*, New York 1995

Balfour, Michael, *Germany: The Tides of Power*, London/New York 1992

Baring, Arnulf (ed.), *Germany's New Position in Europe. Problems and Perspectives*, Oxford/Providence R.I. 1994

Bark, Dennis L. and Gress, David R., *A History of West Germany*, 2 vols, 2nd edn, Oxford/Cambridge Mass. 1993

Barker, Elizabeth, *Britain in a Divided Europe, 1945–1970*, London 1971

Barraclough, Geoffrey, *The Origins of Modern Germany*, New York/London 1984

Bell, P. M. H., *The Origins of the Second World War in Europe*, 2nd edn, London 1997

Berghahn, Volker R., *Germany and the Approach of War in 1914*, New York 1993

—— *Imperial Germany 1871–1914. Economy, Society, Culture and Politics*, Providence R.I. 1994

—— *Modern Germany. Society, Economy and Politics in the Twentieth Century*, Cambridge 1982

Bertram, Christoph, 'The German Question', *Foreign Affairs* 69 (1990), pp. 45–62

Beschloss, Michael R. and Talbott, Strobe, *At the Highest Levels. The Inside Story of the End of the Cold War*, Boston 1993

Bessel, Richard, *Germany after the First World War*, Oxford/New York 1993

Billinger, Robert D., *Metternich and the German Question: States' Rights and Federal Duties, 1820–1834*, Newark/London/Cranbury N.J. 1991

Black, Jeremy, *Convergence and Divergence? Britain and the Continent*, New York 1994

Blackbourn, David, *The Long Nineteenth Century. A History of Germany, 1780–1918*, New York 1998

Blanning, Tim, *The French Revolution in Germany*, Oxford 1984

Boadle, Donald Graeme, *Winston Churchill and the German Question in British Foreign Policy, 1918–1922*, The Hague 1973

Bourne, Kenneth, *The Foreign Policy of Victorian England*, Oxford 1970

Brechtefeld, Jörg, *Mitteleuropa and German Politics. 1848 to the Present*, New York 1996

Breuilly, John, *The Formation of the First German Nation-State, 1800–1871*, New York 1996

—— (ed.), *The State of Germany. The National Idea in the Making, Unmaking and Remaking of a Modern Nation-State*, London/New York 1992

Bridge, F. R., *The Habsburg Monarchy among the Great Powers, 1815–1918*, New York 1990

—— and Bullen, Roger, *The Great Powers and the European States System, 1815–1914*, London/New York 1980

Brose, Eric Dorn, *German History 1789–1871. From the Holy Roman Empire to the Bismarckian Reich*, Providence R.I. 1997

Broszat, Martin, *Hitler and the Collapse of Weimar Germany*, Leamington Spa 1987

—— *The Hitler State. The Formation and Development of the Internal Structure of the Third Reich*, London/New York 1981

Bullock, Alan, *Hitler and Stalin. Parallel Lives*, London 1991

Bulmer, Simon and Paterson, William, *The Federal Republic of Germany and the European Community*, London 1987

Byrd, Peter (ed.), *British Foreign Policy under Thatcher*, Oxford/New York 1988

Calleo, David, *The German Problem Reconsidered. Germany and the World Order, 1870 to the Present*, Cambridge/New York 1978

Carr, William, *The Origins of the Wars of German Unification*, London 1993

—— *A History of Germany 1815–1990*, 4th edn, London 1991

—— *Schleswig-Holstein 1815–48. A Study in National Conflict*, Manchester 1963

Carroll, E. Malcolm, *Germany and the Great Powers 1866–1914. A Study in Public Opinion and Foreign Policy*, 2nd edn, Hamden Conn. 1966

Cate, Curtis, *The Ides of August. The Berlin Wall Crisis 1961*, London 1978

Chamberlain, Muriel E., *'Pax Britannica'? British Foreign Policy 1789–1914*, London/New York 1988

Clarke, John, *British Diplomacy and Foreign Policy 1782–1865. The National Interest*, London 1989

Cole, Alastair, *Franco-German Relations*, London 1999

Cowling, Maurice, *The Impact of Hitler. British Politics and British Policy 1933–1940*, London 1975

Craig, Gordon A., 'Churchill and Germany', in Robert Blake and W. R. Louis (eds), *Churchill*, Oxford 1993, pp. 21–40

—— *Germany and the West. The Ambivalent Relationship*, London 1982

—— *The Germans*, Harmondsworth 1982

—— *Germany 1866–1945*, Oxford 1978

Dahrendorf, Ralf, *Society and Democracy in Germany*, London 1968

Davies, Norman, *Europe. A History*, Oxford/New York 1996

Davis, John R., *Britain and the German Zollverein, 1848–66*, London 1997

Davy, Richard, 'British Views on the German Question', *Europa-Archiv* 45 (1990), pp. 139–44

Deighton, Anne, *The Impossible Peace. Britain, the Division of Germany and the Origins of the Cold War*, Oxford 1990

—— (ed.), *Britain and the First Cold War*, Basingstoke 1990

De Porte, A. W., *De Gaulle's Foreign Policy, 1944–1946*, Harvard 1968

Dockrill, Michael L. and Young, John W. (eds), *British Foreign Policy, 1945–56*, Basingstoke 1989

Dockrill, Michael L. and Goold, J. Douglas, *Peace without Promise. Britain and the Peace Conferences 1919–1923*, London 1981

Dockrill, Saki, *Britain's Policy for West German Rearmament, 1950–55*, Cambridge 1991

Dülffer, Jost, *Nazi Germany 1933–1945. Faith and Annihilation*, London 1995

Dunbabin, John, *International Relations since 1945, vol. 1: The Cold War. The Great Powers and their Allies*, London/New York 1994

Elbe, Frank and Kiessler, Richard, *A Round Table with Sharp Corners: The Diplomatic Path to German Unity*, Baden-Baden 1996

Ellwood, David W., *Rebuilding Europe. Western Europe, America and Post-war Reconstruction*, London 1992

Embree, George D. (ed.), *The Soviet Union and the German Question: September 1958–June 1961*, The Hague 1963

Eubank, Keith, *Summit at Teheran*, New York 1985

Feis, Herbert, *Churchill – Roosevelt – Stalin. The War They Waged and The Peace They Sought*, Princeton N.J. 1957

—— *Between War and Peace. The Potsdam Conference*, Princeton N.J. 1960

Feuchtwanger, Edgar J., *From Weimar to Hitler. Germany 1918–33*, Basingstoke 1993

Fischer, Fritz, *Germany's Aims in the First World War*, 2nd impression, London 1977

Frankel, Joseph, *British Foreign Policy 1945–1973*, London 1975

Freund, Michael, *From Cold War to Ostpolitik. Germany and the New Europe*, London 1972

Fritsch-Bournazel, Renata, *Europe and German Unification*, New York/Oxford 1992

Fulbrook, Mary, *Germany 1918–1990. The Divided Nation*, London 1991

—— *The Two Germanies 1945–1990: Problems of Interpretation*, London 1992

—— (ed.), *German History since 1800*, London 1997

Gall, Lothar, *Bismarck. The White Revolutionary*, 2 vols, London 1986

Garton Ash, Timothy, *In Europe's Name. Germany and the Divided Continent*, London 1993

Geiss, Imanuel, *The Question of German Unification 1806–1996*, London/New York 1997

Glees, Anthony, *Reinventing Germany. German Political Development since 1945*, Oxford 1996

Grenville, J. A. S., *Europe Reshaped, 1848–1878*, Hassocks 1976

Gruner, Wolf D., 'The British Political, Social and Economic System and the Decisions for Peace and War. Reflections on Anglo-German Relations 1800–1939', *British Journal of International Studies* 6 (1980), pp. 182–218

Hancock, M. Donald and Welsh, Helga A. (eds), *German Unification. Processes and Outcomes*, Boulder Col. 1994

Heiber, Helmut, *The Weimar Republic*, Oxford/Cambridge Mass. 1993

Heisenberg, Wolfgang (ed.), *German Unification in European Perspective*, London 1991

Henderson, William O., *The Rise of German Industrial Power, 1834–1914*, London 1975

—— *The Zollverein*, 2nd edn, London 1959

Heurlin, Bertel (ed.), *Germany in Europe in the Nineties*, Basingstoke 1996

Hiden, John, *The Weimar Republic*, 2nd edn, London 1996

—— *Germany and Europe 1919–1939*, 2nd edn, London 1993

Hildebrand, Klaus, *Reich – Nation-State – Great Power. Reflections on German Foreign Policy 1871–1945* (The 1993 Annual Lecture of the German Historical Institute London), London 1995

—— *German Foreign Policy from Bismarck to Adenauer. The Limits of Statecraft*, London 1989

—— 'Great Britain and the Foundation of the German Reich', in idem, *German Foreign Policy from Bismarck to Adenauer. The Limits of Statecraft*, London 1989, pp. 3–42

Hildebrand, Klaus, *The Third Reich*, 2nd edn, London 1985

Hillgruber, Andreas, *Germany and the two World Wars*, Cambridge Mass. 1981

Hobsbawm, Eric J., *Age of Extremes. The Short Twentieth Century 1914–1991*, London 1995

Holborn, L. W. *et al.* (eds), *German Constitutional Documents since 1871. Selected Texts and Commentary*, London 1970

Holbraad, Carsten, *The Concert of Europe. A Study in German and British International Theory 1815–1914*, London 1970

Hope, Nicholas, *The Alternative to German Unification. The Anti-Prussian Party, Frankfurt, Nassau and the Two Hessen, 1859–1867*, Wiesbaden 1973

Howard, Michael E., *The Franco-Prussian War. The German Invasion of France, 1870–1871*, London 1961

Hucko, Elmar M. (ed.), *The Democratic Tradition. Four German Constitutions*, Leamington Spa 1987

Hughes, Michael, *Early Modern Germany, 1477–1806*, Basingstoke 1992

Jacobson, Jon, *Locarno Diplomacy. Germany and the West, 1925–1929*, Princeton N.J. 1972

James, Harold, *A German Identity 1770–1990*, London 1989

—— and Stone, Marla (eds), *When the Wall Came Down. Reactions to German Unification*, New York/London 1992

James, Robert Rhodes (ed.), *Winston S. Churchill. His Complete Speeches 1897–1963, vol. 7: 1943–1949*, New York/London 1974

Jarausch, Konrad H., *The Rush to German Unity*, Oxford/New York 1994

—— and Gransow, Volker, *Uniting Germany. Documents and Debates, 1944–1993*, Providence R.I./Oxford 1994

Jelavich, Barbara, *A Century of Russian Foreign Policy 1814–1914*, Philadelphia/New York 1964

Joll, James, *The Origins of the First World War*, 2nd edn, London/New York 1992

—— 'War Guilt. A Continuing Controversy', in Paul Kluke and Peter Alter (eds), *Aspekte der deutsch-britischen Beziehungen im Laufe der Jahrhunderte*, Stuttgart 1978, pp. 60–80

Kaiser, Karl and Morgan, Roger (eds), *Britain and West Germany. Changing Societies and the Future of Foreign Policy*, London 1971

Katzenstein, Peter J. (ed.), *Mitteleuropa: Between Europe and Germany*, Providence R.I. Oxford 1997

—— *Disjoined Partners. Austria and Germany since 1815*, Berkeley Calif. 1976

Kennan, George F., *The Fateful Alliance. France, Russia and the Coming of the First World War*, Manchester 1984

Kennedy, Paul M., 'Idealists and Realists. British Views of Germany, 1864–1939', *Transactions of the Royal Historical Society*, 5th ser., 25 (1975), pp. 137–56

—— 'The Kaiser and German Weltpolitik. Reflections on William's Place in the Making of German Foreign Policy', in J. G. C. Röhl and Nicolaus Sombart (eds), *Kaiser Wilhelm II: New Interpretations*, Cambridge 1982, pp. 143–86

—— *The Rise of the Anglo-German Antagonism 1860–1914*, London 1980

—— 'The Tradition of Appeasement in British Foreign Policy, 1865–1939', in idem, *Strategy and Diplomacy 1870–1945. Eight Studies*, London 1983, pp. 13–39

Kershaw, Ian, *Hitler. 1889–1936*, London 1998

—— *The Nazi Dictatorship. Problems and Perspectives of Interpretation*, 3rd edn, London 1993

Kettenacker, Lothar, 'The Anglo-Soviet Alliance and the Problem of Germany, 1941–1945', *Journal of Contemporary History* 17 (1982), pp. 435–58

—— 'Britain's Policy Towards Germany', in Gerhard Krebs and Christian Oberländer (eds), *1945 in Europe and Asia. Reconsidering the End of World War II and the Change of the World Order*, Munich 1997, pp. 67–78

—— 'British Post-War Planning for Germany: Haunted by the Past', in Ulrike Jordan (ed.), *Conditions of Surrender. Britons and Germans Witness the End of the War*, London/New York 1997, pp. 13–25

—— *Germany since 1945*, Oxford/New York 1997

Kissinger, Henry A., *A World Restored. Metternich, Castlereagh and the Problems of Peace, 1812–22*, London 1977

Kitchen, Martin, *Europe Between the Wars. A Political History*, London 1988

Koch, H. W., *A Constitutional History of Germany in the Nineteenth and Twentieth Centuries*, London/New York 1984

Kolb, Eberhard, *The Weimar Republic*, London 1988

Kraehe, E. E., *A History of the German Confederation 1850–1866*, New York 1948

Langer, William L., *European Alliances and Alignments 1871–1890*, reprint Westport Conn. 1977

Larrabee, F. Stephen, *Two German States and European Security*, New York 1989

Larres, Klaus (ed.), *Germany since Unification. The Domestic and External Consequences*, Basingstoke 1998

—— and Panayi, Panikos (eds), *The Federal Republic of Germany since 1949. Politics, Society and Economy before and after Unification*, London 1996

Lee, W. R. (ed.), *German Industry and German Industrialization. Essays in German Economic and Business History in the Nineteenth and Twentieth Centuries*, London/New York 1991

Leiby, Richard A., *The Unification of Germany, 1989–1990*, Westport Conn. London 1999

Lewis, Derek and McKenzie, John R. P. (eds), *The New Germany. Social, Political and Cultural Challenges of Unification*, Exeter 1995

Lewis, Paul G., *Central Europe since 1945*, London/New York 1994

Lowe, John, *The Great Powers, Imperialism and the German Problem, 1865–1925*, London/New York 1994

McAdams, Arthur J., *Germany Divided. From the Wall to Reunification*, Princeton N.J. 1993

McCauley, Martin, *Russia, America and the Cold War 1949–1991*, London 1998

—— *The Origins of the Cold War 1941–1949*, 2nd edn, London 1995

McDougall, W. A., *France's Rhineland Diplomacy 1914–1924. The Last Bid for a Balance of Power in Europe*, Princeton N.J. 1978

Mander, John, *Our German Cousins. Anglo-German Relations in the Nineteenth and Twentieth Centuries*, London 1974

Marsh, David, *Germany and Europe. The Crisis of Unity*, London 1994

—— *The New Germany: At the Crossroads*, London 1990

Marshall, Barbara, *The Origins of Post-War German Politics*, London 1988

Martel, Gordon, *The Origins of the First World War*, 2nd edn, London 1996

—— (ed.), *The Origins of the Second World War Reconsidered. The A.J.P. Taylor Debate after Twenty-Five Years*, Boston 1986

Massie, Robert K., *Dreadnought. Britain, Germany and the Coming of the Great War*, London 1992

Mastny, Vojtech, 'Soviet War Aims at the Moscow and Teheran Conferences of 1943', *Journal of Modern History* 47 (1975), pp. 481–504

May, Alex, *Britain and Europe since 1945*, London 1999

Mayer, Arno J., *Politics and Diplomacy of Peacemaking. Containment and Counterrevolution at Versailles 1918–1919*, New York 1967

Medlicott, W. N., *Bismarck, Gladstone and the Concert of Europe*, London 1956, reprint New York 1968

—— *Bismarck and Modern Germany*, London 1955

Mee, Charles L., *Meeting at Potsdam*, New York 1975

Meyer, Henry Cord, *Mitteleuropa in German Thought and Action 1815–1945*, The Hague 1955

Middlemas, Keith, *Diplomacy of Illusion. The British Government and Germany 1937–1939*, London 1972

Millman, Richard, *British Foreign Policy and the Coming of the Franco-Prussian War*, Oxford 1965

Milward, Alan S., *The Reconstruction of Western Europe 1945–1951*, London 1984

Minnerup, Günter, *The German Question after the Cold War*, London 1993

Mommsen, Hans, *The Rise and Fall of Weimar Democracy*, Chapel Hill N.C. 1996

Mommsen, Wolfgang J., *Imperial Germany 1867–1918. Politics, Culture and Society in an Authoritarian State*, London 1995
—— *Two Centuries of Anglo-German Relations. A Reappraisal*, London 1984
—— and Kettenacker, Lothar (eds), *The Fascist Challenge and the Policy of Appeasement*, London 1983
Moreton, Edwina, *Germany between East and West*, Cambridge 1987
Mosse, W. E., *The European Powers and the German Question, 1848–71, with Special Reference to England and Russia*, Cambridge 1958
—— *The Rise and Fall of the Crimean System*, London 1963
Müller, Klaus-Jürgen, *Adenauer and de Gaulle – de Gaulle and Germany. A Special Relationship*, Oxford 1993
Myers, Duane P., 'National Self-Determination in 1918–1919. The Case of Austria', in Norbert Finzsch and Hermann Wellenreuther (eds), *Liberalitas. Festschrift für Erich Angermann*, Stuttgart 1992, pp. 45–66
Nettl, J. P., *The Eastern Zone and Soviet Policy in Germany, 1945–1950*, London 1951
Newton, Douglas J., *British Policy and the Weimar Republic 1918–1919*, Oxford 1997
Nicholls, A. J., *The Bonn Republic. West German Democracy 1945–1990*, London/New York 1997
Nipperdey, Thomas, *Germany from Napoleon to Bismarck, 1800–1866*, Dublin 1996
Northedge, F. S., *Descent from Power. British Foreign Policy 1945–1973*, London 1974
Palmer, Alan, *Metternich*, London 1972
Pflanze, Otto, *Bismarck and the Development of Germany*, 3 vols, Princeton N.J. 1963–90
Pittman, Avril, *From Ostpolitik to Reunification. West German–Soviet Political Relations since 1974*, Cambridge 1992
Pond, Elizabeth, *Beyond the Wall. Germany's Road to Unification*, Washington D.C. 1993
Porter, Ian and Armour, Ian D., *Imperial Germany 1890–1918*, London 1991
Pulzer, Peter, *Germany 1870–1945. Politics, State Formation and War*, Oxford 1997
—— *German Politics 1945–95*, Oxford 1995
Ramsay, A. A. W., *Idealism and Foreign Policy. A Study of the Relations of Great Britain with Germany and France, 1860–1878*, London 1925
Reading, Brian, *The Fourth Reich*, London 1995
Reynolds, David, *Britannia Overruled. British Policy and World Power in the Twentieth Century*, London 1991
Robbins, Keith, *Churchill*, London 1992
Robson, Stuart, *The First World War*, London 1998
Rodman, Barbee-Sue M., *British Public Opinion and the German Question 1918–1920*, Cambridge Mass. 1958

Röpke, Wilhelm, *The German Question*, London 1946

Ross, Graham, *The Great Powers and the Decline of the European States System 1914–1945*, London 1983

Rotfeld, Adam Daniel and Stützle, Walther (eds), *Germany and Europe in Transition*, Oxford 1991

Rothwell, Victor, *Britain and the Cold War, 1941–1947*, London 1982

Sainsbury, Keith, 'British Policy and German Unity at the End of the Second World War', *English Historical Review* 94 (1979), pp. 786–804

—— *Churchill and Roosevelt at War*, Basingstoke 1994

Sandiford, K. A. P., *Great Britain and the Schleswig-Holstein Question, 1848–64. A Study in Diplomacy, Politics and Public Opinion*, Toronto 1975

Schoenbaum, David and Pond, Elizabeth, *The German Question and Other German Questions*, Basingstoke 1996

Schöpflin, George and Wood, Nancy (eds), *In Search of Central Europe*, Cambridge 1989

Schroeder, Paul W., 'Britain, Russia and the German Question, 1815–1848. Emerging Rivalry or Benign Neglect', in Adolf M. Birke and Hermann Wentker (eds), *Deutschland und Rußland in der britischen Kontinentalpolitik seit 1815*, Munich 1994, pp. 15–30

—— *The Transformation of European Politics, 1763–1848*, Oxford 1994

—— 'Did the Vienna Settlement Rest on a Balance of Power?' *American Historical Review* 97 (1992), pp. 683–706

Schulze, Hagen (ed.), *Nation-Building in Central Europe*, Leamington Spa 1987

—— 'Europe and the German Question in Historical Perspective', in *Nation-Building in Central Europe*, Leamington Spa 1987, pp. 183–95

Schwabe, Klaus, *Woodrow Wilson. Revolutionary Germany and Peacemaking 1918–1919*, Chapel Hill N.C. 1985

Schwarz, Angela, 'British Visitors to National Socialist Germany: In a Familiar or in a Foreign Country?' *Journal of Contemporary History* 28 (1993), pp. 487–509

Schwarz, Hans-Peter, *Konrad Adenauer, vol. 2: The Statesman, 1952–1967*, Oxford 1997

Serfaty, Simon, *France, De Gaulle and Europe. The Policy of the Fourth and Fifth Republics, towards the Continent*, Baltimore 1968

Sharp, Tony, *The Wartime Alliance and the Zonal Division of Germany*, Oxford 1975

Sheehan, James J., *German History, 1770–1866*, Oxford 1989

Sheehan, Michael, *The Balance of Power. History and Theory*, London/New York 1996

Showalter, Dennis E., *Railroads and Rifles. Soldiers, Technology and the Unification of Germany*, Hamden Conn. 1986

Shumaker, David H., *Gorbatchev and the German Question. Soviet–West German Relations, 1985–1990*, Westport Conn./London 1995

Sked, Alan, 'Britain and the German Question, 1848–1890', in Adolf M. Birke and M.-L. Recker (eds), *Das gestörte Gleichgewicht. Deutschland als Problem britischer Sicherheit im neunzehnten und zwanzigsten Jahrhundert*, Munich 1990, pp. 49–63

—— *The Decline and Fall of the Habsburg Empire 1815–1918*, London/New York 1989

—— (ed.), *Europe's Balance of Power 1815–1848*, London 1979

Smyser, W. R., *The Diplomacy of the German Question 1945–1989*, London 1995

Sontag, Raymond James, *Germany and England. Background of Conflict 1848–1894*, New York 1938 (reprint 1964)

Sowden, J. K., *The German Question 1945–1973. Continuity in Change*, London 1975

Sperber, Jonathan, *The European Revolutions, 1848–1851*, Cambridge 1994

Stares, Paul B. (ed.), *The New Germany and the New Europe*, Washington D.C. 1992

Steefel, L. D., *The Schleswig-Holstein Question*, Cambridge Mass. 1932

Steininger, Rolf, *The German Question. The Stalin Note of 1952 and the Problem of Reunification*, New York 1990

Stern, Fritz, *Dreams and Delusions. The Drama of German History*, New York 1987

Stevenson, David, 'French War Aims and the American Challenge', *Historical Journal* 22 (1979), pp. 853–77

Szabo, Stephen F., *The Diplomacy of German Unification*, New York 1992

Taylor, A. J. P., *The Struggle for Mastery in Europe 1848–1918*, Oxford 1954 (reprint 1977)

—— *Bismarck: The Man and the Statesman*, London 1955

Turner, Henry Ashby, *Germany from Partition to Reunification*, New Haven/London 1992

—— *The Two Germanies since 1945*, New Haven 1987

Turner, Ian D. (ed.), *Reconstruction in Post-War Germany: British Occupation Policy in the Western Zones, 1945–55*, Oxford 1989

Urwin, Derek W., *A Political History of Western Europe since 1945*, 5th edn, London 1997

Verheyen, Dirk, *The German Question. A Cultural, Historical and Geopolitical Exploration*, Boulder Col. 1991

Watson, Alan, *The Germans – Who are they Now?* 2nd edn, London 1995

—— 'Thatcher and Kohl – Old Rivalries Revisited', in Martyn Bond, Julie Smyth and William Wallace (eds), *Eminent Europeans. Personalities who Shaped Contemporary Europe*, London 1996, pp. 264–84

Watt, Donald C., *How War Came About. The Immediate Origins of the Second World War, 1938–1939*, London 1989

Wawro, Geoffrey, *The Austro-Prussian War. Austria's War with Prussia and Italy in 1866*, Cambridge 1996

Webster, Charles K., *The Congress of Vienna, 1814–1815*, Oxford 1919
—— *The Foreign Policy of Castlereagh 1815–1822*, London 1925
—— 'Palmerston, Metternich, and the European System 1830–1841', in idem, *The Art and Practice of Diplomacy*, London 1961, pp. 152–80
Wegs, J. Robert and Ladrech, Robert, *Europe since 1945. A Concise History*, 4th edn, New York 1996
Wehler, Hans-Ulrich, *The German Empire, 1871–1918*, Leamington Spa 1985
Weigall, David, *Britain and the World 1815–1986. A Dictionary of International Relations*, London 1987
Wettig, Gerhard, *The Soviet Union and German Unification*, Köln 1990
Wheeler-Bennett, John and Nicholls, A. J., *The Semblance of Peace. The Political Settlement after the Second World War*, New York 1972
Williamson, D. G., B*ismarck and Germany 1862–1890*, 2nd edn, London 1997
—— *The Third Reich*, 2nd edn, London 1995
—— *Germany from Defeat to Re-Union, 1945–90*, London 1999
Willis, F. Roy, *The French in Germany, 1945–1949*, Stanford Calif. 1962
—— *France, Germany and the New Europe 1945–1967*, Stanford Calif. 1968
Woodward, Llewellyn, *British Foreign Policy in the Second World War*, 5 vols, London 1962–76
Young, John W., *Britain, France and the Unity of Europe, 1945–1951*, Leicester 1984
—— (ed.), *The Foreign Policy of Churchill's Peacetime Government, 1951–55*, Leicester 1988
Zelikow, Philip and Rice, Condoleezza, *Germany Unified and Europe Transformed. A Study in Statecraft*, Cambridge Mass. London 1995

Index of names

Adenauer, Konrad (1876–1967) 69, 92, 120, 126, 152, 157–8
Alexander I (1777–1825) 16–17, 19, 21
Alexander II (1818–81) 67–8
Andreotti, Giulio (b 1919) 124
Arndt, Ernst Moritz (1769–1860) 15, 25
Attila (395–453) 96
Attlee, Clement R. (1883–1967) 118
Augustus (63 BC – 14 AD) 96

Baden, Max von (1867–1929) 88
Baker, James A. (b 1930) 131, 133, 138, 141
Baldwin, Stanley (1867–1947) 95
Bastide, Jules (1800–79) 50
Bender, Peter (b 1923) 144
Bethmann Hollweg, Theobald von (1856–1921) 13, 78, 81, 87
Bevin, Ernest (1881–1951) 118, 120, 122, 125
Bidault, Georges (1899–1983) 109, 126
Bismarck, Otto von (1815–98) 1, 3–4, 16, 30, 55, 57–60, 62, 66–73, 78, 82, 88–9, 119, 155
Bourdet, Claude (b 1909) 109
Bracher, Karl Dietrich (b 1922) 87
Brandt, Willy (1913–92) 158
Brüning, Heinrich (1885–1970) 95, 156
Bülow, Bernhard von (1849–1929) 76, 95, 146, 155
Bush, George W. (b 1924) 134, 141, 159

Byrnes, James F. (1879–1972) 117, 122

Castlereagh, Robert Stewart (1769–1822) 17–18
Cecil, Lord Edgar Algernon Robert (1864–1958) 96
Chamberlain, A. Neville (1869–1940) 95, 97, 99
Churchill, Winston S. (1874–1965) 84, 96–7, 99, 101, 104–7, 110, 120–2, 124–6, 151–2, 156–7
Clausewitz, Karl von (1780–1831) 84
Clemenceau, Georges (1841–1929) 69, 83
Craig, Gordon A. (b 1913) 4
Cripps, Sir R. Stafford (1889–1952) 102
Crowe, Sir Eyre (1864–1925) 73–4

Dahrendorf, Ralf (b 1929) 10
Dean, Patrick (1909–94) 128
Deighton, Anne (b 1949) 119
Derby, Edward Geoffrey Stanley, Earl of (1799–1869) 67
Disraeli, Benjamin, Lord Beaconsfield (1804–81) 45, 63–4
Doering-Manteuffel, Anselm (b 1949) 9
Dumas, Roland (b 1922) 142
Duncan-Sandys, Duncan Edwin (1908–87) 126
Duroselle, Jean-Baptiste (b 1917) 11–12

Ebert, Friedrich (1871–1925) 88

Eden, R. Anthony, Earl of Avon
  (1897–1977) 95, 102–3, 106–7,
  120–2
Eksteins, Modris (b 1943) 72
Eliot, George (1819–80) 66
Elizabeth II (b 1926) 135
Engels, Friedrich (1820–95) 59

Favre, Jules (1809–80) 70
Fischer, Fritz (1908–99) 79
Foch, Ferdinand (1851–1929) 82–3
Francis II/Francis I (1768–1835)
  German Emperor 1792–1806,
  Emperor of Austria 1804–35 12,
  14, 21
Frantz, Constantin (1817–91) 1, 6, 8
Franz, Ferdinand (1863–1914) 156
Frederick III (1831–88) 155
Frederick William IV (1795–1861) 48,
  54–5, 58, 154

Garton Ash, Timothy (b 1955) 141
Garvin, James (1868–1947) 67
Gaulle, Charles de (1890–1970) 69,
  108–19, 115, 126, 158
Geiss, Imanuel (b 1931) 14, 29
Genscher, Hans-Dietrich (b 1927) 136,
  138–41
Gentz, Friedrich von (1764–1832) 28
Gillespie, Paul (b 1933) 129
Gladstone, William E. (1809–98) 63,
  66
Goebbels, Joseph (1897–1945) 95
Goethe, Johann Wolfgang von
  (1749–1832) 2
Gorbacher, Mikhail (b 1931) 124,
  129, 131, 138–9, 151–2, 158–9
Görres, Joseph (1776–1848) 25
Granville, George Leveson-Gower,
  Lord (1815–91) 63

Haffner, Sebastian (1907–99) 8, 70
Haldane of Cloan, Richard Burdon
  Viscount (1856–1928) 156
Hardenberg, Karl August Baron
  (1750–1822) 17
Heath, Edward (b 1916) 133
Heeren, Arnold Hermann Ludwig
  (1760–1842) 1
Herder, Johann Gottfried (1744–1803)
  51
Herter, Christian A. (1895–1966) 122
Hildebrand, Klaus (b 1941) 70
Hillgruber, Andreas (1925–89) 52

Hindenburg, Paul von (1847–1934)
  87, 89, 93, 95, 156
Hitler, Adolf (1889–1945) 1, 12, 52,
  86, 90, 93–7, 99,103, 105, 110,
  117, 119, 156–7
House, Edward M. (1858–1938) 83
Hubatsch, Walther (1915–84) 9–10
Humboldt, Wilhelm von (1767–1835)
  30
Hurd, Douglas (b 1930) 133, 136, 142

James, Harold (b 1956) 37, 42
John, archduke (1782–1859) 46

Kennan, George F. (b 1904) 8, 78
Kennedy, Paul M. (b 1945) 97
Kohl, Helmut (b 1930) 4, 124, 139,
  158–9
Kruger, Stephanus Johannes Paulus
  (1825–1904) 155

La Garde, Pierre Auguste de
  (1759–1837) 21
Lamoricière, Christoph Léon de
  (1806–65) 54
Ligne, Karl Joseph de (1735–1814) 21
Lloyd George, David (1863–1945)
  82–3
Louis XVIII (1755–1824) 19, 21
Ludendorff, Erich (1865–1937) 87,
  156
Lytton Bulwer, Henry (1801–72) 66

MacDonald, James Ramsay
  (1866–1937) 95
Macmillan, Harold M. (1894–1986)
  119, 125
Maisky, Ivan M. (1884–1975) 102
Maizière, Lothar de (b 1940) 136
Marshall, George C. (1880–1959) 157
Marx, Karl (1818–83) 33, 59
Mazzini, Giuseppe (1805–72) 51
Metternich, Prince Klemens
  (1773–1859) 17–19, 21–2, 28,
  32–3, 36, 39, 41
Millman, Richard (b 1932) 63
Mitterand, François (1916–96) 124,
  131, 134, 143
Molotov, Vyacheslav M. (1890–1986)
  102, 117
Morgenthau, Henry (1891–1967)
  104
Mosse, Werner E. (b 1918) 64
Mussolini, Benito (1883–1945) 5

Namier, Sir Lewis B. (1888–1960) 50
Napoleon Bonaparte (1769–1821)
    14–18, 20, 23, 29, 32, 54, 154
Napoleon III (1808–73) 61–2
Naumann, Friedrich (1860–1919) 80,
    149
Nicholas I (1796–1855) 55
Nipperdey, Thomas (1927–92) 42

Osmond, Jonathan (b 1953 139

Palacky, Frantisek (1798–1876) 51
Paléologue, Maurice (1859–1944) 81
Palmerston, Henry John Temple, Lord
    (1784–1865) 50, 63
Papen, Franz von (1879–1969) 92
Pericles (c 495 BC – 429 BC) 96
Pitt, William (1759–1806) 16

Reagan, Ronald (b 1911) 158
Ridley, Nicholas (1929–93) 133
Ritter, Gerhard (1888–1967) 10
Roosevelt, Franklin D. (1882–1945)
    99, 101, 104–7, 156
Röpke, Wilhelm (1899–1966) 1–2, 9
Rothermere, Harold Harmsworth,
    Lord (1868–1940) 95
Rumbold, Sir Horace (1869–1943) 95

Salisbury, Robert Cecil, Marquess of
    (1830–1903) 64
Scheidemann, Philipp (1865–1939) 88
Schieder, Theodor (1908–84) 10–11
Schiller, Friedrich von (1759–1805) 2
Schuman, Robert (1886–1963) 127,
    157
Schwarzenberg, Felix zu (1800–52)
    52–3, 55–6, 154

Shevardnadze, Eduard (b 1928) 131
Simson, Eduard (1810–99) 48
Smith, Adam (1723–90) 41
Spengler, Oswald (1880–1936) 84
Stalin, Josef V. (1879–1953) 99,
    101–4, 106–9, 120, 122
Steffens, Henrik (1773–1845) 35
Stein, Karl Baron vom (1757–1831)
    15, 25
Sybel, Heinrich von (1817–95) 3
Szabo, Stephen F. (b 1943) 141

Talleyrand-Périgord, Charles Maurice
    (1754–1838) 21–2
Tamerlane (1336–1405) 96
Taylor, A. J. P. (1906–90) 12
Thatcher, Margaret (b 1925) 124,
    132–5, 138, 142
Thiers, Adolphe (1797–1877) 61
Tocqueville, Alexis de (1805–59)
    53–4
Treitschke, Heinrich von (1834–96)
    32, 38, 75

Vandenberg, Arthur (1884–1951)
    120
Victoria (1819–1901) 30, 38, 50, 66,
    72

Washington, George (1732–99) 96
Weber, Max (1864–1920) 75–6
Weizsäcker, Richard von (b 1920)
    140
William I (1797–1888) 58–9, 63, 67,
    155
William II (1859–1941) 12, 72–3, 75,
    87–9, 155
Wilson, Woodrow (1856–1924) 83